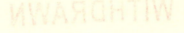

RADICALISM AND FREETHOUGHT IN NINETEENTH-CENTURY BRITAIN

Contributions in Labor History

RADICALISM AND FREETHOUGHT IN NINETEENTH-CENTURY BRITAIN

The Life of Richard Carlile

JOEL H. WIENER

CONTRIBUTIONS IN LABOR HISTORY, NUMBER 13

Greenwood Press
Westport, Connecticut • London, England

Library of Congress Cataloging in Publication Data

Wiener, Joel H.
  Radicalism and freethought in nineteenth-century
Britain.

  (Contributions in labor history, ISSN 0146-3608 ;
no. 13)
  Bibliography: p.
  Includes index.
  1. Carlile, Richard, 1790-1843.   2. Labor and
laboring classes—Great Britain—Biography.   3. Radicals
—Great Britain—Biography.   4. Liberty of the press—
Great Britain—History.   I. Title.   II. Series.
Z325.C28W53   320.5'1'0924 [B]   82-6168
ISBN 0-313-23532-5 (lib. bdg.)   AACR2

Library of Congress Catalog Card Number: 82-6168
ISBN: 0-313-23532-5
ISSN: 0146-3608

First published in 1983

Greenwood Press
A division of Congressional Information Service, Inc.
88 Post Road West
Westport, Connecticut 06881

Printed in the United States of America

10 9 8 7 6 5 4 3 2 1

For Paul, Debbie, and Jane

CONTENTS

INTRODUCTION

Richard Carlile (1790-1843) is one of the most important British working-class reformers of the nineteenth century. He was the leader of an "infidel challenge" against orthodox religion, a propagandist for birth control and republicanism, and a journalist who influenced the development of the popular press. He fought hard to vindicate the principle of free discussion. Carlile is described in the *Dictionary of National Biography* as having done "more than any other Englishman in his day for the freedom of the press" and is characterized by G. D. H. Cole as having "made the greatest stand . . . in the nineteenth century for freedom of speech and writing." He is featured prominently in every history of reform. In addition to brief biographies by Cole (*Richard Carlile, 1790-1843* [1943]) and by a radical contemporary, George Jacob Holyoake (*The Life and Character of Richard Carlile* [1849]), he is the subject of books by his daughter, Theophila Campbell Carlile (*The Battle of the Press as Told in the Story of the Life of Richard Carlile* [1899]) and by the Scottish freethinker, Guy Aldred (*Richard Carlile, Agitator: His Life and Times* [1941]).

Yet controversy has obscured Carlile's achievements up to the present day. Few of his contemporaries were able to agree on precisely what it was he accomplished or (particularly in his later years) what it was he stood for. He was berated by many working-class freethinkers for abandoning infidelity and atheism; written off by Francis Place and other reformers as a "single minded honest hearted fanatic"; and criticized by some who worked closely with him for being "harsh" and "losing his way" about the midpoint of his political life. When members of the London Secular Society tried to build a monument in his memory at Kensal Green Cemetery in 1849, they were unable to raise sufficient funds. And in 1943, on the centenary of his death, only a handful of freethinkers and secularists attended a public commemoration in his memory.

This biography, the first full-length study of Carlile, is intended to clarify his legacy and to present a rounded picture of the man. It is a personal as well as a political biography. Many working-class reformers remain indistinct "names" whose contributions to history are glossed over with little more than a footnote. It is hoped that this book will rectify this situation insofar as Carlile is concerned and will also serve as a pioneering effort in the study of other reformers.

Over the course of years I have acquired innumerable debts while writing this biography. Many librarians have courteously assisted me, particularly at the following institutions: the British Museum, Public Record Office, New York Public Library, Manchester Central Reference Library, Co-operative Union Library, Goldsmith's Library, Dorset County Record Office, Columbia University Library, and the Bishopsgate Library. I am grateful also to friends and acquaintances for information, assistance, and encouragement. These include Dr. Gordon Stein, Dr. I. Prothero, Professor Gwyn A. Williams, Ms. Mary Bostetter, Mr. G. B. A. M. Finlayson, Dr. Edward Royle, Dr. Brian Harrison, Professor J. F. C. Harrison, Professor Joseph Hamburger, Mr. James Epstein, and Professor George Schwab. Most of all I owe a debt of gratitude to my wife, Suzanne. As on so many other occasions she has been a source of intellectual stimulation to me. I could not have completed this book without her.

RADICALISM AND FREETHOUGHT IN NINETEENTH-CENTURY BRITAIN

1

THE BEGINNINGS

Richard Carlile's quest for a better world began unremarkably enough in the small market town of Ashburton, Devon, where he was born on December 8, 1790, and where he spent the first twelve years of his life. By the end of the eighteenth century, history had begun to pass Ashburton by. It had once been a major tin-mining district; then for a time, a center for the manufacture of woolen cloth. Now it was a backwater: its economic base was in decline; its daily life untouched by the first stirrings of industrial and commercial activity that within the next fifty years was to transform drastically the landscape and social structure of modern Britain.[1]

Ashburton was an attractive place to grow up in. It had an ancient market square at the intersection of three principal streets; a Bull Ring where butchers and other local traders gathered on weekdays to exchange their wares; and a majestic fifteenth-century church whose solid oak roof and stone piers contrasted sharply with the crumbling headstones that adorned its churchyard. There was, too, Lawrence Lane, a tree-shaded thoroughfare where Carlile's mother owned a shop and near which (on "Steave-ahead Lane") the future radical reformer was born.

Carlile and his boyhood friends attended the markets and fairs held in Ashburton, frolicked in adjacent country lanes, and, infrequently, visited the bustling metropolises of Exeter and Plymouth, each about twenty-five miles away. (Ashburton was located on the coach road that linked these two cities.) Regrettably, to the freethinker of later years recounting early memories, they also participated in many "wasteful" adolescent activities: badger baiting, squirrel chasing, the wearing of "the gilt on the nauseous oak-apple" on the twenty-ninth of May, in celebration of the escape of Charles II from his parliamentary pursuers, and, most galling, the burning of effigies of Guy Fawkes and Tom Paine.[2] All together, these were satisfying times for a poor country boy with few prospects of improving his economic status. And, as time softened their blemishes, they began to typify for Richard Carlile small-scale, preindustrial society, worth preserving at all costs.

Richard's father, also named Richard, was a man of ability whose forebears had settled in Devon generations before and had made some contributions to the commercial history of Ashburton. The elder Carlile had been a shoemaker by trade and then, successively, an exciseman, a teacher, and a soldier. His intellectual pursuits had borne fruit in the publication of a book of mathematical adages. Yet, as his son was to asseverate frequently, his father had wasted himself on drink and, a few years after 1790, had abandoned his wife and children.[3] The latter, in addition to Richard, included two daughters: Mary-Anne, whose loyalty in the 1820s became a celebrated chapter in the annals of reform, and an older sister who lived with him during the final months of his life, after an estrangement lasting many years.

Elizabeth Brookings, Richard's mother, was a "kind, tender, and indulgent" woman, dour by temperament and conventionally pious.[4] Her view of life was circumscribed almost entirely by the beliefs and practices of the Church of England. She compelled her children to attend church and Sunday school regularly and conducted daily readings at home from the Scriptures and from a popular German verse narrative called *The Death of Abel*. Such family activities were part of the fabric of the life of the rural poor in preindustrial England (though observed with particular seriousness in the Carlile home), and Richard went along with them. But according to his later accounts, he was modestly affronted by some of these duties, which he caustically described as "learning to repeat from memory a prayer and a creed."[5] Still, inward rejection does not equal mental erasure, and the reformer of later years who was to be denounced regularly by churchmen and pamphleteers as an "apostle of infidelity," was deeply conventional by temperament. The imprint of his Ashburton years and of his mother's personality—willing to concede little to life's frivolities—were permanently engrafted on him.

Like other working-class boys of the late eighteenth and early nineteenth centuries, Carlile's formal schooling was skimpy. It comprised, in addition to Sunday school, attendance at two local free schools up to the age of twelve. Both schools were specks in that line of charity institutions, which, in aggregate, laid the foundation for the working-class's "leap into literacy." Such schools were of mixed quality: some transmitted little more than the rudiments of literacy or numeracy to their pupils; others, including the Bourne School attended by Carlile, were slightly more advanced.[6] (Ashburton also boasted a thirteenth-century grammar school whose alumni included a former dean of Westminster and a future editor of the *Quarterly Review*. But Carlile had no connection with it.)[7]

At these free schools Richard Carlile imbibed the foundations of an education. He learned to read and write by means of the catechism and a horn book, the latter being a sheaf of paper mounted on wood and protected by a layer of horn whose pointer indicated appropriate symbols. By rote drilling his teachers sought to instill in him the precepts of a "Christian and Useful Education." One schoolmistress, morosely recollected as "Old Cherry Chalk," sat her charges in concentric circles and compelled them to exchange passages of Scripture verbally with each other throughout the day. A smattering of mathematics, as well as some Latin and grammar, was conveyed by similar means.[8]

Charity institutions like Bourne School brought segmented rural cultures into contact with the expanding world of print in the late eighteenth and early nineteenth centuries. But the cost was sometimes high. Even by the least enlightened standards of the time, Carlile's education was minimal, and he was fully aware of this. In subsequent years he propounded the message that applied intellectual effort, more than anything else, was needed to bring about radical reform. Yet how difficult it was to give effect to such ideas from a base as circumscribed as his. Some working-class reformers of the early nineteenth century overcame educational deficiencies by early, sustained efforts at self-instruction. These included Thomas Cooper, the Lincolnshire shoemaker turned "Shakespearean Chartist," who despite a failure to "master the elements of Latin, Greek, Hebrew, and French," by the age of twenty-four had prodigious achievements to his credit; and William Cobbett, the most successful plebeian journalist of the early nineteenth century.[9] But Carlile's path was different. Not until his late twenties did he begin to compensate for the inadequacies of his schooling, and by then, though he overcame many shortcomings, it was too late to achieve intellectual distinction. He possessed an inquisitive, tenacious mind. But his conception of knowledge—formed by years of schooling in charity institutions— was that of a useful tool whose contours rarely transcended the limits of a debating technique.

To criticize Carlile's schooling in this way is, however, unfair. Eighteenth-century charity schools were not intended to prepare their pupils for careers in political agitation. They trained them instead to be farm laborers, mechanics, and, occasionally, skilled artisans. And it was in the latter capacity—as a journeyman tinplate worker—that Carlile passed the formative years of his life. When his schooling ended in 1802, he worked briefly in a chemist's shop in Exeter, trying to put to use the sciolism of Latin that he had acquired.[10] A sojourn in his mother's shop in Ashburton followed, as he attempted to adjust to a lifetime of routine work. The experiment, fortunately, failed. Mildly rebellious by his own account, he gratefully accepted assistance from his father's relatives and, in 1803, became a tinplate worker, an unremunerative, frustrating occupation that, nonetheless, absorbed his energies for the next fifteen years.

Tinplate working was a parlous trade even in the best of times. It involved molding sheets of tinplate (a mixture of iron and tin) into household articles such as candlesticks, kettles, pots, pans, and ladles. Skilled artisans worked under the same roof, sharing tinplate with each other as well as the tools of their craft: shears, hammers, and solder. It was a small-scale economic activity that had taken root in the West Country and the Midlands in the seventeenth century, and then had spread slowly to other parts of the country. By the first decade of the nineteenth century, when Carlile took it up, it was in precipitous decline, at least in its artisanal form. The margin of profit among tinplate masters had shrunk, and small entrepreneurs, the backbone of the trade, were being challenged successfully by manufacturers in the north of England who were creating a mechanized industry. The wars with France, which began in 1793 and continued for a quarter of a century, further damaged traditional tinplate working by dampening home demand and upsetting normal trading patterns.[11]

The first decade of the nineteenth century was, then, an unpropitious time for a young tinplateman to be entering the trade. Conventional anticipations of income and social mobility were ceasing to be valid. And as Carlile moved from job to job between 1802 and 1817, he did so with diminishing confidence; short-time working and the possibility of a total loss of employment were constant sources of anxiety to him. Years later, when he was settled comfortably into the full-time occupation of a political reformer, he told his readers that he had started as a lowly apprentice and had become a tinplate master before deciding to give up the trade. He was not being truthful. For almost fifteen years Carlile struggled to eke out a bare living—working in villages and towns in Devon, in cities like Portsmouth and Plymouth, and, finally, in London. Never did he advance beyond the position of a journeyman tinplate worker nor had he at any time concrete prospects for doing so.[12]

These years "in the wilderness" are frustrating ones for a biographer of Carlile because it is as if a personal dark ages had descended upon him. Such shadowy outlines are familiar to many historians of the poor, who face the problem of uncovering sufficient documentation for their tasks. But the difficulty is compounded in the case of Carlile because of his efforts to gloss over the waste and "indiscretion" of these prepolitical years. After becoming a reformer at the age of twenty-seven, in 1817, he preached hard work, perseverance, moral earnestness. Yet how, having taken up the burden of popularizing such virtues, could he confess to the irredeemable loss of so many years of his own life?[13] Likewise, his later political and theological convictions, so strongly held, were predicated on the existence of a chasm between light and darkness—right and wrong. Such a mentality was common to many other reformers, but in this instance the "sin" to be eradicated was Carlile's own equivocal past. By blurring its contours, he was slaying it mentally. Had not Tom Paine and Jesus Christ, two future models, been late bloomers?[14]

Such a personal obfuscation of the past, combined with the opaque texture of many aspects of early nineteenth-century working-class culture, makes it difficult to resurrect Carlile's early years. At best, his writings yield glimpses of him: in rebellion against the dictates of a benevolent employer, so presaging a lifelong hatred for any kind of submission; as a sexually charged young man whose chastity is placed in danger by the advances of the wife of another employer; and, in 1811, as a first-time resident of London, overwhelmed and discomfited by a city that sanctioned public executions and other indelicate forms of amusement.[15] Carlile also engaged in youthful indiscretions during these years, though how and under what circumstances he did so remain unclear.

Tinplate working occupied almost all of his waking hours between 1802 and 1817 (at a time when other workingmen were beginning to express their support for political reforms), and it was time, in retrospect, poorly spent. In terms of his attitude to work, Carlile was not a typical artisan. He could never be accused of indifference to the fate of the preindustrial artisan class, now caught up increasingly in the process of economic and industrial change; on the contrary, the radicalism that he espoused can be viewed as a threnody on the age of craftsmanship slowly but inevitably nearing its end. Yet his hands, perhaps surprisingly, offered him no creative satisfaction. The routine of artisan life offended Carlile, and he felt contempt for his workmates, who, caught up occasionally in pastimes such as drinking, subjected him to taunts and insults.[16] In later years he expressed satisfaction that few of these "brutish" tinplatemen became his followers (though, fortunately for him, other artisans were not as hesitant to extend their support to him). What he seems to have learned most profitably during these years was not pride in his craft but how to preserve his individuality in the face of pressures to conform. It was a peculiar lesson for a reformer to imbibe but one that became integral to the kind of reform that he advocated.

During these years of itinerant artisanship and, seemingly, little involvement in politics, an incident took place that may have had some effect on Carlile's development. In 1812 or 1813, while living near Portsmouth, he contemplated taking orders in the Church of England. Briefly he came under the influence of Dr. Lant Carpenter of Exeter and David Bogue of Gosport, advocates of a moderate deism that was reconcilable with Anglican doctrine.[17] It is doubtful that he ever became a true disciple of either man— more likely this was whispered about years afterward to discredit him—but he listened intently to the sermons of Carpenter and Bogue and was influenced by their ideas and by other mildly unorthodox theological views that were circulating in the West Country in the second decade of the nineteenth century. If this was a moment of personal crisis it passed quickly, and the future freethinker was spared the indignity of a close entanglement with the Church of England. Yet the incident, interestingly, reveals disquietude in Carlile's mind, contrary to his characterization of himself as living in a state of "blackness" during these years. Probably, like other discontent artisans he was beginning to be affected by the political currents that, in response to the transformation of the economic system, reflected increasing demands for reform.

In 1813, an important, as opposed to a merely speculative, episode occurred in Carlile's life. He got married. Jane Carlile (her maiden name is unknown) was the daughter of a poor Hampshire cottager. After a brief courtship, she married Richard in Gosport, possibly because she was expecting a child at the time, more likely because of the economic pressures that were undermining tinplate working and forcing her husband to move from job to job.[18] Jane and Richard had nearly twenty years to rue their impetuosity. The marriage, which ended in an acrimonious public separation in 1832, hurt him politically as well as personally. Jane accepted the traditional woman's role of subordination in marriage, but she lacked the suppleness necessary to accommodate her husband's imperious ways. She may not have been "violent and ill-tempered," as he repeatedly informed his readers, and to her credit she gave him invaluable political assistance.[19] But she was unable to provide the emotional stability that he needed. The marriage also increased the financial pressures on Carlile, for within five years he had to support three sons: Richard and Alfred, born, respectively, in 1814 and 1816, and Thomas Paine, who died in the spring of 1819, a year after he was born.[20] Even during this early, relatively smooth period of his life, the gods seemed to be refraining from treating the future freethinker with consideration.

Marriage brought an important change in Carlile's life: it caused him to transfer his activities to London. In 1811 he had lived briefly in the "great wen" (near the Old Bailey), and his experience had not been a happy one. But shortly after their marriage, he and Jane took lodgings in Bloomsbury where, assisted by friends, they tried to improve their economic status.[21] The move was profoundly significant for Carlile. For with the exception of several lengthy stays in Lancashire and more than a decade of enforced residence in prison, he lived and worked nearly all of the remainder of his life in London, becoming a spokesman for that city's discontented working classes and, from his perspective, a victim of its inhospitalities.

From 1813 to 1817, London, like the rest of the nation, was experiencing disaffection among the poor. Economic unrest was widespread, as a result of the wars with France and the social and industrial changes of these years. Reformers like Sir Francis Burdett, William Cobbett, Henry "Orator" Hunt, and Major John Cartwright were expressing the disparate grievances of the working classes. On public platforms and in the pages of a gestating cheap press, they bruited about schemes for reform that received a wide measure of popular support. Numerous tracts were published, political meetings convened, and petitions drafted for transmission to Parliament.[22] To paraphrase Wordsworth, the second decade of the nineteenth century was (for those who could afford political dreams) a blissful—if disquieting—dawn in which to be alive. The poorer districts of the city resounded with intoxicating rhetoric while its more elegant sections reflected the glitter and poverty of diverse social classes.

Political aspirations were beginning to take shape during these years. And although according to his own sketchy accounts, Carlile remained aloof from this agitation until the winter of 1816-1817, his insecure job prospects, combined with qualities of stubbornness and obduracy, made him ripe for political activism. He could not have avoided reading Cobbett's *Political Register* or some of the other cheap radical papers that were being hawked about in the streets of London; nor could he have remained immune for long from the ideas of Burdett, Cartwright, and the militant followers of Thomas Spence who advocated a form of land nationalization. Personally Carlile distrusted authority; while from choice of vocation his future seemed bleak. Political commitment was, surely, a matter of time.

Or was it? One must resist the temptation to anticipate events. Whatever political dreams Carlile may have been beginning to harbor, he spent much of his time at his workbench and in his poorly furnished Bloomsbury lodgings, outwardly unaffected by the events transpiring about him. From 1813 to 1817, he worked for two London firms: Benham and Sons, a small company located on Blackfriars Road near the south bank of the Thames River, and Masterman, Matthews and Company, a Holborn establishment for which he had worked previously.²³ No evidence survives to indicate the nature of his relationship with either employer. But some clues offer an insight into his daily routine. He walked each morning from his rooms to his place of work; and while traversing Holborn and the Inns of Court, he was exposed to the patterings of the tractsellers who advertised their political wares in and around Fleet Street and the Strand. His imagination was stimulated by the nooks and crannies of the City of London, filled as they were with centuries of history. Likewise, the taverns and public houses beckoned him (unsuccessfully), their snug, comfortable interiors calling workmen inside for political conviviality and drink.²⁴

The sights and impressions of a great city were everywhere to be absorbed—and resisted. For Carlile believed strongly in the "respectable" artisanal virtues: diligence, sobriety, thrift, cleanliness, hard work. Such restraints, with their political implications, worked against the enjoyment of urban life because they meant a shunning of the theater and some other social and cultural activities (assuming that these could be afforded). But they illuminate a tension in the lives of many politically involved workingmen: between a striving for improvement by moral, restrained means, and a conviction that reform, political change, and, occasionally, fun, were badly needed.

By the winter of 1816-1817, Carlile and many other artisans faced a future that was, seemingly, hopeless. Part-time working had become a way of life that for some of them was likely to be transformed into permanent unemployment. The options confronting Carlile were limited: he could turn to a precarious craft such as glassmaking or brickmaking or opt for lesser status as a semiskilled or unskilled worker, by taking a factory job in London or, more probably, in the industrial north. His lack of enthusiasm for the workshop made the former alternative unattractive, while factory labor, if taken up, would have extinguished the spark of independence that he clung to and that, within a few years, was to become the firmament of his credo of political rebirth. That, given the hopelessness of such a situation, he discerned a third way is a testament to his obstinacy. It is also a reminder that the web of history is often too complex to allow for easy predictions.

Notes

1. *White's Devonshire Gazette* (1850), p. 462; Charles Worthy, *Ashburton and Its Neighbourhood* (Ashburton, Devon: L. B. Varder, 1875).

2. *Gauntlet,* 17 February 1833; *Carlile's Political Register,* 23 November 1839.

3. Carlile described his father as "much too talented to apply himself to any of the ordinary business of life." Quoted in Theophila C. Campbell, *The Battle of the Press as Told in the Story of the Life of Richard Carlile* (London: A. & H. B. Bonner, 1899), p. 8. His father's relatives produced a local Ashburton soda. *Universal British Directory of Trade, Commerce, and Manufacture* (1796), p. 62.

4. The words were penned by him on hearing of her death (*Republican,* 31 March 1820).

5. Richard Carlile, *Church Reform: The Only Means to That End: Stated in a Letter to Sir Robert Peel, Bart, First Lord of the Treasury, etc.* (London: Richard Carlile, 1835), p. 43.

6. The Bourne School was founded in 1754 by two local MPs. (*London and Provincial New Commercial Directory,* 1823-1824, p. 203.) For historical background on schools of this type, see M. G. Jones, *The Charity School Movement: A Study of Eighteenth Century Puritanism in Action* (Cambridge: Cambridge University Press, 1935); R. R. Sellman, *Devon Village Schools in the Nineteenth Century* (Newton Abbot, Devon: David & Charles, 1967).

7. It is stated incorrectly that Carlile attended the Ashburton Grammar School, in William H. Wickwar, *The Struggle for the Freedom of the Press, 1819-1832* (London: George Allen & Unwin, 1928), p. 68, and W. S. Graf, *Ashburton Grammar School: The Story of Six Hundred Years* (Ashburton, Devon: S. T. Elson, 1938), p. 52.

8. *Carlile's Political Register,* 14 December 1839; *Republican,* 5 May 1820, 28 January 1825.

9. Cooper asserted: "Mine has been almost entirely self-education, all the way through life." *The Life of Thomas Cooper, Written by Himself* (London: Hodder and Stoughton, 1869), p. 43. Another formidable autodidact was William Lovett, the Chartist leader, who was educated at a charity school before being apprenticed to a ropemaker. *Life and Struggles of William Lovett, in his Pursuit of Bread, Knowledge & Freedom* (London: MacGibbon & Kee, 1967, reprint), pp. 1-17. Alexander Somerville tells of a quarrier, unable to read until after his marriage, who walked twenty miles every Sunday to borrow books on astronomy. Somerville, *The Autobiography of a Working Man, by "One Who Has Whistled at the Plough"* (London: Charles Gilpin, 1848), pp. 17-18.

10. *Republican,* 3 March 1820. His employer was a druggist named Edward Lee.

11. The best description of tinplate working is in *The Book of Trades; or, Library of the Useful Arts,* 6th ed. (London: R. Phillips, 1815), pp. 104-10. See also F. W. Gibbs, "The Rise of the Tin-Plate Industry: 1. The Tinplate Worker," *Annals of Science,* 6 (1948-1950), pp. 390-403; W. E. Minchinton, *The British Tinplate Industry: A History* (Oxford: Clarendon Press, 1957).

12. *Republican,* 9 May 1823.

13. He later wrote: "I consider that I rescued myself from the perpetual labour of a mechanic's bench, solely by temperate and studious habits." *New Year's Address to Reformers of Great Britain,* 1 January 1821.

14. Helpful in understanding this aspect of Carlile's mind have been R. K. Webb, *Harriet Martineau: A Radical Victorian* (New York: Columbia University Press, 1960); Norman Cohn, *The Pursuit of the Millennium* (London: Secker & Warburg, 1957); J. F. C. Harrison, *The Second Coming: Popular Millenarianism, 1780-1850* (New Brunswick, New Jersey: Rutgers University Press, 1979), chs. 7-8.

15. See *Isis,* 23 August 1832; Carlile to William Holmes, 24 August 1825, Carlile Papers, Henry E. Huntington Library, San Marino, California (henceforth referred to as C.P.). "The whole of my apprenticeship," Carlile wrote, consisted of "nothing but conspiracies, rebellions and battles." *Republican,* 3 March 1820.

16. *Republican,* 30 May 1823; *New Year's Address to the Reformers,* 1 January 1821. His fellow tinplate workers remained, as he expressed it, "much more fond of beer and gin, then of infidelity." *Lion,* 17 October 1828.

17. *Besley's Devonshire Chronicle,* 18 August 1840; *Republican,* 26 November 1824. See Allen Brockett, *Nonconformity in Exeter, 1650-1875* (Manchester: Exeter University Press, 1962), pp. 172-75; Isaac Carter, *The Unguarded Atheist* (Portsea, 1823).

18. *Scourge for the Littleness of "Great" Men,* 18 October 1834.

19. The words are in a petition from Carlile to the Lord Mayor of London, 11 March 1831, C.P.

20. The dates are: Richard, 25 March 1814; Alfred, 25 February 1816; Thomas Paine, 14 April 1818. All three boys were born in London and baptized in St. George, Bloomsbury. Baptismal Register of St. George. Bloomsbury, London County Record Office.

21. *Republican,* 28 January 1825.

22. For a discussion of this discontent, see E. P. Thompson, *The Making of the English Working Class* (London: Victor Gollancz, 1963);

R. J. White, *Waterloo to Peterloo* (London: William Heinemann, 1957); Olive Rudkin, *Thomas Spence and His Connections* (London: George Allen & Unwin, 1927).

23. *Republican,* 28 January 1825. Stanley J. Benham, *Under Five Generations: The Story of Benham and Sons Ltd* (London, 1937).

24. For the impact of public houses on the cultural life of the nineteenth-century artisan, see Brian Harrison's brilliant essay, "Pubs," in H. J. Dyos and M. Wolff (eds.), *The Victorian City: Images and Reality* (Leicester: Leicester University Press, 1973), vol. 1, pp. 161-90; and Brian Harrison, *Drink and the Victorians: The Temperance Question in England, 1815-1872* (London: Faber and Faber, 1971), pp. 37-63.

2

THE MAKING OF A
RADICAL REFORMER

In December 1816 Carlile was still an obscure tinplateman, not yet ready to identify his situation with that of other workingmen. He was aloof from the demands for political reform that were beginning to attract many artisans and unskilled workers. Within three years all had changed. He had become a spokesman for the politically conscious poor, a journalist of influence in working-class circles, and, to boot, a convicted blasphemer who faced the prospect of a lengthy period of imprisonment.

How and why did these changes occur? What enabled Carlile to gain a leading position in radical politics? Why did he become involved in politics in the first place? The answers to these questions are not obvious, for initially luck and determination had as much to do with them as inner conviction. Carlile was the sort of man (not unusual among reformers) for whom emotional commitment precedes intellectual zest. When aroused, for whatever reason, he became a formidable combatant. Those who called his integrity into question or attempted to circumscribe his freedom of action induced in him a powerful response. At such times his stubbornness increased in intensity, and personal grievances became transmuted into political consciousness. A series of such changes, sketched against a background of social and political unrest, shaped Carlile's life between 1817 and 1819, as well as those of many of his working-class contemporaries.

A spate of reform activities characterized these formative years in British history. There were processions by torchlight on windswept Yorkshire moors; crowded gatherings in public houses in London and the provinces; confrontations with constables and magistrates in northern textile villages; military drills; whispered contacts between small groups of radical reformers. In June 1817, local magistrates suppressed an insurrection of stockingers and day laborers in Pentrich, Derbyshire. In the same month two political trials took place in London: those of the journalist Thomas J. Wooler for seditious libel and of the Spencean reformer, Dr. James Watson, for high treason. Both resulted in acquittals. Informers—paid and self-appointed—attended political meetings, seeking to uncover traces of sedition and blasphemy.[1]

In this alternative world of radical print and exuberant speechmaking, aspiring leaders of reform jostled for advantage. From public platforms Thomas Spence's followers urged the parish control of land, while in the cheap radical press erudite and semiliterate scribblers, with noms de guerre such as "Brutus" and "A Friend to Radical Reform," propounded schemes for national regeneration. The tapestry of reform was woven of many threads. There was the venerable Major Cartwright, whose support for universal suffrage derived from his belief in a mythical Anglo-Saxon past; Robert Owen, just then beginning to disseminate a message of universal cooperation; and Robert Wedderburn, a former Jamaican slave who established several "chapels" where radical sermons were preached and dissident works of theology discussed.[2] William Cobbett and "Orator" Hunt were the two leading advocates of parliamentary reform. The former was a disputatious journalist whose *Political Register* trumpeted the evils of paper money and inequitable taxation, the latter a gifted speaker who presented the case for political democracy in simplistic, though compelling, terms. Portents of change were everywhere and opportunities rife for young men to make their marks as reformers. A willingness to run risks for the cause of reform was requisite for success, as were perseverance and the ability to articulate some facet of the public discontent. Most useful were unlimited reserves of moral indignation.

Carlile's temperament suited this situation perfectly, and in the winter of 1816-1817, when Masterman, Matthews and Company reduced his hours of work, his political convictions began to crystallize. For the first time he commenced reading political tracts and attending reform meetings. The latter included two gatherings held in Spa Fields, London, which were addressed by Hunt and widely publicized in radical journals. Both meetings were charged with tension, and incidents of violence occurred after each, including an attack on a gunsmith's shop in Smithfield and some disturbances in the Minories.³ Still a passive spectator, Carlile was content to absorb the rhetoric around him, but he rapidly began to espouse the grievances of the disaffected poor, especially their demands for equal political rights and a reduction of taxation. At the beginning of 1817, he wrote several short essays, the first that he attempted. These mixed crude sloganizing with unsophisticated analysis and are a pastiche of working-class writing of the time. One piece by Carlile included the hackneyed observation, "Gold and silver have I none, but such as I have I give unto thee"; another was rejected by Cobbett with the acerbic comment, "A half-employed mechanic is too violent." None of these early essays were published.⁴

Several weeks later, in March 1817, Carlile made what was to be the most important decision of his life: he gave up tinplate working and began to devote himself full time to radical reform. Many penny and two-penny political journals were circulating in London and the provinces, and he plunged enthusiastically into the thicket of this excitement. He hawked in the streets Cobbett's *Political Register*, William Hone's *Reformists' Register*, a two-penny newspaper that published accounts of reform meetings, and, with particular fervor, Wooler's *Black Dwarf*, a popular journal that advocated radical political changes, including an extension of the suffrage. "Many a day," Carlile subsequently observed, he "traversed thirty miles for a profit of eighteen pence."⁵ His tale was embellished in its retelling, but there is a nub of truth to it. For as soon as his political convictions began to take shape, stubborn and hostile to authority as he was, he gave effect to them with total commitment.

Shortly after becoming a vendor of tracts and journals Carlile began to make the acquaintance of working-class journalists and publishers and to learn some of the techniques of political communication from them. Thomas Wooler, trained as a printer and skilled in legal controversy, proffered technical advice to him about publishing (which became particularly useful in March 1817, when the government headed by Lord Liverpool suspended the common law protection of habeas corpus), while two other struggling writers, Thomas Dolby and Thomas Davison, shared their more aggressive political attitudes with him.⁶ The most important contact that Carlile made, however, was with another young journalist, William T. Sherwin. Sherwin was his junior by eight years. An exceptionally able writer who had been dismissed for political reasons from a minor office in Northamptonshire, Sherwin had come to London in the winter of 1816-1817 and in March 1817 had launched the *Republican,* a short-lived weekly whose chief claim to fame is to have revived the flagging "radical" reputation of the poet laureate, Robert Southey, by reprinting a cheap edition of his celebrated political poem "Wat Tyler." In April, after the demise of the *Republican,* Sherwin commenced a more substantial and influential paper, *Sherwin's Weekly Political Register,* which continued to circulate until the summer of 1819.[7]

Shortly after he began to publish the *Weekly Political Register,* Sherwin concluded an informal business agreement with Carlile that enabled both men to make a more effective contribution to radical journalism. Sherwin undertook to print and edit the journal and to support it financially; Carlile, eager to make a name for himself, became its nominal publisher (although his name did not appear in print) with legal responsibility for it in the event of a prosecution. The risks he took were considerable because the home secretary, Lord Sidmouth, issued a circular in March 1817, urging magistrates to apprehend publishers who sold "blasphemous and seditious" writings. As the publisher of an aggressively radical journal, Carlile had also to take into account the possibility of a prosecution for seditious libel, a common method of dealing with political opponents.[8] Yet all of this seemed worthwhile to him. For one thing, prison appeared no worse than starvation or the workhouse, the other alternatives awaiting many of the unemployed poor. More important, Sherwin gave Carlile the use of a portion of his premises at 183 Fleet Street where he could pursue the independent calling of a "printer and publisher." This fortified him for the daunting political tasks that lay ahead by conferring "respectable" status upon him.[9]

Thus steeled from the spring of 1817 on, Carlile devoted himself unreservedly to the cause of reform. The contrast with Sherwin was clear. The latter had a fine intellect and some journalistic talent, but he was unable to match his enthusiasm to his objectives. For Carlile the reverse was true. Able to identify viscerally with whatever cause he took up, he shaped vistas out of unpromising material and brought energy to bear upon seemingly intractable enterprises. From the outset of their relationship Sherwin demurred in the face of political pressures, while Carlile grew strong even on the craggiest political terrain. Between 1817 and 1819 the two men worked closely together, but it was Carlile who invariably took the lead in their enterprises. He published tracts under his own imprint: with Sherwin's backing whenever possible, without it (by paying a contract printer) when the circumstances warranted. Only infrequently did he earn more than a small profit from the sale of his pamphlets. But his willingness to commit all of his financial and emotional resources to publishing, and his determination to conquer all, gave him a decided advantage over other radical journalists.

By 1818 the streets of Westminster and the City of London were awash with cheap tracts published by Carlile. These included a reprint of Southey's *Wat Tyler*; a volume of Tom Paine's collected political writings; a precis of *The Principles of Government*, an eighteenth-century political tract by Sir William Jones written in the form of a dialogue between a peasant and a scholar; reprints of three political parodies by William Hone; and miscellaneous pamphlets, which, among other things, advocated emigration to the United States as a means of alleviating economic distress and promoted the ideas of radical luminaries such as Cobbett, Hunt, and Sir Francis Burdett.[10] Carlile wrote introductions to several of these pamphlets, avowing his belief that "despotism trembles at the thought of being resisted" and that Britain was a "continued mass of Corruption, Falsehood, Hypocrisy, and Slander," whose inhabitants were "struggling under a corrupt administration, a corrupt legislation, executed by corrupt and partial men, and a base system of espionage."[11] But his primary objective was to create a favorable climate for reform by, if necessary, publicizing the views of other writers. These early tracts therefore demonstrate little consistency of vision. What was striking about them was their appearance in impressive quantity and variety, heralding a new name in London journalism.

Between 1817 and 1819, Carlile also devoted considerable time to *Sherwin's Weekly Political Register*, composing many of that paper's leaders (though these were all formally signed by Sherwin), writing articles under the pseudonym "Plebeian," and helping to put weekly copy together. His retrospective judgment that "Sherwin was bold, because I was responsible for all his writings and urged him to be bold" has the smack of truth about it.[12] But Sherwin was not a cipher. It was from him that Carlile learned the techniques of political writing that were to serve him so well in future years. And it was with the encouragement of the younger man that his radicalism began to acquire a distinctive shape.

Most of the opinions expressed by Sherwin and Carlile were very similar. In common with other working-class journalists, they attacked kings, boroughmongers, lawyers, fundholders, priests, magistrates, "consumers of taxes," and, in Carlile's magniloquent phrase, the "despotism, which seeks at once to destroy, and which has nearly destroyed everything that is valuable amongst us."[13] High taxation and an unfair distribution of goods in relationship to labor were adjudged by them to be among the country's most besetting evils. The mass of poor people, intoned Sherwin, will not be "content that the greater half of the produce of their labour should be taken from them and given to the CONSUMERS OF TAXES."[14] Particularly singled out for condemnation were savings banks (then being introduced in London and other cities), which they described as "affiliated branches of the funding system" whose purpose was to transform the laborer into a fundholder.[15]

The Sherwin-Carlile critique of the status quo was rooted in their belief that political and economic equality were necessary underpinnings of national prosperity. Reflecting the grievances of the working classes during these years, it drew for sustenance upon the writings of Cobbett on bureaucracy and taxation, Hunt on universal suffrage, and, increasingly, Tom Paine for almost everything else. Paine's political analyses were refashioned in almost every page of the *Weekly Political Register*. "The people," wrote Sherwin, "have no other choice than OPEN RESISTANCE, or UNCONDITIONAL SLAVERY." "All power, whatever it may call itself, which does not emanate from the People, is unjust, and contrary to the RIGHTS OF MAN," he observed in words nearly identical with those of Paine in the *Rights of Man*.[16] Carlile and Sherwin likewise affirmed that "the People of every nation have a right to make what alteration or amendment they think proper, either in their form of Government, or in anything else, with which their welfare is concerned, or connected."[17] Though phrased abstractly, these expressions of working-class sentiment occasionally struck resonances of class feeling, as in this comment on the plight of the poor: "If the *rich* treat the *poor* with inhumanity they must take the consequences, and as the poor have not the privilege to avail themselves of the 'vengeance of the law', their enemies ought not to complain when they sometimes exercise the vengeance of their passions." In a similar vein is this Carlile-Sherwin comment on a strike by Manchester cotton spinners: "There may be some of the masters who are not as bad as the others, but viewing the case generally, it is a conspiracy not merely of the employers, but of the employees and the agents and tools of the Government for the purpose of robbing the Labourer of the fair fruits of his industry."[18]

Given Carlile's subsequent interest in theological reform, it comes as something of a surprise that the *Weekly Political Register* virtually ignored religion. To be sure, the paper contained allusions to "black slugs" and "drones" (priests), common enough in the radical press, and it attacked clerical "gluttony" and "corruption." But Christianity as such was immune from criticism as it was not, for example, in the militantly deist *Theological Comet*, a one-and-a-half penny weekly, or in the popular *Cap of Liberty*, a paper that condemned "the absurdity of the Christian, and the immorality and absurdity of the Jewish religions, or rather doctrines."[19] Almost certainly, Sherwin enforced a policy of restraint in this area. But it is also the case that Carlile, committed as he was to radical political reform, did not begin to engross himself in antichristianity until December 1818, by which time he and Sherwin were drifting apart.

From March 1817, Carlile may be characterized as an energetic foot soldier in the ranks of a miscellaneous army of working-class reformers. His obduracy was beginning to mark him out for advancement, but as yet he did little more than to repeat the ideas of others. Feelings of inferiority weighed heavily on him. He had a dumpy physical appearance; his West Country speech sounded awkward to London workers on those infrequent occasions when he attempted public oratory; and he was conscious of the inadequacies of his formal education. Yet singleness of purpose could, as he realized, compensate for many defects. And by becoming the champion of free speech and, less loftily, a conduit for transmitting Paine's ideas to the working classes, he was able within a short period of time to make considerable strides.

Some of Carlile's initial successes as a reformer resulted from his involvement with the blasphemy prosecutions of William Hone in 1817, which are a significant episode in the evolution of a free press. Hone was an unlikely candidate for political martyrdom. He was a Tottenham bookseller whose links to reform were primarily entrepreneurial. His journalistic activities—as editor of the *Reformists' Register* and collaborator on political squibs with the celebrated caricaturist George Cruikshank—expressed, at best, a tempered radicalism. However, he had the good fortune to be the object of a misconceived prosecution and to have a mantle of public integrity thrust upon him.[20]

Hone wrote and published three political parodies in December 1816: *John Wilkes's Catechism, Political Litany*, and *Sinecurist's Creed.* These fulminated against bishops, placemen, fundholders, "corruptionists," and "place-givers everlasting," but they were not particularly controversial other than in their liturgical formulation.[21] Furthermore, as he zestfully demonstrated at his trials, political parodies had been used innumerable times by reformers and had come to be regarded as no more threatening to those in power than critical newspaper articles. The decision to prosecute him for blasphemous libel, therefore, for spreading "impiety and irreligion" among the masses, understandably surprised many reformers.

Hone's response was conciliatory. He agreed to withdraw the offending parodies from sale, which almost certainly would have led to the dropping of charges against him. But Carlile intervened in August 1817, precipitating a bitter rift with the Liverpool government and creating a cause célèbre. He did this by reprinting the parodies, notwithstanding Hone's threats to sue him for breach of copyright. Carlile's aims were political. He wanted, by training the "clear light" of criticism on the "National Plunderer," to challenge the Tory government to do battle.[22] He was also seeking to exploit a market for radical journalism. The one thing he assuredly was not trying to do was what he was accused of: making a "blasphemous" statement about religion.

Taken into custody almost as soon as the parodies were placed on sale in his Fleet Street shop, Carlile, like Hone, was incarcerated in King's Bench Prison, on the south side of the Thames. He was accused of blasphemy and also of seditious libel for having published an article in the *Weekly Political Register* in which it was maintained that the poor were being enslaved politically.[23] But the similarity of treatment of the two reformers ended at this point. Hone, less "plebeian" than Carlile and much better placed politically, was freed on his own recognizances, and, in December 1817, he gained renown by winning three successive acquittals in the Guildhall. He defended himself skillfully against charges that the parodies were, in the words of Chief Justice Abbott, "highly scandalous, and irreligious."[24] With much wit he persuaded the jurors that "Old Bags" (Nicholas Vansittart), "Derry Down Triangle" (Viscount Castlereagh), and the "Doctor" (Viscount Sidmouth)— were political, not religious, butts.[25] When the acquittals were announced reformers took to the streets, shouting accolades for Hone and contempt for a government that in their view had distorted the objectives of its critics.

For Carlile, the results of incarceration were considerably less gratifying. Unknown except to a small number of working-class reformers, he was, legally speaking, discarded; after four months of imprisonment the charges against him were dropped when the verdicts on Hone became known.[26] He had prepared for an imagined moment of judicial triumph when, as with Hone, London's reformers would shout huzzahs for his integrity and fortitude. But the time never came. His name was not mentioned at Hone's trials, and his release from the King's Bench Prison was accompanied neither by publicity nor public cheers. Only a handful of activists accompanied him to his Bloomsbury lodgings on a cold December day, while the bulk of London's reformers were caught up in the rejoicing for Hone.[27]

Carlile's initial contact with prison had a significant effect on him. For the first time he experienced full blown the ups and downs of political fortune, and he could barely hold back feelings of resentment. Why, he asked himself, were the rewards so disproportionate for himself and Hone? How could the government have brought charges of blasphemy against him when he had not even begun to read seriously the writings of freethinkers or to disseminate ideas about religion? He felt miffed, but he resolved—however fickle the "mob"—to champion free expression and to overcome "CORRUPTION'S HOST." Nothing but fixity of purpose and his own integrity, he told himself, would be allowed to affect his future actions.

As a token of his renewed sense of purpose, Carlile published a parody of his own devising from "Law's Hole, Surrey" (King's Bench Prison), which was intended to complement those of Hone. Entitled *The Order for the Administration of the Loaves and Fishes,* it was a creditable effort. Carlile never possessed a talent for subtle analysis, his instrument of attack invariably being the bludgeon rather than the scalpel. But in this parody, he reworked whimsically a familiar litany of radical grievances. His language was rhythmic and his peroration not unduly strident. Here, for example, is his "Creed for the Use of Corruption's Host": "I believe in Lord Castlereagh, the Supreme Director of all our affairs, maker of treaties for all nations, for the benefit of none; and in the excellence of his features, fundamental and unfundamental." And his comments on financial policy: "I believe in the stability of the funds, I look not for a remission of taxes, no, not till the Resurrection of the Dead."[28]

While composing *The Order for the Administration of the Loaves and Fishes,* Carlile began to develop an interest in theology. If he could amuse his readers with the form of antichristianity, why not attempt its substance? The Tories had willfully confused legitimate political criticism with blasphemy. Was there not a case for investigating the relationship between the two and sharing the results with his readers? The question was tentative as yet because by his own admission he had only just begun to read Paine and other "infidel" writers such as Volney, Edward Gibbon, and the American deist, Elihu Palmer. But Carlile's evolution as a radical freethinker stems, to some extent, from the Hone episode. Not for the first time had a government, in its eagerness to suppress dissent, produced results that were the reverse of those intended.

Shortly after gaining his freedom, Carlile plunged into a maelstrom of political and journalistic activities. He made the acquaintance of many working-class agitators, some of whom talked wildly about revolution while a few tried tentatively to put their plans into effect. Disaffection was widespread during 1817 and 1818 (as the reports of Home Office informers record so indelibly) and Carlile was an excited, if marginal, participant in its manifestations. He participated in many political meetings, while continuing to forgo an active role. Prior to his imprisonment he had attended the famous meeting at the London Tavern where Robert Owen had enunciated publicly for the first time his views on social cooperation. Carlile was unimpressed by Owen (he described him as a "fame-seeking opinionate" who "by far exceeds all other fanatics") and was drawn to meetings with a distinctively political rather than economic flavor, including several organized by Hunt, and by Dr.

James Watson, Arthur Thistlewood, and other Spencean agitators whom he knew personally.[29]

More important, Carlile became a working journalist, adding considerably to his output of tracts and pamphlets and making a tangible, if still limited, contribution to the evolution of a radical press. In addition to *Sherwin's Weekly Political Register*, he published two newspapers in 1818: the *Gracchus*, a moderate reform journal edited by John Whitehead, which survived for only one number, and the much better-known *Gorgon*, edited by John Wade, Francis Place, and John Gast, which combined support for trade unionism with an advocacy of capitalist political economy. Carlile published the first eight numbers of the *Gorgon* (one additional number appeared), while disassociating himself from "the [economic] tendency of the journal," which he regarded as too sympathetic to the middle classes.[30]

In June 1818, he participated in Hunt's abortive campaign in Westminster for a seat in the House of Commons. This was the only electoral contest that ever absorbed Carlile's energies fully, and it is an interesting, though unduly neglected, political event. Hunt was the first candidate for a seat in Parliament to run on a platform of universal suffrage and annual elections, and his soliciting of support among the unenfranchised artisans and workingmen of Westminster attracted considerable attention in radical circles. The contest tugged fiercely at the loyalties of reformers because Hunt's two leading opponents, Sir Francis Burdett and Major John Cartwright, had significant working-class backing. T. J. Wooler, subsequently a staunch ally of Hunt, opposed his candidacy in the pages of his influential *Black Dwarf*, while Cobbett, a lifelong opponent, supported him from Long Island, New York, where he had taken refuge several months before to avoid a prosecution for seditious libel.[31]

Carlile was a diligent member of Hunt's entourage, churning out numerous placards and tracts from his shop at 183 Fleet Street. He helped to advertise Hunt's many speaking engagements and to solicit support among the poorer inhabitants of Westminster. He also supervised the preparation of political banners, including one that bore the exhilarating slogan "Hunt and Liberty," and which, in August 1819, was ostentatiously borne aloft by reformers at Peterloo.[32]

Notwithstanding the enthusiasm of many workingmen (most of

whom were unable to vote), Hunt was beaten decisively after a campaign lasting three weeks. A derisory eighty-four votes were cast for him; two pro-reform rivals, Burdett and Sir Samuel Romilly, were returned to Parliament instead. But for Carlile these were invigorating weeks. In his own mind he was transformed from a tractseller and publisher of ephemeral works into an "agent" for Hunt, an inspiring event for a young reformer.[33] Hunt's name was a byword among reformers, and to appear at his side in the historic streets of Westminster, attracting applause and support, was uplifting. Political millennialism was in the air, and Carlile absorbed bits and pieces of it, while infusing it with a moral energy particular to himself.[34] He collected radical ideas as if they were pieces of a jigsaw puzzle to be cobbled together at his leisure. Cobbett's hatred for taxation, Hunt's democratic slogans, the haphazard conversations of street agitators: these and other strands of discontent contributed to his development as a radical reformer.

Above all, there was the overarching figure of Paine. From the summer of 1817 on, Carlile began to treat Paine's writings with reverence and to use them to sharpen his theological and political insights. They were, he stated, "the only standard political writings that are worth a moment's notice." By reading Paine, "I assumed courage," he told his associates. "The more I read the more I was convinced of their importance."[35] Although he subsequently employed Paine's ideas in different ways to fit changing circumstances, his enthusiasm for them never flagged. More than any other reformer of the early nineteenth century, Carlile popularized Paine, making him accessible to a working-class audience that was becoming literate.

Even before Paine's death in 1809, his writings had come under attack. In the *Rights of Man*, written in the 1790s, he had challenged Edmund Burke's conservative interpretation of the French Revolution and produced a book of seminal importance in the history of popular reform. Part Two of the *Rights of Man*, in particular, by its plea for republicanism and political democracy, inspired a generation of artisans and laborers.[36] Other of Paine's writings were equally contentious. The *Decline and Fall of the English System of Finance*, published in 1797, attacked the use of paper money and gave intellectual sustenance to reformers like Cobbett who were searching for arguments to be used against taxation.[37] *Agrarian Justice*, published in the same year, was likewise fiercely radical. Its major theme was that uncultivated land was "the common property of the human race" and that, therefore, a ground-rent, or inheritance tax, should be levied on landowners for the support of the poor.

Most unsettling to conservatives, however, was the *Age of Reason*, the book in which Paine condemned the "superstitions" and inconsistencies of the Christian scriptures in language understood by working-class readers. (He did this largely from memory since much of the book was written while he was confined in Paris's Luxembourg prison during the French Revolution.) Ironically, his purpose in advocating a "revolution in the system of religion" was to defend the outworks of theistic belief against atheism. But neither his Christian detractors nor his "infidel" supporters regarded him in this light, and the book's three parts, published between 1793 and 1795, were denounced and praised with equal vehemence— and suppressed repeatedly.[38]

Carlile believed that the lineaments of Paine's writings offered a framework for radical reform. But he discovered that because of prosecutions, the bulk of Paine's writings was available only in limited editions or not at all. As early as 1817, therefore, he took it upon himself to rectify this. Previous working-class publishers of Paine, including Daniel Eaton and Thomas Williams, had been fined and imprisoned for their efforts, and so his decision was a difficult one.[39] But Carlile believed that cheap editions of Paine's writings would generate a strong momentum for reform and pose a decisive challenge to the government.

In August 1817, at the outset of his incarceration in King's Bench Prison, he began to reprint Paine's political essays. He published *Common Sense, Rights of Man, Crisis, Address to the Addressers*, and other well-known tracts; initially these appeared in parts in the *Weekly Political Register*, then in two-penny sheets under separate cover. Beginning in the following January, he also issued these essays in bound volumes. These varying methods of distribution, all at popular prices, were effective. Paine's political writings (and, subsequently, his theological works) appeared with Carlile's imprint in 1818, 1819, 1820, and thereafter at irregular intervals. No effort was spared to make them as complete and accurate as possible, and for a time Carlile virtually cornered the market. But increasingly he had to contend with competition from William Hone, B. D. Cousins, James Watson, and other radical publishers, none of whom recognized Paine as Carlile's exclusive "moral property."[40]

To complement the publication of Paine's writings, Carlile and Sherwin (who assisted in the publication of several early editions) wrote biographies of Paine, which made their way onto nineteenth-century radical and freethought publishing lists. Sherwin's more substantial *Memoir of the Life of Thomas Paine* appeared first, in July 1819. Drawing upon correspondence with Paine's friends and acquaintances, it competed for the support of reformers with Clio Rickman's impressionistic memoir that was published at about the same time.[41] Sherwin was the first writer to rebut accusations of personal weakness and of a deathbed "recantation" against Paine. "In political enquiry he was without an equal," commented Sherwin, "and in theological discussion he . . . laboured more efficiently than any other man to free the world from the trammels of intolerance, prejudice, and superstition."[42] Notwithstanding its moderate tone, the biography formed the basis for a successful prosecution of Jane Carlile by the Society for the Suppression of Vice in February 1820.

Carlile's *Life of Thomas Paine,* published in November 1820, was less ambitious than Sherwin's, and it reveals nearly as much about its biographer as about the subject of his study. Carlile praised Paine lavishly: he was "the first and best of writers on political economy"; a man of incorruptible character; a "child of nature" who had warred unceasingly against privilege and superstition.[43] The most readable passages of the *Life,* though, are those in which he drew parallels between himself and Paine. Both men had been prosecuted unjustly, he maintained (the *Life* appeared after Carlile's conviction for blasphemy in October 1819), and both were abandoned by friends and supporters. Oversimplified as this theme was, it nonetheless helped to make Carlile's biography a popular one with American as well as British radical reformers.[44]

The reprinting of Paine's political writings enhanced Carlile's reputation in working-class circles, and he now became determined to attract publicity to himself even at the cost of imprisonment. He saw himself as an astringent critic of authority who was rapidly acquiring influence and reputation. The best way to keep up the offensive was, he believed, by means of theological controversy.

Several London acquaintances, including Clio Rickman, Paine's biographer, pushed him in this direction, and in December 1818 he issued a cheap edition of the *Age of Reason*, which had not been sold legally in Britain since 1797. Repetitive, simplistic in structure, unabashedly popular in style, it had aroused the feelings of workingmen in the revolutionary decade of the 1790s. Hoping once more to stir the embers of controversy, Carlile threw himself wholeheartedly into its publication.

Notes

1.See the accounts in Thompson, *Making of the English Working Class*, pp. 607-69; White, *Waterloo to Peterloo*, pp. 55-133; and T. M. Parsinnen, "The Revolutionary Party in London, 1816-20," *Bulletin of the Institute for Historical Research*, 45 (1972), pp. 266-82.

2. Wedderburn, an obscure reformer, is of some interest. He was convicted of blasphemy in 1820 and imprisoned for two years in Dorchester Gaol, where he was treated more harshly than Carlile. He published several tracts and gave lectures on theology until as late as 1828. There is an account of his blasphemy trial in *Wooler's British Gazette*, 27 February 1820. See also *People*, 28 June 1817; *Republican*, 5 July 1822; Carlile to William Holmes, 14 May 1822, C.P.

3. Carlile wrote: "I shared the general distress of 1816, and it was this that opened my eyes." *Republican*, 1 March 1822. On the Spa Fields meetings, see *The Meeting in Spa Fields* (London: William Hone, 1816) and *The Riots in London* (London: William Hone, 1816).

4. *Republican*, 1 March 1822, 28 January 1825; Campbell, *Battle of the Press*, p. 13.

5. *Republican*, 3 March 1820.

6. On Thomas Davison, who edited the *Medusa* (1819-1820) and the *London Alfred* (1819), and was Carlile's printer before being imprisoned for blasphemy in 1820, see Joel H. Wiener, "Thomas Davison," in Joseph O. Baylen and Norbert J. Gossman (eds.), *Biographical Dictionary of Modern Radicals*, vol. 1: *1770-1830* (Hassocks, Sussex: Harvester Press, 1979), pp. 114-16. For Dolby, see *Memoirs of Thomas Dolby, Formerly of Sawtry, in Huntingdonshire, Late Printer and Publisher, of Catherine Street, Strand, London* (1827). Files of the *Black Dwarf*, *Wooler's British Gazette*, and other radical newspapers contain useful information about all these journalists.

7. The most detailed account of Sherwin's life is by Joel H. Wiener, "William T. Sherwin," in Baylen and Gossman, *Biographical Dictionary*, vol. 1, pp. 445-46.

8. A summary and analysis of the legal actions taken against the press is to be found in Wickwar, *Struggle for the Freedom of the Press,* pp. 13-48.

9. Carlile could not afford to buy a printing press, and all of his printing was done by others. But he registered himself as a printer, a common practice among radical journalists. His earliest printers were Sherwin, Thomas Davison, and Thomas Moses. See Carlile to William Holmes, 24 August 1824; Carlile to Thomas Turton, 10 December 1822, C.P.

10. The Wat Tyler reprint, according to Carlile, "decided the success of my attempts to become a bookseller." *Republican,* 3 November 1826; *Isis,* 7 July 1832. Other publications by Carlile include: John Knight, *The Emigrant's Best Instructor* (1818); *Mr. Cobbett's Address to His Countrymen, on His Future Political Works* (1817); *The Speech by Sir Francis Burdett, Bart., in the House of Commons, on Tuesday, May 20, 1817* (1817).

11. Introduction by Carlile to his two-volume edition of Thomas Paine, *Political and Miscellaneous works* (1818); Introduction to *Contrast, or the Two Speeches* (1818), p. 2.

12. *To the Reformers of Great Britain,* 13 October 1821. Carlile's first piece as "Plebeian" appeared in *Sherwin's Weekly Political Register,* 31 May 1817. His contributions to the paper are filled with clichés of popular radicalism such as "corrupt and profligate system" and "Hospital of Incurables" (House of Lords).

13. *Sherwin's Weekly Political Register,* 31 May 1817.

14. Ibid., 7 June 1817.

15. "Plebeian" (Carlile) in ibid., 16 May 1818. Attacks upon savings banks were common among radicals. See, for example, ibid., 22, 29 August 1818.

16. "The operation of government is restricted to the making and administering of laws; but it is to a nation that the right of forming or reforming, generating or regenerating constitutions and governments belongs." Thomas Paine, *Rights of Man, Part Two* (Harmondsworth, Middlesex: Penguin, 1969), p. 170.

17. *Sherwin's Weekly Political Register,* 21 May 1817.

18. Ibid., 8, 29 August 1818.

19. *Cap of Liberty,* 6 October 1819. The objective of the *Theological Comet* was "TO ADVOCATE REASON, TO INQUIRE FOR TRUTH, TO DESTROY ILLUSION, AND TO SUPPRESS THE VILLAINOUS MANEUVRES of you, ye hypocrites!" *Theological Comet,* 24 July 1819.

20. The best biography of Hone is Frederick W. Hackwood, *William Hone: His Life and Times* (London: T. Fisher Unwin, 1912).

21. The full titles of Hone's parodies are: *The Political Litany, Dili-*

gently Revised to Be Said or Sung until the Appointed Change Come; The Late John Wilkes's Catechism of a Ministerial Member, Taken from an Original Manuscript in Mr. Wilkes's Handwriting Never before Printed, and Adapted to the Present Occasion; and The Sinecurist's Creed, or Belief, as the Same Can or May Be Sung or Said Throughout the Kingdom.

22. Carlile's challenge to the government was set out in his introduction to the second edition of Hone's *Political Litany*, which appeared in December 1817.

23. This number of *Sherwin's Weekly Political Register* (2 August 1817) also included a reprint of Cromwell's famous speech on the dissolution of the Long Parliament.

24. *The Three Trials of William Hone for Publishing Three Parodies* (London: William Hone, 1818), p. 48.

25. These famous characters perform in the *Sinecurist's Creed*, a hilarious parody on the doctrine of the trinity.

26. Several detained vendors were released when Hone was acquitted. But in 1819 Joseph Russell, a Birmingham printer, was tried and convicted for selling the parodies. *Black Dwarf*, 14 January 1819; William Hone to William Pare, 31 March 1819, Hone papers, Add. Ms. 40,108 f. 7, British Museum, hereafter B.M. Carlile was released on a recognizance of £100 in December 1817 although the charges against him were never officially withdrawn. T.S. 11, Box 945, Bundle 3465, Public Record Office (hereafter P.R.O.); *Sherwin's Weekly Political Register*, 18 April 1818.

27. Speakers at a congratulatory dinner in Hone's honor made no reference to Carlile. *Trial by Jury and Liberty of the Press: The Proceedings at the Public Meeting, Dec. 29, 1817, at the City of London Tavern* (London: William Hone, 1818). According to an informer, the Spencean agitators, Dr. James Watson and Arthur Thistlewood, gave Carlile support. 18 Dec. 1817, Home Office 40/8, P.R.O.

28. Richard Carlile, *The Order for the Administration of the Loaves and Fishes; on the Communion of Corruption's Host* (London: Richard Carlile, 1817), p. 8. The parody is reprinted in Guy Aldred (ed.), *Jail Journal* (Glasgow: Strickland Press, 1942), pp. 41-44.

29. For his criticisms of Owen, see the article by "Plebeian," *Sherwin's Weekly Political Register*, 20 September 1817.

30. *Gracchus*, 27 June 1818; *Gorgon*, 18 July 1818.

31. There is considerable material on the election in *Collection of Addresses, Pamphlets, Posters, Squibs, etc. Relating to the Election, 1818*, B.M., and the Place Newspaper Collection, vol. 20, f. 192, B.M. See also J. M. Main, "Radical Westminister, 1807-20," *Historical Studies* (Australia and New Zealand), 12 (1966), pp. 186-204.

32. On the banner, see Henry Hunt, *Addresses* (1820-1822), 11 February

1822. This is an appendix to *The Memoirs of Henry Hunt, Esq., Written by Himself*, 3 vols. (London: T. Dolby, 1820-1822); *Carlile's Political Register*, 7 December 1839.

33. *Lion*, 7 November 1828. Subsequently he wrote of Hunt: "Of all the quacks who ever quacked, since quackery commenced, Henry Hunt is the greatest." *Republican* 10 January 1823.

34. On the millennialism of this early period, see J. F. C. Harrison, *Robert Owen and the Owenites in Britain and America* (London: Routledge & Kegan Paul, 1969), pp. 91-139; Harrison, *Second Coming*; W. H. Oliver, "Owen in 1817: The Millennialist Moment," in S. Pollard and J. Salt (eds.), *Robert Owen: Prophet of the Poor* (London: Macmillan, 1971), pp. 166-87.

35. *Prompter*, 27 November 1830; *Republican*, 25 February 1820.

36. Thompson, *Making of the English Working Class*, pp. 87-115; Gwyn A. Williams, *Artisans and Sans-Culottes* (London: Edward Arnold, 1968), pp. 58-80; Moncure D. Conway, *The Life of Thomas Paine* (London: Watts & Co., 1909), pp. 228-47.

37. Cobbett's reworking took the title *Paper against Gold.*

38. For a moderate view, see Franklin K. Prochaska, "Thomas Paine's *The Age of Reason* Revisited," *Journal of the History of Ideas*, 33 (1972), pp. 561-76. Moncure Conway's assessment of the *Age of Reason* as "the uprising of the human HEART against Religion of Inhumanity" is, despite its ornateness, closer to the spirit of Paine. Conway, *Paine*, p. 235.

39. Eaton was made to stand in the pillory and imprisoned for eighteen months for publishing part three of the *Age of Reason* in 1812.

40. He ceased to have further dealings with William Benbow when the latter undersold him with an 1821 edition of Paine's political writings. *To the Reformers of Great Britain*, 13 October 1821, 20 December 1821.

41. The appearance of Rickman's *Life of Thomas Paine* led to a bitter feud with Sherwin that can be traced in the pages of *Shadgett's Weekly Review*, 24 April, 8, 15 May 1819.

42. W. T. Sherwin, *Memoir of the Life of Thomas Paine* (London: Richard Carlile, 1819), p. 228.

43. Richard Carlile, *Life of Thomas Paine*, 2d ed. (London: Richard Carlile, 1821), pp. 5, 12.

44. There were at least three editions of Carlile's *Life* (1820, 1821, c. 1824), as well as an American reprint.

3

BLASPHEMY AND SEDITION

The year 1819 was one of anticipation and setback for working-class reformers. Images abound: the portly figure of Cobbett disinterring Tom Paine's bones from a field in New Rochelle, New York, and carrying them back to England, only to lose them once again; Scottish weavers assembling on Glasgow Green to petition the prince regent for passage money to Canada; Lancashire cotton spinners drilling unarmed on the high moors above Saddleworth, "with a steadiness and regularity which would not have disgraced a regiment on parade."[1] At one meeting after another, radical workingmen in northern textile districts and in London's poorer quarters put forth demands for an extension of the franchise and a rectification of economic grievances. But their expectations of reform were dampened by the Peterloo Massacre in August, which created a sense of oppression that was not to be erased for many years. The enactment of the Six Acts at the end of the year—placing restraints on public meetings and almost extinguishing the radical press for a decade—exacerbated the plight of reformers and increased class tensions.

Carlile's activities during this year can best be explored within this framework of expectation and setback. At the outset of 1819 he was a publisher of radical tracts who was beginning to make a contribution to the reform movement; by the end of the year he was recognized as a standard-bearer of free expression. He had begun to articulate the political and religious grievances of workingmen; and, by his defiance of authority, to express their independence of spirit. Just as Peterloo dashed immediate prospects for reform, however, so too did Carlile fail to hold his supporters together. Popular freethought—the issue that he increasingly came to be identified with in 1819—was to be a solvent of radicalism and not its savior.

The publication of Paine's *Age of Reason* in December 1818 (part of a larger edition of his *Theological Works*), followed a month later by Elihu Palmer's American deist book *The Principles of Nature*, brought Carlile into conflict with the law. It once more unloosed the specter of blasphemy, a crime which, in the opinion of conservatives and many reformers, was destructive of the moral harmony of society. Other forms of political opposition—the advocacy of seditious ideas, for example—might under certain circumstances be tolerated. But blasphemy was too dire in its consequences. In the words of the Whig reformer, Thomas Erskine: "There was nothing for it but to crush the blasphemer at any hour."[2]

This was particularly true of the *Age of Reason*. It was a book, churchmen insisted, whose appeal was to "the level of the meanest capacity." To give sanction to the doctrines of the "infidel" Paine, especially at a time of political unrest, was to transcend the boundaries of acceptable behavior. "All the respectable part of society," commented one clergyman on the appearance of Carlile's edition of the *Age of Reason*, "should testify their abhorrence of those attempts now making to unsettle all the principles of mind."[3] With several blasphemy prosecutions having been commenced successfully in the years before 1819, there seemed little reason to suppose that Carlile would avoid a similar fate.

In legal terms he had to contend not only with the unsympathetic Tory government but with crusading private associations that were determined to suppress blasphemy, if need be with the help of paid informers and agents provocateurs. The best known of such groups was the Society for the Suppression of Vice and the Encouragement of Religion and Virtue, which had been established in 1802 to counteract the "poisonous effects of infidelity" and, in its inimitable phrasing, to curtail "undue freedom of thinking."[4] Since 1802 its activities had been aimed at the work of "infidel" publishers like Daniel Eaton, whom it prosecuted in 1812 for selling the *Age of Reason*, and at destroying all the "subsidiary" effects of blasphemy: obscenity, gambling, cruelty to animals, brothel keeping, profanation of the Sabbath. Carlile's action persuaded it to give its attention almost exclusively to radical journalism, however, and between 1819 and 1823 it was to initiate about 200 prosecutions of vendors and publishers, many of them aimed directly at Carlile.[5]

In January 1819, an intensive legal struggle began, involving the Vice Society, the Liverpool government, and Carlile. In an opening salvo, the Vice Society brought a common law indictment against Carlile, for being an "evil disposed and wicked person" and for selling the *Age of Reason*, a work containing "the foulest and most horrible blasphemy." Sir Samuel Shepherd, the attorney-general, then followed with an ex officio information couched in similar terms.[6] Private indictment and government information followed one another in almost vertiginous fashion until, by September, Carlile had become the target of between eight and a dozen prosecutions, at least four of them for blasphemous libel (passages cited were from the *Age of Reason* and Palmer's *Principles of Nature*) and four for seditious libel (offending passages were drawn from *Sherwin's Weekly Political Register* and the *Republican*, a journal that Carlile began to publish in August).[7] Because the Vice Society and the government were moving in tandem, Carlile and his supporters correctly inferred a symbiotic relationship between the two. But such a relationship was a common feature of criminal law in the early nineteenth century, at a time when many prosecutions were initiated privately and there were few constraints on the powers of magistrates.

Carlile's "blasphemy" was compounded in January 1819 when he began to issue the *Deist: or Moral Philospher*, a four-penny journal that initially appeared weekly and, thereafter, in an irregular format. The *Deist* was intended to "exterminate prejudice from the human mind" and to propagate a "genuine spirit of philosophy and free inquiry." But as its lengthy subtitle indicated— *Being an Impartial Inquiry After Moral and Theological Truths: Selected from the Writings of the Most Celebrated Authors in Ancient and Modern Times*—it was not a typical journal of opinion. Carlile wrote little for it; instead he filled its pages with reprints of freethought tracts, including Palmer's *Principles of Nature* (for which the Vice Society filed an information against him); Samuel Francis's *Watson Refuted: Being an Answer to the Apology for the Bible. In a Series of Letters to the Bishop of Llandaff*, a combative defense of Paine's deist views published initially in 1796; and Baron d'Holbach's *Christianity Unveiled: Being an Examination of the Principles and Effects of the Christian Religion*, an atheist pamphlet dating from the 1750s. Two important French tracts also appeared in English translation for the first time in the *Deist:*

d'Holbach's *Letters to Eugenia, on the Absurd, Contradictory, and Demoralizing Dogmas and Mysteries of the Christian Religion* (1768), and Voltaire's *Important Examination of the Holy Scriptures* (1736).[8] On a personal level, the *Deist* reinforced Carlile's growing interest in antichristian propaganda. Although he did not fight a personal battle in its pages, he took advantage of its publication to immerse himself in freethought literature. By the time he reluctantly placed the publication aside at the end of 1820 (it was revived briefly in 1826), he had become a freethinker in the fullest sense of the term, committed to extending the perimeters of anticlerical feeling and theological controversy at almost any cost.

The likelihood of imprisonment, which intimidated many reformers, merely strengthened Carlile's resolve. He reveled in the legal and political tribulations to which he was subjected during 1819. His hatred for the Vice Society and the Liverpool government was undiluted. He believed that the growing struggle for reform was between "all that can render life desirable or worth preserving" and "tyranny, fraud, and superstition." Priests, he asserted, were the "very bane of morality and civilization," their purpose being to strengthen the power of privileged groups in society at the expense of the poor. "Let us gird on the shield of reason, and drive those drones from our hives," he told his readers.[9]

In February, because he refused to stop selling the *Age of Reason* while charges were pending against him, Carlile was imprisoned for several days in Newgate Gaol at the behest of the Vice Society. His reply was a spirited four-penny tract entitled *A Letter to the Society for the Suppression of Vice, on Their Malignant Efforts to Prevent a Free Enquiry after Truth and Reason*. Christianity, he stated in this pamphlet, is "now experiencing its decay. . . . There is no hope of its regenerating or reviving." He described the radical press as a "dreadful park of artillery" that "will continue to open its destructive fire on superstition, bigotry, and religious despotism." What shall "check its career?" he asked. And, in words that were to serve as a prod to him during some of the dark days that followed, he averred: "Nor the fear of imprisonment, nor the fear of death shall deter me from a perseverance."[10]

His obstinacy was increased by the realization (understood by other journalists) that financial pickings were to be had from prosecutions. As his notoriety grew in the early months of 1819—

with conservative and radical newspapers placing the spotlight on him in differing ways—Carlile began for the first time to enjoy the fruits of journalism. A pamphlet that was likely to atrophy under ordinary circumstances might, he perceived, gain a renewed lease on life by prosecution; at the same time controversial books such as the *Age of Reason* could usefully be resuscitated. As he observed subsequently: "Prosecutions are life to me. I really enjoy them. They are intellectual banquets. I wish I could contract for all the harassment that may arise from them."[11]

The initial printing of the *Age of Reason,* in December 1818, was limited to 1000 copies. However, as soon as the prosecutions against him were commenced in January 1819, every copy was sold, and in the spring, without any assistance from Sherwin, Carlile brought out a second edition of 3000 copies. This too sold out before the end of the year despite the persistent harassment of booksellers and vendors by local magistrates. Weekly numbers of the *Deist* were sold in large quantities in the streets of London and provincial cities, as were "infidel" pamphlets such as the *Letter to the Society for the Suppression of Vice.* Profits—the most fulsome of Carlile's life—approached £50 weekly by the summer of 1819 (and may, briefly, have exceeded that sum), a princely income for a radical publisher.[12] Still, Carlile was more intent on selling his ideas than in deriving a profit from them. He even parceled out the *Age of Reason* and other tracts to wholesale agents at a substantial loss so as to increase their visibility among reformers.

Improved income brought with it tangible rewards. In February 1819, Carlile transferred his publishing business from Sherwin's cramped quarters to a new "Temple of Reason," at 55 Fleet Street. During the next three years the latter became a fulcrum of political resistance and the pivot of his publishing activities. The premises, which contained ample living quarters and carried an annual charge of more than £150, greatly increased his "respectable" status.[13] He became a "Bookseller" (in the parlance of the day) with a position of standing in the reform movement. Yet, ironically, he never enjoyed the personal rewards of this social renaissance since his own stay at 55 Fleet Street was terminated within a year by his conviction and imprisonment.

With indictments and profits cascading around him, Carlile's career as a radical journalist moved into an accelerated phase during 1819. The inefficiencies of the legal system produced substantial delays in his trials, which he added to by several times imparling to the following judicial sessions. Meanwhile he worked furiously to get his message of political and theological reform across to the working classes. Distribution of his tracts would under no circumstances be halted, he stated. During the spring and summer months sporadic seizures of his tracts were carried out at the initiative of the Vice Society and local magistrates. Several vendors were charged with hawking his publications without a license, or selling books that were under indictment. A few were imprisoned; others, including James Cahuac, a London bookseller of some reputation, succumbed to legal pressure and agreed to stop selling "deistical" or blasphemous works.[14] But the majority of vendors and booksellers who handled Carlile's publications continued to do so. There existed a network of London wholesalers and distributors who were willing to run the risk of imprisonment for political reasons and, since a small profit could be earned from the sale of radical publications, as an alternative to poverty. Carlile's publishing arrangements were never in any danger, therefore, although he suffered considerable stock losses. Sales of the *Age of Reason*, the *Principles of Nature*, and other freethought tracts generally escalated in proportion to the excitement generated by the prosecutions.

As publicity on his behalf increased, reformers of miscellaneous backgrounds began to assist Carlile. Many moderate reformers backed him in his opposition to arbitrary government. For them, in the words of a participant in a series of debates held at the "British Forum" in the spring of 1819, the issue was not the truth or falsity of his ideas or whether he was asking "immodest or offensive questions"; it was the fundamental issue, "whether men shall be at liberty to inquire for themselves?"[15]

More radical reformers took a different approach. Hunt's supporters, for example, endorsed the essence of Carlile's political challenge to the government—his advocacy of extended voting rights and reduced taxation—while refusing to underwrite his anticlericalism. "Extreme" proponents of theological reform, on the other hand—deists, freethinkers, and working-class "infidels"—gave him unqualified support. They believed Paine's ideas to be more worthy of consideration than those of Anglican and Nonconformist clergymen and commended Carlile for attacking priests, "the staunchest blood-hounds of the corrupt, borough-mongering system."[16] Such reformers cheered the *Democratic Recorder,* a one-and-a-half-penny political journal, for endorsing the stand of "the brave, the persecuted" Carlile, and *Wooler's British Gazette,* a companion publication to the *Black Dwarf,* for prophesying that his trial would be "one of the most stirring . . . that ever occurred."[17]

By the summer of 1819, 55 Fleet Street had become the chief mart in London for the distribution of radical and freethinking tracts. "Such was my situation and connexion with all classes of Reformers in point of business," Carlile recalled, "that I knew the face of almost every public man in London, by their coming to my shop for pamphlets."[18] Those who congregated there included Arthur Thistlewood, James Ings, and William Davidson, all of whom were executed in 1820 for participating in the Cato Street Conspiracy to assassinate members of the British cabinet Although Carlile distanced himself from these Spencean street revolutionaries at the time of their trials, accusing them of "folly and madness," he was an injudicious participant in some of their conversations. His opinions were malleable, and he was responsive to the utterances of a variety of radical agitators, especially to those who showed some sympathy with freethought.

During the spring and summer, Carlile began for the first time to regard himself as capable of influencing events. The recipient of considerable publicity, he was (as he saw it) on the way to becoming a household name in radical reform circles. Yet, as he was well aware, pitfalls lurked everywhere. Informers were busily taking notes of all that transpired at his shop, while magistrates and Home Office employees were regularly apprised of what he and his associates were up to. At the Cato Street trials in April 1820, the perils of contact with street agitators were made clear. A neighbor of Carlile who had cast a statue of Paine for him, was revealed to be a police spy. His testimony against Thistlewood and the younger James Watson provided the basis on which both men were executed for treason. Fortunately for Carlile, he was in prison at the time and so could not be linked even tangentially to these events.[19]

With his trials postponed repeatedly on technical grounds, he continued to publish radical and freethinking tracts. Writing was becoming a passion for Carlile, one that ideally matched his temperament. The committing of ideas to paper enabled him to make contact with reformers scattered throughout the country, while the favored alternative method of political propaganda, speechmaking, was personally discomforting to him and more limited in scope. In intellectual terms he recognized the need for public debate if his ideas were to be disseminated widely. But he shied away from a conspicuous role at public meetings, preferring to protect himself from the unpredictable responses of the "mob." By dint of practice and hard work, he eventually became a competent platform speaker. But to the end of his life he was essentially a journalist rather than a speaker, an agitator molded out of the clay of Cobbett and not of Hunt.

Only once did Carlile play a major role at a public meeting in 1819, and that, fortuitously, was on the occasion of the Peterloo Massacre. The event was of considerable importance to his career. By the summer of 1819, working-class demands for political reform were beginning to reach unprecedented proportions. Large meetings were being convened in the north of England to petition for a democratic suffrage; and in July, in Birmingham, several thousand artisans and mechanics elected Sir Charles Wolseley, a patrician reformer, to "represent" them in the House of Commons. Resolutions advocating universal suffrage and the summoning of a national convention were widely discussed. And an enormous gathering was planned for St. Peter's Fields, Manchester, in August, where annual elections and universal suffrage were to be demanded and parliamentary delegates selected on the Birmingham model. Weavers, artisans, and factory workers from Manchester and its surrounding towns and villages were urged to attend this "monster meeting" to support demands for reform.[20]

Such was the background to Peterloo, and it was by chance that Carlile became a conspicuous participant. He had not previously taken an active part in the agitation for political reform, his major preoccupations being theological reform and the need for a free press. But as a result of the success of his pamphlets and the prosecutions pending against him, he had become something of a radical celebrity. Several leading public personalities, including Burdett and Cartwright, had turned down invitations to speak, and it was believed by some reformers that Carlile's presence would add lustre to the occasion. Accordingly, John Knight, a veteran Lancashire agitator, invited him to attend the St. Peter's

Fields meeting on behalf of a "Patriotic Union Society" of Manchester. He accepted with alacrity. Although still hesitant about public speechmaking, he regarded the occasion as a special one. It would be his first trip to the north of England, and, if all went smoothly, it would strengthen his reputation as a radical reformer.

The St. Peter's Fields meeting was advertised for Monday, August 16, and on the preceding day, after stopping briefly in Birmingham, Carlile traveled by coach to Manchester, carrying with him the text of resolutions adopted at several London reform meetings. He met Knight, Hunt, and other reformers on the morning of August 16 about three miles from the center of Manchester, and from there a procession, appropriately bedizened, set off for the hustings in the center of the city. Thousands of admirers lined the route of march as the landau in which Carlile and Hunt were seated wended its way slowly past New Cross and Shude Hill toward St. Peter's Fields. The accolades of passersby were intended mostly for Hunt (Carlile's face was unknown in Lancashire), but all reformers in positions of prominence could bask in the splendor of the occasion. As the party arrived at the hustings and began to prepare its speeches, Carlile felt a sense of exhilaration. The morning had been full of hopeful stirrings for the future, more so perhaps than any other he had experienced.

Without warning, promise was transformed into tragedy. As banners were being unfurled amid shouts of "Hunt and Liberty," the sound of trampling horses could be heard moving closer. From his vantage point atop the hustings, Carlile saw the sabres of the yeomanry "cutting very near" to him, and within minutes, many men, women, and children were lying wounded and dying in the grass. As he and other reformers scurried to positions of safety, the meeting place became a scene of carnage: eleven persons were dead and several hundred wounded, many seriously. The agitation for universal suffrage by means of "monster meetings" and petitions came suddenly and decisively to an end.[21]

Carlile left Manchester as expeditiously as possible. Unrecognized by the local constabulary who were seeking Hunt and Knight, he returned to London where several days later he began to publish detailed accounts of the "Peterloo Massacre." These appeared in the final number of *Sherwin's Weekly Political Register* (on August 21) and in the early issues of Carlile's own journal, the *Republican*, which appeared for the first time on August 27. Couched in the form of epistles to the home secretary, Lord Sidmouth, these narrations of the day's events formed the basis for the standard history of Peterloo as seen through the eyes of its victims. And as such, they contributed significantly to the shaping of a working-class consciousness, a process dependent as much upon cultural symbols and common political memories as theoretical analysis.[22]

In maintaining that the carnage had not been provoked by the reformers, Carlile condemned the yeomanry. "All prospect of rec-onciliation must now be considered as being effectively destroyed," he wrote, "and the People have now no recourse left but to arm themselves immediately, for the recovery of their rights, and the defence of their persons, or patiently to submit to the most un-conditional slavery." He told readers of the *Republican* that "retaliation is become a duty, and revenge an act of justice." "I will never attend a public meeting on any political question of Reform, without arms," he avowed. "Once having narrowly escaped with life is to me a sufficient justification."[23]

Such rhetoric—commonplace in radical reform circles in the months after Peterloo—increased the discontent of the working classes and made Carlile an object of renewed government atten-tion. The attorney-general brought additional charges of seditious libel against him for the offending Peterloo articles. And after attending a protest meeting held at the Crown and Anchor Tavern in the Strand, he was taken into custody on a warrant issued by the lord mayor of London and held for five days in the Giltspur Street Compter. This was his third period of incarceration and the second that year. Bail proceedings at the Mansion House were attended by a large, "motley" crowd of reformers who gathered to provide support. Responding to their applause, Carlile confirmed his reputation for obstinacy. "I shall continue to sell the [pamph-lets]," he stated. "I will not be intimidated."[24] Freed on bail, he remained true to his word. The Peterloo articles, accompanied by a copperplate engraving of "the bloody attack," were sold in large quantities in the following weeks, notwithstanding that several of their vendors were apprehended by the authorities.

Amid this crescendo of political events now moving toward a climax, Sherwin took fright and abandoned the *Weekly Political Register*. This was not entirely unforeseen because for the better part of a year, he had been distancing himself from Carlile. But Carlile took maximum advantage of the opportunity now available to him. A week after *Sherwin's Weekly Political Register* appeared for the last time, carrying the account of the "Horrid Massacre at Manchester," a new two-penny journal, the *Republican*, commenced its existence, avowing its determination to defend the poor and the politically unenfranchised, and, as well, the willingness of its editor to seek "even martyrdom in the cause of liberty."[25] The transition from *Register* to *Republican* was a smooth one. The journals were similar in content and style, and several contributors—including Augustus St. John, a political essayist who subsequently achieved fame as a travel writer, and Allen Davenport, an advocate of the theories of Thomas Spence—moved from one to the other.[26] But from the beginning Carlile imparted a much more decisive personal energy to the *Republican* than Sherwin had given to the *Weekly Political Register*. He espoused the grievances and aspirations of his readers in ways that the more cautious Sherwin never came close to doing. By the end of 1825, when the *Republican* finally ran its course after six contentious years, it had established itself as one of the premier working-class journals of the early nineteenth century, a companion to outstanding radical papers such as Cobbett's *Political Register*, Henry Hetherington's *Poor Man's Guardian*, and Feargus O'Connor's *Northern Star*.

Editing the *Republican* took up much of Carlile's time in the late summer and early autumn of 1819, but within a few weeks of the paper's debut, preparations for the approaching trials, now scheduled for the second week in October, had to take priority over all else. Carlile's trials provide an important link in the chain of events stretching from the 1790s to the 1840s that helped to define the political consciousness of a generation of British workingmen. They are a benchmark in the struggle for a free press, a token of working-class dissatisfaction with the political and economic system. But they were not, as might have been anticipated, exciting. The long delays, while whetting public interest in the trials, paradoxically diminished their impact. Had the trials taken place in the spring or early summer, when the reform movement was at its crest, their significance would have been spotlighted. As it was, in the aftermath of Peterloo reformers were no longer as interested in the plight of one recusant journalist. Though still of considerable interest, therefore, the trials of Richard Carlile had to compete for attention with a bevy of other activities: the formation of political unions to demand an extension of the suffrage, demonstrations and disturbances in the industrial north, and meetings to protest against the Liverpool government's repressive policies and to consider the feasibility of a boycott of excisable goods. Hunt, awaiting trial separately for his part at Peterloo, generated much more publicity than did Carlile. And to make matters worse, some reformers began to jib at the latter's determination—indicated in the early numbers of the *Republican*—to emphasize antichristianity in his defense rather than the more attractive, general issue of free expression.

The setting for the trials was London's Guildhall, where William Hone and other reformers had done battle previously with the law. It was a magisterial fourteenth-century building, imposing and stately, but likely to make a legal novice feel somewhat nervous. Nor (other than in political terms) was Carlile made to feel comfortable by the hundreds of prospective spectators who converged on the courtroom on the morning of October 13, when the first of his two trials began, hoping to be present at a historic confrontation. There was excitement in the streets, and when the doors were opened at a few minutes before nine, a portion of the crowd broke ranks and forced its way inside. Within minutes the courtroom was filled to "suffocation."

Given the central place of political trials in the public consciousness in early nineteenth-century Britain, at a time when newspapers provided extensive coverage, the drama of the morning was predictable. By his defiant stand, Carlile had aroused an interest in his fate, and the charges against him could not help but produce an eruption of feeling. "Blasphemy, by itself, is disgusting to the generality of minds," wrote a contributor to the *Edinburgh Review*, "but when it is accompanied by a bold defiance, it becomes attractive."[27] Expectations were increased, too, by the presence in the courtroom of Hunt, Wooler, and many other prominent radical reformers. They accompanied Carlile to his seat and remained near him during the proceedings. William Hone was also there, resurrecting memories of his acquittals in 1817.

Yet, notwithstanding this myriad of feelings, Carlile did the improbable: he bored his audience. There is sufficient testimony on this point, and one instance (admittedly untypical) may be offered. Henry Crabb Robinson was a prominent essayist and man about town who resented Carlile's "pert and insolent" attack upon the judicial system and hoped for a conviction. But when he mingled with the "vast crowd" outside the Guildhall on the morning of October 13, he was anticipating political entertainment of a high order. Robinson's hopes were soon dashed. By the afternoon of the second day (with, as it turned out, two more days yet to come) he was vexed by the dullness of the proceedings and he decided to retire to gentler pursuits at his club in Pall Mall. When he left the courtroom Carlile had finished subjecting the jurors to a verbatim reading of the *Age of Reason* that was interrupted frequently by prosecuting counsel; spectators were shuffling in and out; and numerous seats were empty.[28]

The problem, as Carlile privately realized, had to do with the ineptness of his defense. His physical assets—a resonant if soft voice, impressive reserves of stamina, unyielding determination— were insufficient guarantors of success. Nor was publicity able to turn the tide in his favor, though *A Report of the Proceedings of . . . the Mock Trials of Richard Carlile,* which he published in two-penny numbers while the trials were taking place, sold several thousand copies. What he needed above all was poise and legal acumen to enable him to cope with a formidable situation. These qualities he did not possess. In the weeks leading up to the trials Francis Place, Jeremy Bentham, and other reformers tried to obtain free legal assistance for him. He spurned their offers, almost as if they were intended to be demeaning. "I am bent, personally, on meeting the Attorney General," Carlile informed Place in a tone of self-assurance that could have come only from one who was unaccustomed to confronting the full power of the law.[29] Yet how, after all, could Carlile's attitude have been different? Hone had vindicated himself unaided in 1817; so too had Wooler in the same year against a charge of seditious libel. The plaudits of the crowd were there for the taking, provided only that they were earned. This could most effectively be done by nourishing the popular symbol of the persecuted individual matched against a powerful government.

As Carlile comprehended, however, there were many obstacles weighing in the balance against him. The jurors who were to decide his fate were drawn from narrow lists of freeholders; the two prosecutors, Sir Robert Gifford, the attorney-general, and John Gurney, the solicitor to the Vice Society, were skilled advocates capable of taking full advantage of the plasticity of common law; and the presiding judge, Sir Charles Abbott, was, notwithstanding the facade of legal neutrality that he maintained, determined to secure a conviction. Furthermore, Carlile could defend himself only narrowly. He was not allowed to vindicate the "truth" of his alleged libel: all that had technically to be proven against him was the fact of publication.

To carry him through, he relied on fixity of purpose and the counselings of a few friends and wellwishers, notably Hunt, Wooler, Hone, and Elton Hamond, an eccentric disciple of Jeremy Bentham.[30] His strategy (such as it was) was to reject outright the foundations of the prosecutor's case: by insisting that a prosecution for blasphemous or seditious libel could not be based upon the ambiguities of the common law and that the truth of a libel was sufficient to extenuate it. Neither proposition had any standing in law. Common law prosecutions were part of the legal system since the mid-seventeenth century, and not until 1843 was the truth of a libel to be accepted in a court of law as a justification for it. Only Carlile's lesser arguments were relevant to the case: that the method of jury selection was unduly restrictive and that the charges against him, by their lack of clarity, endangered freedom of political expression. His inadequate understanding of the common law, however, combined with a tendency to ramble, reduced him to ineffectualness throughout most of the proceedings.

The first of the two trials, lasting three days, was based on the publication of the *Age of Reason*, a work of "impiety," which according to the attorney-general, was "flung out against the happiness and peace" of the people. Brushing aside Carlile's assertion that the law was being manipulated to buttress the position of Christianity, Sir Robert Gifford maintained that religion was "a part of the common law of the land, and therefore, a part of the constitution of the country." Nobody—especially, by implication, a person of humble background—could be allowed to "defame and revile" religion without being made to suffer the consequences. The gravamen of Carlile's offense, it was implied, was his attempt to undermine the religious beliefs of the "lower and illiterate" classes and to diminish their ability to "bear up against the pressure of misery and misfortune."[31]

In a lengthy, discursive defense speech Carlile stated that his objective in reprinting Paine had been to present "a fair, candid, honest, calm, and argumentative enquiry into the origin of the religious establishments of this and other countries." What, he asked the jurors, was theological disputation but an "honest difference of opinion"? In an effort to illustrate the arbitrary nature of religious belief, he solicited testimony from the archbishop of Canterbury, the chief rabbi, and the astronomer royal.[32] When this ploy failed (through adverse rulings by Justice Abbott), he was reduced to positing the falsity of Scripture by, in effect, proclaiming the truth of Paine. He read the text of the three parts of the *Age of Reason*—"a body of truth," he told the jurors, "to which I subscribe." As well as strengthening his case, the reading was intended as a way of getting the *Age of Reason* into the public record (though no newspapers availed themselves of the opportunity to print it). But it induced a feeling of tedium in his auditors.[33] When he began to cite numerous authorities furnished by Hone and Elton Hamond to support his antiscriptural arguments, the effect became numbing. For nearly two days Carlile read excerpts from Bolingbroke, Gibbon, Hume, Locke, Drummond, Volney, and other critics of Christianity, so that as his trial neared its end, his defense became little more than a roll call of freethinkers without any effective legal exegesis to underpin it.

About halfway through these proceedings Carlile's position collapsed, at least symbolically. The support of reformers began ineluctably to drain away from him and, if only indistinctly, he understood that he could no longer hope for an acquittal. In pandering tones that did his reputation little good, he appealed to the jurors for sympathy. "What have I done more than others?" he asked. "What have I done that I should be crushed? I am crushed." His expostulations fell on deaf ears. The attorney-general, sensing a conviction, presented his case to the jury quickly, making, as he did so, the revealing statement that "deism was . . . as bad as atheism." He was supported by Justice Abbott who admonished those present to recall that the *Age of Reason* was "a work of calumny and scoffing, and therefore [is] an unlawful publication."[34] Months of hope unraveled rapidly for Carlile as, within half an hour, the jury returned a verdict of guilty on eleven counts of blasphemous libel. Several speakers harangued a small crowd outside the Guildhall shortly after the verdict was announced. But their protests were unavailing.[35]

With Hunt, Sherwin, Wooler, and other associates, Carlile retired to a coffee house nearby to plan strategy for the following day, when he was to be tried for publishing Palmer's *Principles of Nature*. This volume was as denigratory of the "absurdities and contradictions" of Christianity as the *Age of Reason*, and even blunter in its advocacy of militant deism. Among other things it referred to Jesus scoffingly as "nothing more than an illegitimate Jew" and to the Scriptures as "a vast variety of fact, fable, principle, wickedness, and error."[36] The Vice Society conducted the prosecution, and its solicitor emulated the attorney-general in the accusations and denunciations that he laid against Carlile. The latter's plea that he be permitted to read the full text of the *Principles of Nature* to the court (as he had done with the *Age of Reason*) was rejected. Likewise, Carlile's claim that, in publishing Palmer, he was seeking merely to stimulate discussion on "matters of speculative opinion," fell on deaf ears.[37] The trial lasted several hours, and the jury took only thirty minutes to bring in a conviction for blasphemous libel. Mercifully, the other pending indictments and informations—about eight of them—were then dropped.

Carlile appealed subsequently against both verdicts in the Court of King's Bench. More effectively than in the Guildhall, he restated his belief that free expression was "the great bulwark of civil and religious liberty," and that it was being endangered by the actions of the Tory government and private pressure groups and by a legal system that gave license to biased judges to sentence impecunious defendents to lengthy prison terms.[38] He presented himself as a modern Jesus shunned and persecuted by those in power yet with his integrity unchallenged. "I have in my humble sphere endeavored to promote the cause of truth," he told the court.[39]

Sir John Bayley, who presided at the appeal and sentencing, possessed, in Carlile's words, a more "dignified, humane, and temperate manner" than Abbott. But his demeanor could not belie the harshness of the punishment he imposed. Rejecting the appeal, he reminded Carlile of the dangers posed to social order by "blasphemous" writers: "If . . . an attack is to be made upon these bonds and rules which embrace together all our moral and social institutions in life, what can be expected as the consequences here and hereafter?"[40] The sentence he imposed—three years in Dorchester Gaol, a fine of £1500, sureties for good behavior—

was much harsher than expected. And because of Carlile's unwillingness to accept the financial provisions, the punishment
proved to be far worse than prescribed.

Reactions to the trials were expressed in vigorous terms. Unlike
Hone, Carlile had championed Paine and Palmer and other infidel
writers aggressively and in so doing had excited many people to
a pitch of indignation. Several spectators in the courtroom applauded the verdicts loudly when they were announced, actions
that were commended privately by the home secretary; other
persons vented their satisfaction in an outpouring of tracts and
newspaper leaders.[41] One commentator linked Carlile with "Deism
and Fanaticism . . . insurrection and rebellion"; another, Charles
Phillips, an Irish barrister not noted for a modest turn of phrase,
praised the legal system for its treatment of "the chief Bacchanal
of [Deist] orgies . . . [who has] literally disseminated the moral
plague, against which even the nation's quarantine can scarce
avail us."[42] The *Times*, consistently hostile to Carlile, echoed the
views of its conservative readers by applauding the conviction of
such a "notorious criminal."[43]

Such responses were anticipated and, if anything, likely to improve Carlile's standing with reformers. But the disappointment
that some of his own supporters felt with his performance could
not be assuaged as easily. Many "respectable" reformers who were
attracted to his cause because they perceived it as involving free
discussion now abandoned him. The *Examiner*, a pro-reform
journal under the editorship of Leigh Hunt, had described his views
on free speech as "the opinions of a great part of the civilized
world." But in the aftermath of the trials, it did little more than
express the tepid conviction that "we must all speak and act
according to the dictates of our conscience."[44] W. J. Fox, a prin-
cipled advocate of freedom of conscience, remained convinced
that Carlile's imprisonment placed every religious dissenter "at the
mercy of every bigot in the country." But his fellow Unitarians
gave him little support. Most agreed with R. B. Aspland, the
editor of the influential *Monthly Repository*, who avowed that
Carlile had imperiled the position of dissenters needlessly by his
advocacy of infidel views.[45]

Most disappointing to Carlile was the muted reaction of some
working-class reformers. All radical reformers, he believed, should
have echoed the judgment of the *Democratic Recorder* that he

would be "immortalized in the pantheon of history" and concurred with the poet Percy Bysshe Shelley's "indignation that will not, and ought not to be suppressed."[46] But this was not the case. Many radicals were aggrieved by his failure to extend his defense into political areas. To be sure, his antichristian rhetoric satisfied some discontented artisans and factory workers. Yet in the months after Peterloo, others found Henry Hunt's call for universal suffrage more attractive. If the twin causes of radical freethought and political equality could not be united under a single oriflamme (the *Black Dwarf* for one took the position that "religion and politics should be entirely separated"), there was little doubt that the bulk of working-class sentiment would gravitate toward Hunt.

Within weeks of his conviction Carlile experienced the bitter aftertaste of the "loser." Friends and acquaintances began to abandon him for more fruitful political pastures. Augustus St. John, a frequent contributor to the *Republican*, ceased to have any dealings with him, while William Hone, untruthfully denying any involvement with his defense, shunned him.[47] Hunt, a reformer of some principle notwithstanding Carlile's acidulous view of him, gave increased voice to his own political commitments, which lacked even a scintilla of antichristian substance.

A much-applauded radical reformer for the better part of 1819, Carlile had now to cope with the reality of a lengthy term of imprisonment. It was not an alluring prospect. But there was still much to be optimistic about: financial resources were sufficient for at least another year; the *Republican* had built up a weekly circulation of several thousand readers; and a coterie of loyal supporters, though reduced in size, remained as admiring of Carlile as ever. On a November morning as he was transferred by coach from King's Bench Prison in London to the more remote environs of Dorchester Gaol, about 150 miles away, Carlile could console himself with these thoughts and with his determination to make infidelity his chosen issue.

Notes

1. Leo A. Bressler, "Peter Porcupine and the Bones of Thomas Paine," *Pennsylvania Magazine of History and Biography,* 82 (1958), pp. 176-85; White, *Waterloo to Peterloo,* pp. 179-80; Samuel Bamford, *Passages in the Life of a Radical* (London: MacGibbon & Kee, 1967 reprint), p. 132.

2. *Hansard's Parliamentary Debates* (henceforth referred to as *Hansard*), House of Commons, 6 December 1819, 41, p. 710.

3. Speech by the Bishop of Llandaff, *Hansard*, House of Lords, 10 December 1819, 41, p. 988.

4. Society for the Suppression of Vice, *Address* (1803), pp. 30-31. For useful critical analyses of this and other societies, see Leon Radzinowicz, *A History of English Criminal Law and Its Administration from 1750*, vol. 3 (London: Sweet & Maxwell, 1956), chs. 6-7; Thomas Donald, *A Long Time Burning: The History of Literary Censorship in England* (London: Routledge & Kegan Paul, 1969), pp. 139-203.

5. In an appeal for subscriptions in 1821, the Vice Society boasted of the prosecutions it had initiated (reprinted in *To the Reformers of Great Britain*, 24 June 1821). See also Vice Society, *Plans and Observations* (1825).

6. *Vice versus Reason: A Copy of the Bill of Indictment, Found at the Old Bailey Sessions, January 16, 1819, against Richard Carlile, for Publishing Paine's Age of Reason* (1819); *A Copy of the Information, Exhibited Ex Officio, January 23, 1819, by His Majesty's Attorney General, against Richard Carlile, for Publishing Paine's Age of Reason* (1819).

7. For a breakdown of the charges pending against him, see *A Return of the Individuals Who Have Been Prosecuted Either by Indictment, Information, or Other Process, for Public Libel, Blasphemy, and Sedition, in England, Wales, and Scotland, from 31st December 1812 to 31 December 1822* in Great Britain, Parliamentary Papers, 1823, 15 (562), pp. 6-8; *A List of the Jurors to Try the Two Informations by the Attorney General and Three Indictments by the Society for the Suppression of Vice, against Mr. Carlile* (1819), pp. 1-4.

8. d'Holbach was identified correctly as the author of *Letters to Eugenia* (rather than "Freret"), but the author of *Christianity Unveiled* was cited as "Boulanger," a pseudonym frequently used by d'Holbach. The translator of the tracts was John Grattan, a farmer who lived near Chesterfield, Carlile to Turton, 22 August 1840, C.P.

9. *Republican*, 1, pp. xiv-xv.

10. Richard Carlile, *A Letter to the Society for the Suppression of Vice, on Their Malignant Efforts to Prevent a Free Enquiry after Truth and Reason* (London: Richard Carlile, 1819), p. 6. See also his petition in *Sherwin's Weekly Political Register*, 27 February 1819.

11. *Prompter*, 16 April 1831.

12. His claim of a £50 weekly profit is in Richard Carlile, *An Abstract Embodying the Evidences, of the Lectures Delivered by Mr. Carlile, at Brighton and Elsewhere in the Year 1836, to Prove that the Bible Is Not a*

Book of Historical Record, but an Important Mythological Volume (London: Richard Carlile, 1837), p. 18.

13. *Times*, 24 August 1819, reported that the rental on the house was £150 annually, while Carlile claimed that rent, rates, and taxes cost him more than £200 annually. *Republican*, 3 November 1820.

14. In Exeter the mayor ordered all copies of the *Republican* to be burned in front of the Guildhall because of the "great number of disaffected individuals in this part of the country." Thomas Flood, the Mayor of Exeter, to Lord Sidmouth, 16 September 1819, Home Office 42/195, P.R.O. For similar incidents during the battle for an untaxed press in the 1830s, see Joel H. Wiener, *The War of the Unstamped* (Ithaca, New York: Cornell University Press, 1969), pp. 195-209.

15. *The Speech of J. Mills, Esq., Delivered at the British Forum, Held at the Crown and Anchor Tavern, in the Strand, on the Following Questions* (London: Richard Carlile, 1819), p. 5. The *Times* labeled all radical reformers as "Infidels and Jacobins." 18 November 1819.

16. *Substance of the Speeches of John Gale Jones, Delivered at the British Forum, March 11, 18 & 22, 1819, on the Following Question.* (London: Richard Carlile, 1819), pp. 15, 19; *The Opening Speech, and Reply, of Mr. Fleming, at the British Forum, Held at the Crown and Anchor Tavern, in the Strand* (London: Richard Carlile, 1819), pp. 7-8.

17. *Democratic Recorder*, 16 October 1819; *Wooler's British Gazette*, 14 February 1819. The *Cap of Liberty* assessed his confrontation as a "culminating struggle between the population of the entire civilized world and their spiritual and temporal rulers." 15 September 1819.

18. *Republican*, 3 March 1820.

19. Carlile claimed that his neighbor was planted as part of a "regular ministerial plot." *Carlile's Political Register*, 7 December 1839.

20. Jeremy Bentham, *The King Against Sir Charles Wolseley, Baronet, and Joseph Harrison, Schoolmaster: Set Down for Trial, at Chester, on the 4th of April 1820* (1820); Donald Read, *Peterloo: The "Massacre" and Its Background* (Manchester: Manchester University Press, 1958), pp. 109-15.

21. This account of Carlile's activities is drawn from the *Republican*, especially 10 March 1820; Bamford, *Passages*, chs. 30-39; Read, *Peterloo*; Robert Walmsley, *Peterloo: The Case Reopened* (Manchester: Manchester University Press, 1969); *Manchester Meeting: An Account of the Dreadful Attack of the Military upon the Reformers* (Birmingham, 1819).

22. The development of class consciousness is a much-debated subject. For some differing interpretations, see Thompson, *Making of the English Working Class*; Wiener, *War of the Unstamped*; Harold Perkin, *The Origins of Modern English Society, 1780-1880* (London: Routledge & Kegan Paul, 1969); Trygve Tholfsen, *Working Class Radicalism in Mid-*

Victorian England (New York: Columbia University Press, 1977); Patricia Hollis, *The Pauper Press: A Study in Working-Class Radicalism of the 1830's* (London: Oxford University Press, 1970).

23. *Republican*, 10 September 1819; *Sherwin's Weekly Political Register*, 21 August 1819.

24. *Times*, 27 August 1819; *Wooler's British Gazette*, 29 August 1819.

25. *Republican*, 27 August 1819.

26. There is a brief sketch of St. John in the *Dictionary of National Biography* and a less flattering description by Carlile in a letter to Thomas Turton, 9 July 1840, C.P. G. J. Holyoake described Davenport as "The anxious poet of Radicalism—the earnest advocate of Agrarian equality— the friend of liberty and the people." "The Late Allen Davenport," *Reasoner*, 2 (1847). p. 17.

27. "Law as to Libels Against Christianity," *Edinburgh Review*, 34 (1834), p. 396.

28. Thomas Sadler (ed.), *Diary, Reminiscences and Correspondence of Henry Crabb Robinson*, 3d ed. (London: Macmillan, 1872), vol. 1. pp. 334-35.

29. Carlile to Francis Place, 28 January 1819, Place Papers, Add Ms. 37,949, f. 241, B.M.; *To the Reformers of Great Britain*, 20 December 1821.

30. For Wooler's assistance, see *A Dialogue of the Approaching Trial of Mr. Carlile for Publishing the Age of Reason (by Thomas Paine)* (1819). For Carlile's contacts with Hamond, see Carlile to "N.D." [Elton Hamond], 28 October 1819, Dr. Williams's Library, London.

31. *The Report of the Proceedings of the Court of King's Bench, in the Guildhall, London, on the 12th, 13th, 14th, and 15th days of October; Being the Mock Trials of Richard Carlile, for Alleged Blasphemous Libels* (London: Richard Carlile, 1822), pp. 5, 13 (subsequently referred to as *Mock Trials*); *Statesman*, 13 October 1819.

32. Robert Owen, rejecting Carlile's request to testify, stated: "I could not at present leave this place without causing an essential injury to the great object in which I am deeply engaged, for which the existence and wellbeing of millions depend."

33. Carlile described the *Age of Reason* as a work that "contains a finer system of ethics . . . than any thing which can be congregated or formed from that Book which it so ably investigates." *Mock Trials*, p. 79.

34. *Statesman*, 15 October 1819.

35. *A Genuine Report of the Two Trials of Richard Carlile, for the Republication of Thomas Paine's Age of Reason and Palmer's Principles of Nature* (London: Duncombe, 1819), p. 33.

36. These quotations are from Carlile's 1823 edition of Palmer's *Principles of Nature*, pp. 23-25.

37. *Statesman*, 15 October 1819.

38. *Republican*, 24 December 1819.

39. Carlile also drew a comparison with Galileo in *The Accusation, Condemnation, and Abjuration of Galileo Galilei, Before the Holy Inquisition, at Rome, 1633*, a tract he published in 1819.

40. *A Letter of Remonstrance to Sir Robert Gifford, Knight, His Majesty's Attorney General* (London: Hayward and Roscoe, 1820), p. 49; *Speech of the Hon. Justice Bayley, in Passing Sentence on Richard Carlile, in the Court of King's Bench, Nov. 16, 1819* (London: Chappell and Son, 1819), p. 6.

41. Lord Sidmouth approved "the marked and predominant feeling against [Carlile] in the court, and even in the streets." Letter to Lord Eldon, 17 October 1819, in Horace Twiss, *The Public and Private Life of Lord Chancellor Eldon, with Selections from his Correspondence* (London: John Murray, 1844), vol. 2, pp. 346-47.

42. *Constitutional Remarks Addressed to the People of Great Britain, Upon the Subject of the Trial of Richard Carlile, for Republishing Paine's Age of Reason* (London: J. Hatchard, 1819), p. 5; *The Speech of C. Phillips, Esq. . . . at the Egyptian Hall, Mansion House, on Thursday, 4th of November, 1819* (London: George Herbert, 1819), pp. 1-2.

43. *Times*, 15 October, 6 November 1819.

44. *Examiner*, 23 May 1819; Carlile to Leigh Hunt, 31 May 1819, Leigh Hunt Papers, Add. Ms. 38,523, f. 48, B.M.; *Examiner*, 25 October 1819.

45. W. J. Fox, *The Duties of Christians towards Deists* (London: George Smithfield, 1819), p. vii. Aspland was unsympathetic in two letters which appeared in the *Times*, 10, 11 November 1819.

46. *Democratic Recorder*, 16 October 1819; Shelley to Leigh Hunt, in Roger Ingpen (ed.), *The Letters of Percy Bysshe Shelley* (London: Sir Isaac Pitman and Sons, 1909), vol. 1, pp. 736-37.

47. Hone wrote a letter to the *Morning Chronicle* (16 October 1819) dissociating himself from Carlile, but part of a draft of Carlile's defense in Hone's handwriting is in the Carlile Papers.

4

THE ADVANTAGES OF PRISON

From November 1819 to November 1825 Richard Carlile joined that select band of reformers who have built upon their prison experiences to shape the flow of history. He converted Dorchester Gaol, his enforced place of residence, into a surrogate school and a "Repository of Reason" from which freethinkers and radical reformers drew inspiration. He also made it the focal point in a continuing struggle to publish "blasphemous and seditious" writings and to secure a free press. By doing so, he made perhaps his greatest contribution to the history of reform.

In the early nineteenth century it was customary for political prisoners to be shunted about the country so as to isolate them from London, from where, it was felt, dangerous ideas could too easily be disseminated. Dorchester Gaol was as favored in this respect as other county gaols—York, Lincoln, Lancaster, Gloucester— all of which were used to house political prisoners.[1] The prison was an ancient foundation that had been reorganized in the 1790s along lines suggested by John Howard, the reformer, in his book *The State of the Prisons* (1777). Physical conditions in Dorchester had been improved considerably and its administration made more efficient. But the reform that Howard placed most stock in, the payment of employees out of public funds, had not been carried out. Day-to-day supervision of the jail remained in the hands of a keeper,who hired a staff and paid them from his own salary and perquisites. In theory the keeper was accountable to the county magistrates meeting in Quarter Sessions who periodically drew up gaol regulations; in practice he was a law unto himself, able to determine the conditions of stay and mode of treatment for prisoners held there.[2]

Shortly after he was incarcerated, Carlile began to attack this capricious system. In a stream of petitions and tracts, he condemned corporal punishment (which was commonly inflicted on prisoners) and urged that "the most perfect cleanliness, sobriety of manners, and useful pastime" prevail in Dorchester and other prisons. The only justification for incarceration, he insisted, was to instruct perpetrators in "respectable" values and prepare them for a return to society.[3]

Yet, paradoxically, the very brutality and inefficiency of the prison system worked to Carlile's advantage. "Rational" administrators almost certainly would have treated him worse than did the keeper of Dorchester Gaol, a bungling minor official whose objective was to keep "dangerous" prisoners like Carlile out of spiritual and political mischief, if need be by separating them from other inmates. Carlile was spared, therefore, the indignity bestowed upon many political offenders (including most of his own shopmen and vendors) of having to co-mingle with "common criminals." He was granted a political status that allowed him to use a "large, light, and airy" room in return for a small weekly payment.[4] The room contained a sink, bed, desk, oddments of furniture, and a set of weights contributed by his friends that were intended to maintain him in fit physical condition. (Stocky to begin with, Carlile became corpulent during his years in Dorchester). His more enthusiastic supporters also plied him with razors, hosiery, "night-caps," and other gifts, which enhanced the relative comfort of his surroundings.[5]

Most important, Carlile did not have to depend on prison rations. He was allowed to make provision for himself, and he met his personal needs for several years by drawing upon the profits of his publishing business and appealing for public and private support. On average, he spent £2 to £3 weekly on food, fuel, and writing supplies during his six years in prison, an expenditure that was more than adequate to his needs.[6] After a dispute with the keeper, he was granted permission to hire two servants: one to do laundry and clean his room, another to make special purchases for him and run errands. Such a seeming indulgence in comfort was attacked by some reformers, including several publishers and vendors whose treatment in prison was much less temperate. But most of Carlile's followers accepted that six years of incarceration in a remote provincial prison was a far cry from paradise and that if he was to maintain his position as a radical journalist, he had to have a modicum of physical well-being. His weekly "indulgences" allowed for this.

More than compensating for the adequacy of his surroundings, however, was the severe "quarantine" to which he was subjected. The keeper of Dorchester Gaol was determined to shield other prisoners from the contagious proximity of a blasphemer. He therefore permitted Carlile a maximum of three hours of outdoor exercise weekly. Employees of the prison were adjured not to speak to him, and he was not allowed contact with other prisoners, including Robert Wedderburn, the black "infidel" for whom he was attempting to collect subscriptions. With the exception of his wife and three sons, visitors were either discouraged from coming to see him or were barred peremptorily at the gates.[7] Even after March 1824, when the visiting magistrates eased his restrictions somewhat, contacts with outsiders were kept to a minimum. A handful of followers made their way successfully into the prison, but most were discouraged by the lengthy coach journey and the obstacles likely to be placed in their way at the last moment by zealous employees.[8]

In the best of circumstances, prison is apt to scar the human psyche deeply. When, as in the case of Carlile, it is conjoined with a regimen of isolation, the effects are almost certain to be permanently damaging. After being at the hub of political events for more than two years, Carlile was suddenly denied physical contact with the outside world. He was compelled to form his observations of events from printed sources and, amid considerable pressure, to fashion these impressions into critical analyses for his readers. It is not surprising that many of his judgments went badly awry. Without yet looking closely at his ideas, suffice it to say that he began to indulge in rhetorical excess during his years in prison and that many of his comments on events were far removed from "reality." There was, for example, his impassioned support for Queen Caroline in 1820, when she attempted to gain a place at the side of her husband, George IV, at his coronation. Other reformers enthusiastically took up the cudgels on behalf of the queen, but few equaled the journalistic license of Carlile, who described her as a "virtuous and true heroine" (even her strongest supporters admitted that her morals were none too impeccable) and observed: "We felt even a yearning of the bowels, and that sympathy, which can start a secret fear on her behalf."[9] His judgments about the revolutions in Spain and Naples in the early 1820s were equally grandiloquent. He interpreted these uprisings as harbingers of "the annihilation of kingcraft and priestcraft throughout Europe." "The annals of history," he stated, "can display nothing more than the present feeling. Such is its effect, that it penetrates the walls of a prison and almost makes the prisoner forget where he is."[10]

"Quarantine" produced in Carlile contrasting emotional states, which became a recurring facet of his personality. Periods of melancholy became interspersed with messianic prophesying. There were plaintive moments shared with readers, as in this comment of August 1820: "So, for keeping a conscience, I am to have three years' imprisonment! Bravo! bravo! christians."[11] Then would follow expressions of doubt about his ability to achieve anything worthwhile. In November 1823, he lapsed into a condition of "muscular and nervous debility," which incapacitated him for several weeks and gave his gaolers the opportunity to remove all "weapons" from his room and to deny him the surfeit of meats and puddings that he pined for.[12] Yet just as events seemed to be rushing toward a personal crisis, Carlile would begin to revel in the constraints of his situation. "I never was happier," he told his supporters. "I never was so well employed for my own future interest before."[13] Insulated from the turmoil of the outside world with its unpredictable shifts of political fortune, he felt serene, even hopeful. He believed at such times that he was a political "Antichrist" come to do good: "The Printing Press has been his forerunner, and to give it the fullest power to which it is equal, [the Antichrist] comes! Finally, to change the condition of the whole of mankind, he comes!" If the moment of redemption for the oppressed had not yet arrived, it was, or so it periodically seemed to him, not far distant.

The "solitude in perfection" of prison strengthened his obdurate temperament, suffusing it with qualities of self-righteousness that were, at times, politically damaging. "I have acquired that degree of mental power, or self-control, as never to suffer an ill-founded or unpleasant imagination to rise or disturb me," he told readers of the *Republican*.[14] Prison, he contended, enabled him to endure the obloquy of commonplace political contact. It also made him "enthusiastic" and tinctured his outlook with apocalyptic elements. "As the oak destroyed the bramble and the brier, these useless absorbers of the earth's juices; so may infidelity destroy kingcraft and priestcraft, these mischievous drains upon the resources and happiness of mankind," he observed in a letter to his followers that can be described most charitably as lacking a "feel" for the political issues of the moment.

There was another, more constructive side to Carlile's prison years: "temperance by example." From the outset of his incarceration he was determined to conform to a strong code of personal conduct. Only by the "proper occupation of time," he believed, could individuals bring events under control. Time was "man's only property"; its effective use was the "great panacea for all human ills."[15] "If moral instruction or moral habitude will not form a good character," he wrote, "religion will not do it."[16] This emphasis on moral improvement and self-discipline was an important facet of working-class reform attitudes in the early nineteenth century. But for Carlile it had a special intensity. "Always recollect," he told one of his shopmen, "that I began to sell books with a borrowed twenty shillings, and everything else I have done by hard labour, close attention and perseverance: up early and laying down late: for a person attached to a bed beyond what health requires for rest makes life, what I call a living death: we may be as well dead as dormant, for what good we do when we sleep away time beyond what the health requires."[17]

His aim was to make his personal behavior correspond to "laws of nature." This meant moderation and balance. "The most delicious draughts when taken to excess are sure to nauseate," he stated, "as nature requires a medium in all things."[18] Benjamin Franklin, who had devoted his life to "mental improvement," was his model; while Confucius, Seneca, Rochefoucault, and other "common sense" moralists were cited frequently by him for their advice on ethical questions. (A favorite apothegm of his was Seneca's statement that "he lives longest who has made the best use of his time.") "Temperance by example" embodied many concrete, respectable virtues. Thus, Carlile bathed regularly at a time when daily ablutions were not customary; made it a point always to be sober and temperate; employed "natural" medical remedies to cure his illnesses; read and wrote ceaselessly; and, most important, worked hard to bring about reforms that he felt to be necessary if the demands of workingmen were to be met.

Cleanliness was a special part of his daily routine. It exemplified "human economy" and discipline: a hot bath, he observed, is not a trivial luxury but a moral necessity.[19] Dirt was the analogue of all those intellectual vices that impeded human effort. Unless such obstacles were removed, reform could not be carried out. Carlile believed—literally—that dirt obstructed the circulation of body fluids by compressing foul air within the system. The body had, therefore, to be purged by bathing and, when illness occurred, by the intake of mercury or another substance that could dissolve impurities.

Similar thinking lay behind Carlile's "rational" ingestion of food and drink. He believed that if a balance between mind and body was to be preserved, eating habits had to be divorced from the sensual pleasures of the moment. (Privately he confessed to a fondness for the gastronomic "elegancies of life.") Therefore, he proscribed meat and alcoholic beverages from his diet—though he was not by conviction a vegetarian or a teetotaler—substituting in their place milk, bread, fruit, fresh vegetables, and a herbaceous, home-brewed "tea." Such a diet was "respectable," and Carlile urged his followers to adopt it. But its observable deficiency was caloric: the intake of milk and bread in large amounts tended, as he reluctantly conceded, to produce corpulence.[20]

No less important than physical discipline was the moral side of "temperance by example," though he confessed to greater obstacles in this area. For one thing he had a penchant for attractive women. "I love philosophically," he told one supporter while offering private advice about the consequences of a seduction. "I think it a piece of cruelty, a horrid barbarity, not to gratify an entreating, agreeable woman. I confess that I could not be so hardhearted, so cruel, so barbarous."[21] He ogled the "pretty wenches" whom he saw from his window and allowed his mind to dally on thoughts of women he had known. A harmless enough diversion, it might seem, though to a reformer like Carlile it was fatuous and time-wasting. His prison writing is replete with sexual imagery, ranging from an obsession with scriptural immorality (as in his reference to the "gross credulity, effeminacy, and foul passions" of Christianity) to a chiliastic description of women as "the most important channel through which virtue can be propagated and the social state be rendered peaceable, prosperous and happy."[22] Clearly, his interest in women fell below the standards of "temperance by example."

Other unbidden factors intruded into Carlile's prison world, disrupting the fine balance between mind and body. The staunchest act of self-will could not obliterate the sympathies he felt for those prisoners who were chained and whipped, and whose moans he heard. "I declare that I would rather suffer seven years imprisonment in the room in which I am locked at present, than a whipping of such a brutal nature as those inflicted in this Gaol," he wrote.[23] He experienced, too, a nostalgic longing for the world of nature. He was a rationalist to his bones, enjoying few pleasures from the physical side of life. But on warm evenings the absence of the "real" world made him pine for the harmonious society he had left behind in Ashburton, where people could, he believed, relate directly to their environment. For him, such a world was a salutary alternative to the tempestuousness of working-class politics (now an integral part of his life) and to the solitude of prison life.

Of Carlile's many "respectable" virtues during these years, self-education was the most significant because it permanently affected his career. A cluster of reforming values adhered to self-education: moral improvement, tenacity of purpose, thrift, a belief in perfectability, even sexual restraint. The worst tyranny, Carlile (and other artisan reformers) believed, was indolence, and self-education was the best remedy for this.[24] Although his accomplishments as an autodidact fell short of those of Cobbett, Thomas Cooper, and other working-class contemporaries, the act of seeking after a "second birth of mind" in prison unleashed creative energies within him. Self-education became a litmus test of personal commitment for Carlile, a means by which he could constantly reassess his fixity of purpose. So long as he was steadfast in his pursuit of intellectual goals—however short of perfection the results were— he would have much to show for his efforts.

As early as 1820 he expressed this attitude in a candidly phrased letter to his four-year-old son Richard. The epistle was modeled on the writings of Lord Chesterfield, whom he much admired. Opportunity, he told his son, was there to be seized, if—and only if—ability was cultivated by intellect. "It is difficult to remedy ill or awkward habits," he wrote. "The beginning to do anything right and well is much better than amendment from bad habits."

By his admission he had wasted fifteen years working at an un-edifying trade. He had irredeemably squandered time and felt a "sense of degradation" about it. Now he was ready to make amends by hard work, and he implored his son to do likewise, by studying and fostering habits of self-discipline at an early age.[25]

Shortly after his imprisonment began, Carlile set out to remedy many of his educational deficiencies. He occupied himself daily with a program of "careful reading, sober, deep, and serious thinking, and industrious application."[26] "I have such an appetite for printed paper, whether printed lies or printed truths," he observed, "that I can never let a book which professes to be philosophical pass me unread."[27] In almost perverse defiance of his creed of temperateness, he read omnivorously. His wife and shopmen were implored to send him printed materials, and with their help he ingested thousands of books, newspapers, tracts, and broadsides during his six years in Dorchester. By day and night he read, sometimes with the cooing of birds or the clatter of horses' hooves on the pavement outside providing melodic accompaniment; at other times in conditions of total silence. And when unexpected difficulties arose—an enigmatic phrase, an un-familiar word—he turned to the tools at hand: Fenning's *Universal Spelling-Book* (a popular book of grammar), the *Oxford Encyclopaedia*, and, increasingly indispensable, two copies of the Scriptures to enable him to check theological references and build up a detailed knowledge of Christian doctrine.[28]

"Decorative" reading matter was eschewed by Carlile. He favored "simple truth and plain reason," not "the madness of mental power," and refused to read fiction or poetry.[29] The former dis-tracted the mind from serious work, he believed; it was at best a timid, indirect way of promulgating "useful truths." "We should, as lovers of truth, war . . . with the novelist and the romance writer, and give [them] no quarter," he told his readers.[30] Poetry was even worse, notwithstanding a lifelong admiration that he had for Byron and Shelley: it was a "trifling with common sense," a "pretty stringing together of words." He described poets as "the precursors of priests,—the syrens of human language, that have lured man to destruction, the general corruptors and the authors of the FALL OF MANKIND."[31] By comparison the theater emerged with its rep-utation intact; it was merely a "school for immorality and scandal."

Nearly all of Carlile's reading was confined to politics and theology. Of the significant political texts that he read in prison (in addition to the works of Paine), James Harrington's *Oceana*, David Hume's *Commonwealth*, and John Locke's *Essay on Toleration* probably influenced him the most, while among contemporary writers he was inclined strongly toward the writings of James Mill, Jeremy Bentham, and Major Cartwright. Mill and Bentham, who corresponded with him from time to time, strengthened his understanding of jurisprudence and his pragmatic political instincts. Cartwright, especially in his book *The English Constitution*, made him aware of some of the complexities of historical change.[32]

More basic to Carlile's development as a reformer, however, was theology. From the time of his reprinting of the *Age of Reason* in December 1818, he had been persuaded of the need to destroy the power and privileges of organized religion. And many of his prison readings were undertaken specifically with this objective in mind. He studied Christian texts carefully because he believed a sound understanding of them to be necessary if he was to combat the claims of his opponents. Thus, he read and analyzed the writings of numerous apologists for Christianity, making their arguments— literal and allegorical interpretations of Scripture, proof from design— part of his intellectual armory. Occasionally he took the offensive against Christianity after reading a particular text. But mostly he bided his time, awaiting a favorable moment before striking.[33]

If a better understanding of Christian theology gave Carlile the self-confidence to engage clergymen in debate, his increasing familiarity with the literature of freethought provided him with the foundations of his beliefs. From 1819 to 1823, he sampled the full range of "infidel" writing, moving from deism to atheism to allegorical readings of Christianity, in search of damaging insights and continually adjusting his interpretations to fit new circumstances. Paine's antiscriptural writings, as inscribed in the *Age of Reason*, remained the altar-piece of his radicalism. But other freethinkers—some of them more hostile to Christianity than Paine—influenced him considerably. Comte de Volney's *Ruins of Empires*, a powerful deist book published in France in 1791 and first translated into English in 1795, shaped his thinking, as it did a generation of working-class freethinkers. Carlile told his readers that Volney's sweeping references to a "universal and identical mover" and to a "secret power that animates the universe" made "the first impression on my mind," and on several occasions he reprinted portions of *Ruins of Empires*.[34] Baron d'Holbach's materialist writings, which dated from the mid-eighteenth century, also shaped Carlile's thinking, and he published several of them for the first time in English translation. Other antichristian works that Carlile studied closely in prison were Hume's *Dialogues Concerning Natural Religion;* Lord Shaftsbury's *Characteristiks of Men, Manners, Opinions, and Times,* an influential seventeenth-century deist volume; Gibbon's *Decline and Fall of the Roman Empire,* particularly those chapters in which the corruptions of Christianity were singled out for ironic treatment; and William Hone's *Apocryphal New Testament* (1821), a volume that underscored the fortuitous nature of religious orthodoxy by reprinting those gospels not part of the official church canon.

Unanticipated events sometimes affected Carlile's studies. He sought confrontations with clergymen, even going so far as to advertise in local newspapers for defenders of the faith to come forth and engage him in verbal or written battle. Most clergymen declined the offer. But a few were unwilling to let slip an opportunity to reclaim a recusant blasphemer. Refusing to meet tête-á-tête with Carlile in Dorchester prison, they plied him instead with unsolicited exegeses of Christian doctrine. Thomas Chalmers's *Evidence and Authority of the Christian Revelation* (1814) and Olinthus Gregory's *Letters to a Friend on the Evidence, Doctrines and Duties of the Christian Religion* (1811) reached him in this way, with the latter book providing the basis for a lengthy refutation of Gregory in a tract entitled *Observations on "Letters to a Friend" . . . by Olinthus Gregory* (1821) in which Christianity was condemned as a "villainous imposture upon the industrious and productive classes of society."[35] Sometimes Carlile's responses took a lighter form, as when he replied to the overtures of the Reverend William Tait of Bristol, an implacable controversialist. After accepting several tracts from Tait, Carlile took inspiration from the biblical patriarchs: since the tracts are "sacred scriptures," he told his readers, "I have put them into the water-closet as an appropriate sacrifice to Jehovah."[36]

Better analytic skills and greater familiarity with theological and political thought brought dividends to Carlile. He became more self-confident, so much so that he began to think of himself as a philosopher who "ranges all over the world in idea, and feels as much or more pleasure from a mental loco-motion, than from a bodily loco-motion." The street agitator and ephemeral publisher became a "sober, quiet, studious man, craving no society"; while prison became for him "an admirable school for study and reflection."[37] And as he reflected upon the weaknesses of his fellow men, who squandered their lives in pursuit of insubstantial goals, Carlile reached the predictable conclusion that only a small number of men and women were capable of meeting the exacting standards of "temperance by example." "Human cattle" predominated in the world, he observed, whether they were convicted debtors and felons like those in the public wing of Dorchester prison; demagogic politicians like Hunt and Cobbett; or ordinary artisans and mechanics who lacked the self-discipline to place their bodies at the service of their minds.[38] "The ignorance arising from superstition," he commented, "is the strong hold of all the unjust distinctions, and of all the splendid idlers, in society." This cynicism—both democratic and elitist in its implications—remained an integral part of his political outlook for the remainder of his life.

Carlile's transformation of the dessicating experience of prison into a stimulus to creative activity provides a conceptual means for understanding his evolution as a radical reformer. But it does not explain how he continued to maintain his position as a leader of working-class reform in the 1820s. For this one must turn to the external man, the radical "blasphemer" who, with uncommon stamina, waged war against the government and those private groups that were bent on destroying him. No more prepared to submit to authority while in prison than he had been in 1819, he was determined to keep his publishing business going at all costs and to keep the *Republican* alive as an influential journal of working-class opinion. There was no alternative available to him. Publishing was the lifeblood of his career. Lacking access to the established press (the *Times* and most other newspapers refused to accept paid advertisements from him), he had no means of circulating his ideas other than by his own publications. If freedom of the press was to be validated on "true and honourable grounds" and as "a matter of public instruction," Dorchester Gaol had to continue to be a fount of journalistic activity.

To publish while in prison was a difficult task. Several journalists had done it in recent years, though in more auspicious circumstances. Cobbett had kept his *Political Register* in circulation while imprisoned for seditious libel in 1810, and Wooler had done the same for the *Black Dwarf* in 1817. But both men were housed in Newgate prison in the center of London, and both could rely on professional help to carry them through. Carlile, as well as being separated from the pulse of radical journalism, had lost the support of several experienced collaborators who had helped him during his incarceration in 1817, including Sherwin and Augustus St. John. He had to rely on the less skilled assistance of his wife and of two close associates: Thomas Davison, a struggling Smithfield printer who edited several freethought tracts and was imprisoned for blasphemy in 1821, and Thomas Moses, a commercial printer based in Clerkenwell who befriended him for several years.

Jane Carlile, Davison, and Moses reopened Carlile's shop at 55 Fleet Street in January 1820 (it had been shut down at the time of his sentencing because of taxes owed), published a second volume of the *Deist* and another edition of Paine's political writings, and continued to print and sell the *Republican* during the winter months of 1819-20, albeit with a circulation reduced from 10,000 to 12,000 weekly in the weeks leading up to the trials to one that no longer exceeded 3000. Carlile worked closely with his three helpers. They forwarded weekly parcels to him, including copies of the *Times* and other newspapers and many of the latest political and religious tracts, and from these materials—supplemented by books that he read at greater leisure—he produced an avalanche of words and phrases for the *Republican*.

Thirty-two octavo pages had to be filled weekly (the size of the *Republican* was doubled in January 1820 when its price was increased to six pence as a result of the imposition of a four-penny stamp duty), a major feat because Carlile rarely solicited contributions. Three or four days before the paper appeared in London on Friday mornings, he sent a batch of hastily written essays to his shopmen. Editorials and political copy had to be reasonably up to date, and he usually composed these under great pressure. He worked during the daylight hours and often by candlelight at night, rarely taking time to ponder his comments before they were forwarded, sometimes—as was painfully clear to his readers—not examining them for infelicities of style.

The technical problems of publishing from Dorchester and London were considerable. Frequent disputes with compositors and shopmen took place; copy went astray; booksellers and retailers of pamphlets refused to handle "blasphemous" publications; and rows with vendors about "irregularities" in the weekly receipts were common.[39] There was also the sheer task of finding enough to say day after day and week after week, given the amount of space that had to be filled and Carlile's insistence that he do most of the writing himself. "Here am I," he confided on one occasion to his readers, "with three pages to fill up in three quarters of an hour and nothing to say!"[40] There were advantages to be had in sharing the burden of composition with others, but these, in his opinion, would be more than counterbalanced by the need to temper his opinions. He alone knew exactly what he wanted to say. Collaborators, if encouraged to participate in the putting together of the *Republican*, were certain to introduce extraneous matter, including "the fiction of novels . . . and the timidity that shelters its desire to promulgate useful truths under the cloak of that fiction."

The strong qualities of the *Republican* as a journal of working-class dissent in fact did derive from the personal imprint of Carlile. Some of its early numbers were crude and vituperative, dubious assets to the radical cause even at a time when working-class journalism was not notably delicate. But the coarseness diminished as Carlile honed his skills—a result of greater writing experience and sharpened abilities. A small heaping of nonsense always clung to the *Republican* (sometimes the paper appeared to be made up of a random combination of drivel and inspiration), but content and style improved significantly over time. The result was a journal that, while veering toward the didactic, contained a fascinating miscellany of radical subject matter.[41]

Editing a weekly newspaper singlehandedly for six years while a political prisoner would alone have assured for Carlile a niche in the history of journalism. But his contribution to the press went much beyond that. In the early 1820s he published many tracts in addition to the *Republican:* some he wrote, others were penned by collaborators, still others were reprints of freethought writings. The last included new editions of the *Age of Reason* and the *Principles of Nature;* several previously unpublished essays by Palmer entitled *Posthumous Pieces;* d'Holbach's *Critical Examination of the Life of St. Paul* (1823), based on Peter Annet's eighteenth-century deist tract of the same name; six-penny reprints of Byron's freethinking poems *Cain* and the *Vision of Judgment* (John Hunt had been prosecuted recently for publishing the *Vision of Judgment*); and an unexpurgated edition of Shelley's verse-drama, *Queen Mab* (1822), which the Vice Society had suppressed up to now.

Carlile also published two atheist tracts by Jeremy Bentham, which appeared in print for the first time: *Analysis of the Influence of Natural Religion on the Temporal Happiness of Mankind* by "Philip Beauchamp" (1822), cobbled together from a Bentham manuscript prepared by George Grote; and *Mother Church Relieved in Bleeding* (1823), an extract from a longer antichristian work entitled *Church-of-Englandism and Its Catechism Examined.*[42] Of some interest too were four political pamphlets written by an unknown author who used the pseudonym "Philanthropos." These tracts attacked kings, lords, and priests for conspiring "to deprive the people of the right of Nature, to deprive them of their liberty and property, by rapine, by treachery, and by usurpation." According to "Philanthropos," these groups had connived at "the operations of each other upon the pockets of the people." He maintained that as soon as the people rejected scriptural religion and adopted a standard of "natural law," they would be able to destroy this privileged triumvirate and establish a better society.[43]

Carlile was still primarily a propagandist for the views of others, but in the early 1820s he began increasingly to publish his own views on a wide variety of subjects. His *Life of Paine*, which appeared in 1820, has been referred to. Other tracts followed in quick succession, including *An Address to Men of Science*, which appeared in May 1820 and in a second edition in the following year, and *Observations on "Letters to a Friend" . . . by Olinthus Gregory*, published in October 1821. In these pamphlets he expounded deist interpretations while demonstrating how, under the influence of d'Holbach, his opinions were becoming impregnated with materialist ideas. The *Address to Men of Science* was, as well, a fascinating compendium of radical ideas about education and science. Carlile urged that "metaphysical" concepts be banished from schools, along with "dead languages" and history, and that pupils be made to study "natural science," a subject, he maintained, that was alone capable of enhancing "the cause of Truth, of

Reason, of Nature and her Laws." He affirmed his willingness to publish original books by men of science as a way of accelerating the progess of intellect; and although he was not successful at this, his *Address* gave an impetus to the popular interest in science.[44]

In 1823, he wrote and published the *Moralist*, a weekly conspectus of aspects of personal morality. Unprepossessing in style, the *Moralist* survived for only nine numbers. Yet its essays set forth the philosophical case for "temperance by example" or, in more formal terms, for "the science of human happiness." Nearly all of the conventional vices were censured in its pages—intemperance, sexual license, gambling ("the most fatal of all passions"), improvidence, idleness—because these allegedly deflected men and women from "mental improvement." "Who but a fool," observed Carlile, "would waste his time in bed, or any other way?"[45] The virtues that he strongly recommended were, he admitted, in short supply because most people were enticed away from "useful production" by the pleasures of the moment. Yet this merely emphasized the seriousness with which matters of personal morality had to be approached since, according to Carlile, "a knowledge of our vices and their effects is half an abandonment."[46] Although hortatory to excess, the *Moralist* is essential reading for students of the history of reform, not only for what it tells about Carlile and his followers but because its insistent comments on self-improvement and respectability provide an insight into a key aspect of working-class radicalism.

In continuing to publish radical tracts and journals while in prison, Carlile had to cope with increasing financial burdens. The year 1819 was beyond all expectations a profitable one for him, and it colored his attitude toward journalism. Henceforth he was an unbridled optimist with a credo about the press that might best be summarized in the words: "Publish and achieve grace!" In true entrepreneurial fashion, his object was constantly to produce new works, constantly to move from one publishing venture to another as soon as funds became available. This may have seemed inconsistent with his exhortation to his followers to husband their resources for future use. But how could Carlile be faulted for optimism? He had issued large quantities of printed matter cheaply between 1817 and 1819 and had become successful beyond his wildest dreams. Why not carry on in similar fashion from Dorchester prison?

Financial problems, stemming from his trials and imprisonment, made such notions fanciful. As soon as Carlile's sentence was handed down, the attorney-general secured a writ of levari facius, which enabled the sheriff of the City of London to close down the Fleet Street shop and sequester a portion of his stock.[47] (Placards, tacked onto the door of 55 Fleet Street by supporters and inscribed "LONG LIVE THE INQUISITION," were ignored by those enforcing the writ.)[48] These actions were undertaken ostensibly because of arrears on the payment of taxes on the house and Carlile's stated intention not to pay the £1500 fine. But their justification was political: to dilute his resources at source, even to terminate his publishing business. If this was not done, his opponents rightly surmised him capable of continuing to publish and sell tracts in the style that he had been accustomed to before his trials.

The closing for several months of the "Temple of Reason" and the seizure of stock imposed heavy losses on Carlile, which he was never able to recover. He initiated proceedings against the sheriff and, in February 1826, after prolonged litigation, managed to regain a portion of his sequestered stock.[49] But it had become damaged in the intervening years and was greatly diminished in value. Thereafter, he never replicated the value of the original stock. In the late 1830s, toward the end of a politically important though financially unremunerative career, he was to be seen in the market squares of northern towns selling off bits and pieces of his original waterlogged stock for miniscule sums in order to raise money for other purposes. Yet Carlile resisted financial adversity as vigorously as he did the legal and political attacks directed against him. Shortly after the sheriff initiated his actions, he asked his associates to remove portions of the stock to avoid confiscation.[50] These were hidden in rooms in central London and in the Clerkenwell premises of Thomas Moses, and were sold with his other publications when his shop was reopened in January 1820.

The shop at 55 Fleet Street remained open for two more years, with the help of Jane Carlile, his sister Mary-Anne, and numerous shopmen, and during that time it became an entrepôt of cheap political and freethought literature to which radical workingmen came on a regular basis. But in February 1822, the Court of Exchequer issued a writ against Carlile for nonpayment of his fines, and a second, more serious, seizure of his stock followed. The "Temple of Reason" at 55 Fleet Street was permanently closed down, much to his chagrin. In the following January about 30 percent of the confiscated stock was sold at auction, notwithstanding that his supporters managed to retrieve some books and personal items for him.[51]

These confiscations gravely weakened Carlile's financial position. During its two years in operation 55 Fleet Street never paid its way, nor did any of his subsequent shops. Publishing became a precarious trial at arms—unlike the heady days of 1819—in which occasional small profits invariably were followed by large losses. Carlile suffered by having to reprint stock that had been confiscated and because of the increased distribution costs necessitated by these seizures. Rival publishers, including unscrupulous men like William Benbow, took advantage of this to undermine his position, though there were few radical publishing lists in the nineteenth century that did not contain books and pamphlets issued by Carlile.

The most serious difficulty he faced was in launching new publishing ventures. These required capital, and although Thomas Moses extended credit to him for printing, such "loans" were insufficient to enable him to do more than move tentatively from one project to the next. After a second volume appeared in May 1820, the *Deist* could no longer be continued; sales of Paine and Palmer were halted between 1819 and 1822 except for remaining stocks; and the *Republican,* the capstone of Carlile's publishing business, ceased to appear during 1821 because of heavy distribution losses. It was replaced temporarily by *Addresses to the Reformers,* pamphlets of similar format, which, because of their irregular appearance, lacked the impact of the original.[52] In January 1822 Carlile recommenced the *Republican,* publishing it for five more years. Yet it failed to turn a profit for him. He could do little more than earn income from it sufficient to pay the expenses on his shops. The confiscations of his stock were, he ruefully maintained, "of more injury to me than double the amount of the fine would have been." To the end of his life he steadfastly asserted that without such seizures he would have "annihilated Christianity"; but because of them his position was one of continuing penury.[53]

Ironically, Carlile's concern to appear "respectable" to his followers compounded his financial difficulties. He was obsessive about maintaining a visible, well-stocked shop. Such a shop, he believed, was a token to his followers that temperance could be made to work, that endurance would overcome the discomforts of the moment. He was determined, therefore, to keep open his "Temple of Reason," and he did so until February 1822, when it was closed down at the time of the second stock seizure. Immediately he undertook a search for quarters of comparable quality. Fleet Street alone would suffice since, as was true of no other street in London, it conveyed an aura of journalistic well-being.

Having acquired in 1821-1823 the leases of two smaller shops with the aid of subscriptions from his followers—one in Water Lane, another in the Strand—he was not content until September 1823, when he took over the lease of a shop and house at 84 Fleet Street. His satisfaction was short-lived. Two fires, one of suspiciously Christian provenance, destroyed this second "Temple of Reason" in November 1824, forcing him to commence yet another lengthy search for a shop.[54] At last, seventeen months later, his quest ended when, with the aid of Francis Place and several private patrons (and after making use of a tiny shop at 135 Fleet Street for about a year), he reopened the third and most capacious of his "Temples of Reason," at 62 Fleet Street abutting Bouverie Lane. Here he remained for nearly a decade, churning out tracts and journals, and attempting tirelessly to harness the aspirations of working-class reformers to the chariot of radical reform and infidelity. The sums needed to maintain such premises placed a continuing strain upon him, however, and they illuminate a central paradox of his character: that he was a modest, even ascetic, private man who was prepared to undergo enormous personal sacrifices to project an image of external solidity.

Financial difficulties cast a shadow across Carlile's prison years, but they could not detract from his many notable achievements. The resonances emanating from Dorchester prison were multifaceted: well-publicized legal and judicial battles with the law; the dissemination of "blasphemous" and "seditious" writings among the poor; and a prolonged struggle for an unshackled press. It is to some of these events that we now turn.

Notes

1. Two prominent reformers, Gilbert Wakefield (1799-1801) and Henry White (1808), had occupied the same prison room as Carlile. Better known were the "Tolpuddle Martyrs," six rural laborers convicted of adminis-

tering illegal oaths to fellow trade unionists, who were imprisoned in Dorchester Gaol in 1834 before being transported to New South Wales.

2. M. B. Weinstock, "Dorchester Model Prison, 1791-1816," *Proceedings of the Dorset Natural History and Archaeological Society,* 127 (1956), p. 97; *A Guide to Dorchester, and Its Neighbourhood* (Dorchester, 1880?), pp. 12-13.

3. Petition of March 1823, reprinted in *Republican,* 28 March 1823; *Republican,* 12 October 1824.

4. The radical journalist James Watson paid five shillings for a coach to take him to Clerkenwell Prison so that he did not have to consort with common criminals. *Working Man's Friend,* 16 February 1833. Radical journals of the period are filled with complaints about prison based as much upon "status" as conditions of treatment. Carlile, for example, wrote privately: "I can pity the inmates of a Prison, but I cannot associate with them unless I was shut up in the same ward and then no further than civility would require." Carlile to William Holmes, 26 June 1822, C.P.

5. *Republican,* 17 March, 8 September 1820; *Morning Herald,* 29 December 1823.

6. In the *Prompter,* 23 July 1831, Carlile claims to have expended two and a half guineas weekly.

7. On the legal aspects of his solitary treatment, see the Report of the Visiting Justices, 20 November 1819, 8 January 1820, and its approval by Quarter Sessions (11 January 1820) in *Dorset Quarter Sessions Proceedings,* 7 (1819-27), p. 44, Dorset C.R.O., Dorchester.

8. On the formal removal of the restrictions, see a letter from the Visiting Justices to George Garland, Sheriff, 20 March 1824, George Garland Papers, Dorset C.R.O.

9. *Republican,* 16 June 1820.

10. Ibid., 11 August 1820.

11. Ibid., 4 August 1820.

12. There are many references to this incident in the *Republican* during November and December 1823. See also two letters by Carlile in the *Morning Herald,* 29 December 1823, attacking "J.H.N.," who had accused him of "insanity."

13. *Republican,* 27 October, 29 December 1820; *Carlile's Political Register,* 19 October 1839.

14. *Republican,* 27 June 1823.

15. The words are Eliza Sharples's, but they express Carlile's sentiments. *Isis,* 14 July 1832.

16. *The Gospel According to Richard Carlile, Showing the True Parentage, Birth, and Life of Our Allegorical Lord and Saviour, Jesus Christ* (London: Richard Carlile, 1827), p. 30.

17. Carlile to William Holmes, 6 July 1823, C.P.

18. *Republican,* 13 October 1820.

19. "Bathing," *Phoenix,* 19 February 1837.

20. *Republican,* 26 May 1820. See also his letter to William Holmes, 13 February 1822, C.P.; *New Year's Address to the Reformers,* 1 January 1821.

21. Carlile to William Holmes, n.d. (c. 1824), C.P.

22. *Republican,* 8 February 1821.

23. Carlile denounced "the inflicting of bodily torture." Ibid., 28 March 1823.

24. Following his lead a group of his imprisoned shopmen announced their intention in 1824 of converting Newgate Prison into "a school for literature, as well as for industry and good habits." Ibid., 26 August 1824.

25. Carlile to Richard Carlile, Jr., 20 July 1820, Print Room, B.M.

26. *Isis,* 28 July 1832.

27. Richard Carlile, *Observations on "Letters to a Friend on the Evidences, Doctrines, and Duties of the Christian Religion; by Olinthus Gregory, L.L.D. of the Royal Military Academy, Woolwich"* (London: Richard Carlile, 1825), p. 55. George Jacob Holyoake described his six months in Gloucester Gaol as "College Days of Learning." Holyoake, *Sixty Years of an Agitator's Life* (London: T. Fisher Unwin, 1906), vol. 1, p. 5.

28. *Republican,* 8 September 1820, 14 June 1822. *Fenning's Universal Spelling-Book* was part dictionary, grammar, and style sheet, an indispensable manual for an aspiring journalist. It went through hundreds of editions.

29. "On Reading," *Isis,* 11 August 1832.

30. *Lion,* 24 October 1828. Carlile wrote: "I had rather bear a year's imprisonment where I now am, then be compelled to read the forty-five volumes of Scott's novels." *Gauntlet,* 10 February 1833.

31. *Prompter,* 1 October 1831; Carlile to William Holmes, 10 April 1823, C.P.; *Isis,* 15 September 1832.

32. There are numerous references in the *Republican* to his political readings as, for example: 2 June, 1 July 1820, 23 August 1822.

33. See *Republican,* 2 May 1823; Carlile, *Observations on . . . Olinthus Gregory,* pp. 55-56; *To the Reformers of Great Britain,* 13 October 1821.

34. *Republican,* 18 February 1820. Carlile stated that the *Ruins of Empires* was a "work that has made more Deists and Atheists than all the other antichristian writings that have been circulated in this country." *Republican,* 15 December 1820. George Houston, an American freethinker, described it as "a book that created in me a thrist after truth and knowledge." *Correspondent,* 26 April 1828.

35. Carlile, *Observations on . . . Olinthus Gregory,* p. 99.

36. *To the Reformers of Great Britain,* 23 April 1821.

37. Ibid., 13 October 1821; *Carlile's Political Register,* 19 October 1839.

38. The phrase "human cattle" appears in the *Republican*, 12 August 1824.

39. On these complaints, see *To the Reformers of Great Britain*, 13 October 1821; Carlile to William Holmes, 4 August 1826, C.P.

40. *Republican*, 1 September 1820, 22 December 1820.

41. G. W. Foote, the freethinker, wrote about Carlile that "his literary ability was never transcendant, but he wrote nervous terse English." *Freethinker*, 30 March 1913.

42. Carlile thanked Bentham for giving him permission to print another tract, *Truth Versus Ashurst*, and assured him that "your kind attentions to me have not been wasted." Carlile to Jeremy Bentham, 22 January 1824, Bentham Papers, University College London.

43. "Philanthropos," *The Character of a Peer* (1821), p. 8. The other tracts, all published in 1821, were: *The Character of a Priest*, *The Character of a Soldier*, and *The Character of the Jew Books; Being a Defence of the Natural Innocence of Man, Against Kings and Priests, or Tyrants and Imposters*.

44. Richard Carlile, *An Address to Men of Science; Calling upon Them to Stand Forward and Vindicate the Truth from the Foul Grasp and Persecution of Superstition* (London: Richard Carlile, 1821), pp. 28-48.

45. *Moralist* (1823), no. 3.

46. Ibid, (1823), no. 1.

47. *Republican*, 17 December 1819. One of the Six Acts of December 1819 had authorized such seizures.

48. See *Wooler's British Gazette*, 21 November 1819.

49. *Oracle of Reason*, 17 September 1842; *Wooler's British Gazette*, 8 December 1822. See also *Drakard's Stamford News*, 6 December 1822.

50. Some of Carlile's property was also held for him in rented rooms in Bloomsbury. See the letter by an informer ("Searcher") to the Treasury Solicitor, 17 February 1822, T.S. 11, Box 945, Bundle 3465, P.R.O.

51. *Prompter*, 29 January 1831; *Phoenix*, 5 February 1837; *Christian Warrior*, 28 January 1843. There is a description of the sale of his stock in the *Republican*, 21 February 1823, and an auctioneer's notice in T.S. 11, Box 945. Bundle 3465, P.R.O.

52. Six of the *Addresses* were issued in 1821, including the *New Year's Address to the Reformers* appearing on January 1. A third volume of the *Deist*, published in 1826, included a reprint of Peter Annet's *Free Enquirer* and d'Holbach's *Bons Sens*.

53. Carlile's estimates of the value of his confiscated stock ranged from £1000 (*Republican*, 30 June 1820) to more than £5000. *Mock Trials*, p. xix.

54. There is an account by James Watson of the "Christian" fire. *Republican*, 19 November 1824. After the second fire Carlile wrote: "The Saints are trying every scheme to get the house down, and I fear they will succeed." Carlile to William Holmes, 21 December 1824, C.P.

5

THE WAR OF THE SHOPMEN

Richard Carlile's warfare with the government and private pressure groups in the early 1820s stemmed, to a considerable extent, from his intense belief in the importance of a free press. His conviction was not based upon legal or constitutional theory, nor did it derive from a concern to vindicate individual rights. He had read Blackstone, Paine, Bentham, and other political writers and had listened to innumerable orations on the merits of "universal liberty." But like most of his radical associates, theory counted for much less with him than practice. He regarded free expression, increasingly, as a means with which to achieve reform, a "grand panacea" that would produce "uniformity of opinion and conduct among the whole human race, by leading them in the path of Nature, and by concentrating all their ideas as in a focus."[1] "I convert not by preaching, or declamation," he told his readers, but by "the silent oratory of the pen, and printing press. Give me the free use of those, and I have nothing to fear from opposition."[2] Without the freedom to discuss and interpret ideas, especially those that challenged conventional opinion, it would be impossible, he believed, to eliminate obstacles to political and theological reform.

Carlile was also determined to vindicate himself personally. He had (as he conceived it) sacrificed freedom and a measure of financial security to publish critical writings. Unless such publication was acknowledged as useful (even at the price of additional hardship for himself and his followers), the rationale for his continuing imprisonment would remain unclear. Above all, Carlile wanted to augment his standing as a spokesman for reform: by publishing Paine, Palmer, d'Holbach, Shelley, and other antichristian writers frequently and cheaply, so as to maintain challenges against privileged power, particularly organized religion. An emancipated press, free of "delusion, error, and falsehood," was, therefore, essential to him.

As in 1819, his determination to publish meant a bitter conflict with authority. The Society for the Suppression of Vice had not abated its intention to stamp out "blasphemous and seditious" writings. To accept any compromise on this point would be for them to accept tacitly that it was impossible to protect church and state from "revolutionary" influences. Members of the Society, and of the even more enterprising Constitutional Association for Opposing the Progress of Disloyal and Seditious Principles (which was founded in May 1821 for the express purpose of curbing the "licentiousness of the press"), were unwilling, therefore, to cede any ground. The Liverpool government was less belligerent because of its need to take into account public opinion. But it too was prepared to launch an attack upon Carlile's publishing ventures. Thus the "war of the shopmen" in the early 1820s may best be described as a renewal of the earlier confrontation, with larger numbers of participants on both sides and greater legal significance attached to it.

Two general strategies, both intended to reduce Carlile's effectiveness as a journalist, comprised the patchwork of private and official actions initiated against him and his supporters from 1820 on. The first was to obstruct or impede his publications at source. The most drastic means for accomplishing this—of doubtful legality—was to prohibit him outright from engaging in publishing activities while in prison. Such a move was urged on the Home Office by solicitors employed by the Constitutional Association, who maintained that Carlile had no prima facie right to pursue "shocking, illegal practises" while in prison, and that he should be barred from using the mails and having access to printing facilities.[3] Reluctantly the Crown's law officers advised that no statutory or common law basis existed for a total ban on Carlile's publishing activities.[4] Journalists had traditionally been allowed to continue their activities while in prison provided, as in this case, they had the resources to do so. When Jane Carlile agreed, in 1819, to cease selling the *Age of Reason* and the *Principles of Nature*, the argument was clinched in Carlile's favor since these were the only publications for which he had been convicted.[5]

A better tactic, it was generally agreed, was to hold forth the possibility of another prosecution of Carlile should he disseminate more "blasphemous" or "seditious" tracts. Thus, Home Office officials kept a close surveillance on him in the 1820s. They collected files of the *Republican* and other pamphlets, marking and collating them, and periodically considered the possibility of a prosecution. In October 1824, Robert Peel, the home secretary, agreed to bring blasphemy charges against Carlile for a series of freethinking pamphlets if the attorney-general and solicitor general consented. Both refused, however, perhaps because another conviction for blasphemous libel would have made Carlile liable for transportation to New South Wales under the provisions of the Blasphemous and Seditious Libels Act of 1819. Instant martyrdom for a prominent reformer without any compensating political advantage was not in the government's best interest. Still, controversy cut both ways. Charles B. Woolaston, a visiting magistrate to Dorchester Gaol, opposed a prosecution of Carlile, unless, as he put it, "it would be followed up by sending the man out of the kingdom." Anything less severe would, Wollaston believed, merely increase his notoriety and the sale of his pamphlets.[6]

If Carlile was to be impeded from publishing radical literature, a more effective approach was to employ a series of legal pinpricks. These included the closing of his shop for three months in the winter of 1819-1820, the confiscation of portions of his stock, and restrictive actions taken by the keeper of Dorchester Gaol, undoubtedly with official backing. The keeper lacked the legal power to confiscate packages exchanged between Carlile and his helpers, but he had many of them opened and, in some instances, the contents arbitrarily removed. Such intrusions did not obstruct Carlile's activities significantly. They irritated him, however, and he frequently complained about them, to no avail.

The second general strategy used against Carlile in the 1820s was to attack those who assisted him. This worked better than interference with the copy at source, because the distribution of radical newspapers and tracts was a cumbersome procedure. Carlile had not only to get the *Republican* and his other publications into print but to oversee their distribution throughout the country. Many persons were involved in this, including shopmen, wholesale distributors, and vendors. In the early 1820s these assistants became sporadic victims of a campaign to drive Carlile out of business. The warfare was conducted by magistrates, legal officers of the Crown, hired attorneys, clergymen, and assorted police officials. Occasionally, the results were impressive; more often than not, they were uncoordinated and of limited impact.

Those who hawked Carlile's publications in the streets were the most likely victims of prosecution, as they had been in 1819 and as they were to be again in the 1830s during the battle to win an unstamped press. From 1819 to the end of 1821, vendors who worked for Carlile were prosecuted in London, Manchester, Oxford, Edinburgh, Nottingham, and elsewhere.[7] Many were poor laborers whose income from the sale of "blasphemous and seditious" literature fluctuated between ten shillings and one pound weekly. Because of their poverty and lack of legal knowledge, they were often unable to defend themselves. Even worse, they could be tried and convicted summarily in police courts on miscellaneous charges, ranging from the sale of printed literature without a license to—in the case of an Exeter agent—vending cider without a license.[8]

Prison terms meted out to street vendors varied from one week to six months, and gaol conditions for such "common criminals" were often wretched. Yet many poor men and women, undeterred by the prospect of incarceration, worked enthusiastically for Carlile. Little capital was needed to become a street vendor, and the rewards—a small income, political involvement, some "fame" (Carlile had begun his career in this way)—acted as a stimulus. For every hawker of radical literature who was prosecuted and imprisoned in Cold Bath Fields Gaol or the Giltspur Street Compter in London or in a provincial "lock-up" during these years, many more continued to be available if needed. It proved difficult, therefore, though not impossible, to make a dent in Carlile's business by focusing on his street vendors.

More effective were the prosecutions directed against his pivotal associates: those who worked in his shops and were responsible for putting together his publications. These shopmen were the cog-wheels of his publishing activities, loyalists without whom he could not have functioned as a journalist for any length of time. They worked in his successive "Temples of Reason," forwarding reading matter to him in Dorchester, receiving copy that they edited and passed on to printers and compositors, and handling distribution arrangements with country agents and wholesalers. They also sold pamphlets sometimes resorting to elaborate contrivances to avoid detection, as in the use of a hole in the ceiling or floor (with an attached drop), or a "silent system." The latter worked as follows: the names of all available publications were listed on a clock, purchasers indicated their preferences by rotating a dial, which was operated by a pulley, and money was then exchanged without any overt communication between the parties to the act.[9]

But the prosecution of Carlile's shopmen was a difficult undertaking because, unlike vendors, they could not be convicted summarily for minor offenses. As "publishers" of newspapers and pamphlets (although their names usually did not appear in print) they were answerable to more serious charges: specifically, that of disseminating "blasphemous and seditious" libels. Jury trials were part of the legal process, with conviction by no means a forgone conclusion. The harshness of the penalties engendered sympathy for the defendants and increased the possibility of an indecisive verdict or outright acquittal.

Between 1821 and 1824, almost two dozen of Carlile's shopmen were prosecuted by the Vice Society, the Liverpool government, and, from 1821 on, by the Constitutional Association, which attacked publications that spread "false and inflammatory statements respecting public institutions and public men . . . and [that offered] direct incitement to violence and crime."[10] The "Bridge Street Gang" (as reformers called the Constitutional Association) survived for less than three years, but it was supported by prominent clergymen and politicians and it possessed considerable financial resources. It also used its legal powers more ruthlessly than did the Vice Society or the government.[11] "If there be an individual who can imagine, that publications subversive of the Constitution, of morality, of decency, or of religion, can be tolerated in a well-regulated society," it warned, "the examples of Curl, Woolston, Wilkes, Paine, Eaton, and Carlile, will furnish a speedy and satisfactory refutation."[12] When its admonition was ignored, it commenced a series of prosecutions against Carlile's shopmen in an attempt to drive them from the field. It hired informers to buy radical pamphlets and to incite illegal acts, and at the ensuing trials its attorneys did their best to obtain convictions, sometimes by using dubious legal tactics. Not surprisingly, the Constitutional Association was condemned by reformers, who accused it of posing as a "genuine Loyalty Company" and of seeking to reduce "the liberty of the press . . . to a mere shadow."[13]

Carlile's response to the prosecutions of his vendors and shopmen was resolute, though less "political" than might have been expected. He did not call upon his supporters in the country to join the battle. Instead he fell back on a tactic that was idiosyncratic even within the context of self-improving radicalism. He affirmed that he would not use outside volunteers until the "spontaneous unity" of his family had been tested and all of its members coaxed into frontline political positions. Thus, he implored his wife, sister Mary-Anne, and three sons (who were not yet old enough to participate meaningfully) to demonstrate their loyalty to him by assuming the risks of radical publishing. Given the lack of affection between him and Jane Carlile, and his somewhat aloof relationship with Mary-Anne, it was an odd appeal. But his conception of reform was quirky, and in this instance he regarded his next of kin as "humble instruments" to do his bidding. He wanted them to become partners in the struggle for justice. His only regret, or so he implied, was that he did not have a larger family to share his suffering and work for the regeneration of mankind.[14]

Jane Carlile was the ballast of family resistance and a loyal associate from November 1819, when Carlile's term of prison began, until February 1821, when she was convicted of blasphemous libel and sent to join him in Dorchester Gaol. Jane was an uneducated country woman who lacked even a patina of radical consciousness. Yet she remained deeply loyal to her husband during his time of greatest need. Her conjugal duty, as she saw it, was to endure hardship and, in poignant phrasing, to "share [Richard's] sufferings as I have shared his prosperity."[15] Personally unenamored by his schemes, she nonetheless gave them full public support. As Carlile awkwardly expressed his feelings on a later occasion: "When she saw I was determined, she would assist, after her fit or anger had passed away."[16]

Carlile denigrated or commended his wife in public depending upon the alacrity with which she carried out his prescribed tasks. "I rejoice to think," he wrote in the *Republican*, that she is "an object virtuous enough for the disapprobation of . . . ministers." Yet when she wavered ever so slightly he did not hesitate to reprove her for lacking "sufficient fortitude." "I trust that she will be sufficiently recovered in time to answer the first call," he told his readers at a time when she was seriously ill. "Any ground of excuse or evasion will be to me extremely painful."[17]

Such sentiments did little to enhance the reputation of a reformer who preached the need for individual morality but did not always put his precepts into action.

In December 1819, shortly after Carlile's incarceration began, Jane gave birth to Thomas Paine, their third son. (A previous son, also named Thomas Paine, had died in the spring.) With the shop temporarily closed down and portions of furniture carted away by order of the sheriff, she endured extreme hardship during these winter months. The account of her visit to her husband in Dorchester, in January 1820, is affecting. As he told his readers: "She wept, held out her infant to speak for her, whom she could no longer support, and sunk down in a chair incapable of uttering a sound."[18] Yet within a few weeks she reopened the Fleet Street shop and for eighteen months worked in it, often at great personal danger to herself. When her efforts brought her imprisonment, she adjured other wives to emulate her example: "Let us, as women, never cease to stimulate and strengthen the minds of our husbands and sons to raise a power above those assassins of virtue that shall bring them to justice for their manifold crime."[19]

In October 1819, even before the sentence against her husband was officially announced, the Vice Society brought an information against Jane Carlile for publishing the first day's proceedings of the *Mock Trials*, containing portions of the *Age of Reason*. She was charged with contributing to "the high displeasure of Almighty God, to the great scandal of the Christian Religion, to the evil example of all others, [and conspiring] against the peace of our said Lord the King, his crown and dignity."[20] Her attitude was flexible. Rejecting the advice of Carlile, who urged her to resist, she pleaded innocent but agreed to desist from selling any tracts that had been or were currently the object of a prosecution.

This response brought her no peace. In February 1820, she became the object of two additional Vice Society prosecutions: for selling Sherwin's *Life of Paine*, a volume not hitherto deemed worthy of prosecution, and for publishing an essay in the *Republican* by a Peterborough correspondent who accused the prince regent of condoning the Peterloo Massacre and blamed clergymen for the "abominable . . . systems of oppression, which have nearly brought the whole nation to destruction."[21] In succeeding months she was harried continually by the Vice Society (being briefly imprisoned on one occasion), and in October she was

tried and convicted on both charges, notwithstanding that
Matthew Davenport Hill, a prominent barrister, defended her. Her
trial in the Guildhall was devoid of excitement, and it received little
coverage in the press. Carlile, relishing the cut and thrust of
confrontation and the political capital to be earned from a well-
publicized clash, urged her to stand firm, to oppose "the venom of
this society." She did not do so. Fortunately for him, however,
both convictions were overturned on technical grounds, enabling
him to gain some publicity for his cause and, briefly, to increase the
output of his publications.[22]

At this point the attorney-general entered the lists against Jane
Carlile. She was accused of a seditious libel for publishing an article
by Carlile in the *Republican*, in which he characterized George IV's
treatment of Queen Caroline as "malignant, treacherous, and
abominable" and attacked him for "studiously [endeavoring] to
break [his wife's] spirits and her heart by the most unmanly and
brutal conduct."[23] Since Caroline's attempts to attend her estranged
husband's coronation in 1820 were supported enthusiastically by
many reformers, it was invidious to single out a passage in the
Republican for prosecution. Yet Jane Carlile was brought speedily
to trial in January 1821 on precisely this charge.

She appeared without counsel in deference to her husband, who
insisted that lawyers were parasites who belonged to an oppressive
political faction. But the orotund speech that he wrote for her was
even less effective than his own defense oration had been in 1819.
The clerk of the court read Jane's lengthy statement, somewhat
diminishing its risibility. Otherwise the circumstance of a barely
educated woman citing learned passages from Tertullian, Saint
Augustine, and Cicero was calculated to evoke mirth rather than
compassion.[24] To nobody's surprise, a special jury rapidly
convicted Jane. Her consolation, tenuous at best, was extravagant
praise from her husband. "I have felt more solid happiness as a
married man, within this last year," he observed, "than [in] all the
former years of my wedded life." Her joy was tempered, too, by the
severity of her sentence: two years in Dorchester prison and
payment of recognizances of £200 upon her release to certify good
behavior for a period of three years. Only her married status gave
her some protection. As a married woman she lacked legal standing
and could not have a fine assessed against her.

With his prison room cramped by his wife's presence, Carlile next induced Mary-Anne to enter the battle. She was even a less promising participant than her sister-in-law because of her minimal education and nonexistent political convictions. Without hesitation, though, she became "the next victim to the propagation of moral and correct theological principles."[25] In October 1820 during Jane Carlile's first trial, Mary-Anne commenced working at 55 Fleet Street. She stayed there for more than nine months, doing everything she could to keep the publishing business going and to uphold the honor of the family.

Mary-Anne Carlile drew down upon herself the wrath of both the Vice Society and the Constitutional Association. In the spring of 1821, the former brought charges of blasphemy against her for publishing *An Appendix to the Theological Works of Thomas Paine,* a modest deist tract that was based on an American publication; simultaneously, the Constitutional Association charged her with seditious libel for selling an essay by Carlile in which he lauded the revolution in Spain (his statement was dated from the "Second Year of the Spanish Revolution from Despotism to Liberty") and implied that a similar upheaval in Britain would usefully eradicate privilege and overcome opposition to reform.[26]

Mary-Anne was tried on both charges in the Guildhall in July 1821 before two special juries. The verdicts were mixed. On the sedition charge, which came on second, the jury failed to reach a verdict after twenty hours of deliberation. A young barrister, Henry Cooper, skillfully presented her case. He facetiously commended the Constitutional Association for its "pure spirit of chivalry" and, more effectively, charged that its actions "kindle feelings of indignation, and hostility, and hatred in large numbers of the people, [and] are of no general benefit to the state." Their only result, he told the jury, was to curtail the boundaries of free expression.[27] Hill's forensic skills impressed Carlile, who praised him for the "very eloquent, very bold, and very honest style of his defense." But the lawyer's quiescent political tone was irritating— as in his statement that the Carliles typified "wild democracy"—and Carlile would have preferred not to have involved him in the case.[28]

Mary-Anne's blasphemy trial on the same day was more to Carlile's liking, though it ended in a conviction and a lengthy prison term. Mary-Anne conducted her own defense. Like Jane Carlile, she read a speech written by her brother that was recondite and unpersuasive on the legal aspects of the trial but which contained some politically trenchant passages. It depicted the common law crime of blasphemy as "a phantom of the brain of a madman," which was used as a tool of oppression, and it referred to Mary-Anne as "a forlorn female, with no other friend or relative than an imprisoned brother."[29] When the presiding judge, Sir William Draper Best, "suppressed" portions of the defense speech on the ground that it was blasphemous, events worked in Carlile's favor. Substantial public sympathy developed on Mary-Anne's behalf. Carlile published her *Suppressed Defence* as a one-shilling tract and attacked the judicial ruling as "a wanton act of illegality and judicial corruption." He was supported by Sir Francis Burdett, Joseph Hume, and other reformers, who presented petitions to the House of Commons on her behalf and took an interest in the case.[30]

Mary-Anne Carlile also commanded support by virtue of the harsh penalty meted out to her. She was sentenced to one year in prison and assessed a fine of £500. But what made the sentence much worse than it seemed was her poverty; other than by a public subscription or an act of private charity, there was no possibility that she could pay her fine. Jane Carlile's marital status protected her against such an "open" penalty, but Mary-Anne had no such defense, and her sentence might be extended at the whim of the home secretary, so long as the fine remained unpaid. As Robert Peel, the holder of the office, remarked offhandedly during a parliamentary debate in 1823: "When the Crown thought [Mary-Anne Carlile] had passed in terms of years, a confinement equal to that fine she was unable to pay, it might extend its mercy to her."[31] In the event, she served twenty-eight months in Dorchester prison, her fines being remitted and her freedom granted in November 1823.

The imprisonment of his wife and sister was personally as well as politically significant for Carlile. Both women were locked up in the same room with him: Jane, from February 1821 to February 1823; Mary-Anne (with separate sleeping quarters), from July 1821 to November 1823. His son Thomas Paine also remained in prison for much of the time, despite a series of illnesses. And in June 1822, a daughter, named Hypatia in memory of a fourth-century Alexandrian "infidel" martyred by Christians, was born in the room in Dorchester Gaol which the family shared. (Hypatia's death from whooping cough in February 1825 was a traumatic event for

Carlile, who blamed the Christians—"those real representatives of all that is religiously foul and bigoted in this country"—for it.) Amid this unwelcome increase in numbers, the only consolation vouchsafed to Carlile was the domiciling of Richard and Alfred, his two older sons, with his in-laws in Dorset where, in theory, they were being groomed for radical warfare. When they periodically visited him, they merely added to the tension.

These unanticipated by-products of family warfare upset Carlile's "philosophical calm." He wanted to be left alone with his books, to ruminate on theology and politics and to write. Instead he had to endure the cloying attentions of his loved ones. "Locked up as I am with wife, sister, and child," he confided to an associate in 1822, "I find it difficult to accomplish the necessary quantity of reading and writing."[32] Disagreements began to rend the fabric of domestic unity, and he had to compromise on minor points. He consented, for example, to take daily walks with his wife and children and to abide by restrictions on his movements imposed by the keeper of the prison, whereas previously he had refused to leave his room in protest at these rules. When, however, he demanded total silence from Jane and Mary-Anne, they maintained that this was "not most agreeable to us."[33] The clash of temperaments was abrasive, and Richard's marriage, already under strain, deteriorated badly, leading to a "moral divorce" ten years later. But he stayed on relatively good terms with his sister, and she returned to Devon and continued to be a "warm partisan" of his after her liberation.[34]

Having exhausted domestic recruits (his older married sister refused to aid him), Carlile turned to volunteers in July 1821. Hitherto he had rejected assistance other than by means of the discreet rendering of gifts and the proffering of rhetoric; now he actively solicited it in the knowledge that there was no choice if he was to continue his struggle. From July 1821 on, therefore, when the first provincial recruits, Joseph Rhodes, a Manchester shoemaker, and Susannah Wright of Nottingham, arrived in London, the "war of the shopmen" can properly be said to have begun. At this point the personal struggle of the Carliles became transformed into an intense political battle. And the issues raised— freedom of expression, radical reform of political and religious institutions, the sale of "blasphemous and seditious" literature—

became an integral part of the cultural and political aspirations of the working classes in the early nineteenth century.[35]

During the "war of the shopmen" Carlile's qualities as a leader became defined. He directed a miscellaneous group of enthusiasts who fought vigorously for their cause. His own contributions were part technical, part political, part inspirational. He worked tirelessly from his prison room: advising his shopmen and vendors how to resist prosecutions, placarding the streets of London with tracts and broadsides, providing legal advice, giving those who were imprisoned a weekly "gaol allowance" of up to 5 shillings each. Few details escaped Carlile's surveillance; few squabbles were too minor for him to attempt to resolve. Though exasperated by the pettiness of political strife, he rarely lost his temper. On the contrary, he corresponded enthusiastically with his followers, in the *Republican* and privately, rarely showing any doubt or hesitation about the likelihood of victory.

The most impressive asset that Carlile possessed as a leader was an animating moral vision. His shops were, he boasted, "[fortresses] unassailable to all the force of corruption . . . [which] will like a moral sun, shed [their] beams upon every extremity of the Island."[36] Vowing to provide "a weekly case for prosecution until all harassment ceased," he described himself as a spokesman for "all mankind, white or black, red or brown, the Asian, the African, the European, and the American." He was prepared to do battle until "the destinies of monarchies are sealed, [and] the people of the earth will them extinct." Such rhetoric may have been excessive, but it acted as a spur to working-class reformers who, like Carlile, were unwilling to compromise and for whom apocalyptic imagery was uplifting. To radical workingmen, he was a "GENERAL who will stand by us, and let us enlist under his banners; and batten down tyranny by words and arguments instead of fire and sword."[37]

The shopmen and vendors who went into battle on Carlile's behalf in the early 1820s were, like the readers of his publications, a microcosm of the thousands of artisans and mechanics who participated in radical reform movements during the first half of the nineteenth century. Of the more than twenty shopmen who were convicted and imprisoned between 1821 and 1824, about half came from Leeds, Manchester, and London, while the remainder were from towns and villages that extended from the rural hinterlands of Lincolnshire to the West Country. A significant number of volunteers were shoemakers or printers by trade, both groups being well represented in radical movements throughout the period. Others who played a visible role in Carlile's struggle included a flax dresser, a carter, a drysalters' warehouseman, and, conspicuous by his singularity, an "itinerant comedian" who brought a love of Shakespeare into reform politics.

The shopmen and vendors also represented a broad spectrum of commitment. They were poetasters, social cooperators, freethinkers, and political agitators. Most were antichristian, though in divergent ways that mirrored Carlile's own intellectual shifts during these years, as he moved from deism to atheism to allegorical rationalism. Nearly all of his volunteers considered themselves to be disciples of Paine, and most supported "republican" government. And the majority passionately believed in self-improvement as a lever of social change. Carlile urged his shopmen to become "bright men" by developing their intellectual skills; and many of them responded to these importunities by reading and studying diligently and by seeking to master the intricacies of politics and theology. By working for a free press and pitting their "mental superiority" against "vice, tyranny, and falsehood," they hoped to extirpate corruption and to enable every man and woman to secure a proper reward in a just society.

The specifics of each of their prosecutions differed. Most of the shopmen brought to trial between July 1821 and July 1824 were accused of blasphemy, while some were charged with seditious libel. The charges depended on the whims of private attorneys and the aggressiveness of the government's legal officers. Several shopmen were prosecuted for selling Palmer's *Principles of Nature* (which Carlile reprinted in May 1822 after a hiatus of more than two years); others were tried for articles that appeared in the *Republican* or in the *Addresses to the Reformers*; still others were accused of blasphemy for selling the *Observations on . . . Olinthus Gregory* or one of Carlile's other freethought tracts. In the only departure from the seeming randomness of these prosecutions, eight shopmen were tried and convicted of blasphemous libel in the spring and early summer of 1824, in a series of actions brought by the attorney-general and the solicitor to the Treasury. The charges were based on the sale of the *Principles of Nature* and Paine's *Age of Reason,* the latter being reissued in 1823 at a time when Carlile was optimistic about his publishing prospects.

Carlile published accounts of many of the shopmen's trials, including those of his wife and sister. These appeared in two- or three-penny weekly numbers in the *Republican,* and were then bound and sold in pamphlet or volume form. Mostly the publications were undertaken at a loss, sometimes amid bickering with shopmen who felt that their trials were not receiving sufficient attention. But because publicity was a primary objective, Carlile gave prominence to those trials that featured strong defense speeches or, in the instances of his sister and a shopman named William Tunbridge, "suppressed" defenses. The shopmen were urged by Carlile to shun counsel. He tried to serve as their factotum attorney, helping to marshal arguments for the defense and frequently writing the speeches. What their orations lacked in legal acumen, therefore, they more often than not compensated for in grit and bravado.[38]

Most of the shopmen made an "open avowal of principle" during their trials. They took as their model Susannah Wright, a poor woman who, when charged with blasphemy in the Guildhall in July 1822, declared: "I have no fear about me for anything that concerns myself. I should enjoy even a dungeon in advocating such a cause as that in which I am now engaged. . . . I am bold to tell these persecutors, they never can, they never will, put down these publications." Humphrey Boyle, a shoemaker, attacked his judge and prosecutors in similar terms: "Silently and ingloriously, I will never succumb to a corrupt power. I may fall before it, but I will first deal it some blows and as many as my strength and ability will admit."[39] Most effective perhaps was the speech of William Haley, a well-educated shopman who told a packed courtroom at the Old Bailey in July 1824: "We are not ignorant; we are not driven by frantic poverty to engage in the sale of these works, far otherwise; we know that we cannot reasonably expect to continue more than a day or two in the employment, and we have every reasonable prospect of being consigned to the company of the Newgate beetles, for some five or six and thirty moons: yet no title in the gift of the proud sovereign of these realms is more eagerly sought, than a situation of so honourable a nature."[40]

Although most of the shopmen were convicted (during three years only one secured an outright acquittal, and this resulted from the failure of a witness to appear), they fought a series of vigorous legal battles. Individually and collectively they attacked a judicial system that appeared to sanction restraints upon free expression and to be weighted heavily against the poor. The selection of special jurors, a practice widely used in political trials in the early nineteenth century, was excoriated: by limiting the choice of prospective jurors to propertied freeholders, it was nearly impossible (or so it was believed) for poor reformers to receive fair treatment.[41] Likewise, the judges who presided at these trials were accused of manipulating the forms of law to fit their conservative prejudices. In the guise of objective charges to the jury, for example, they frequently pronounced the accused to be guilty, by declaring passages from tracts to be libelous. Nor were Mary-Anne Carlile and William Tunbridge the only defendants to have their speeches "suppressed." At her trial, Susannah Wright was interrupted repeatedly by the judge as she attempted to demonstrate the "falsity" of the Thirty-nine Articles; when she described the Vice Society as "modern Herods, and Pilates, and High Priests," she was prevented from continuing.[42] Similar treatment was doled out to another shopman, James Watson, who was tried in the spring of 1823 for selling Palmer's *Principles of Nature.* Watson was not permitted to make substantive comments on Palmer nor was he allowed to cite passages from the book in extenuation of his act.[43]

Following the example of Carlile in 1819, many shopmen attacked the vagueness of the common law crime of blasphemy. William Tunbridge, who subsequently quarreled with Carlile and became an associate of William Cobbett, maintained at his trial in January 1823 that "there could be no such law as would compel men to admit the truth of any system of religion," while William Holmes, another shopman, asserted: "I deny the right of any earthly being to prevent the free expression of human opinions."[44] A temperate statement by a Lancashire shoemaker, William Campion, at his trial at the Old Bailey in June 1824, was most eloquent on this point. "What is blasphemy?" Campion asked.

Is it blasphemy to suggest, that Tobias's dog was perhaps a poodle, when others assert that it was a grey-hound? Is it blasphemy, to insinuate, that a serpent's talking to a woman must be understood allegorically, and not literally? Is it blasphemy to assert that the great unknown cause of all things could never have commanded one of his trusty servants, to feed upon bread buttered with human feces? Alas! Gentlemen, I known not what blasphemy is.[45]

With Carlile's encouragement many shopmen interjected political themes. Watson and Haley maintained that the common law protected pre-Reformation Christianity but that it "can know nothing of reformed Christianity, but as an heresy." Others challenged the "truth" of Christianity. Haley spoke of "my perfect belief of the falsehood of the Christian religion," while Campion voiced the opinion that all religious systems were exploitive and self-serving. At his trial James Watson tried unsuccessfully to "prove" that Moses was a murderer.[46]

Hostile judges sometimes declared the comments about religion to be out of order. Thomas Denman, who in his capacity as common serjeant of the City of London presided at the trial of Humphrey Boyle in May 1822, allowed Boyle to make a lengthy speech, which included a reference to the Bible as "an obscene book . . . not worthy of being called the word of a God." (He did this after requesting that women and children leave the courtroom.) But Denman, a former Whig politician with pro-reform sympathies, did not typify the attitudes of the bench.[47] More characteristic was the ruling by the chairman of Clerkenwell Sessions, who told Watson at his trial: "You may read the Bible, but not make any comment upon it; it is both immoral, irreligious, and illegal. Let the case be what it may I shall stop you."[48] Discussion often centered on what constituted a "fair and temperate" discussion of religion. As defined by judges and prosecutors, theological controversy was lawful so long as it was "reasonable." But "gross and indecent attacks" of the kind made upon Christianity by many of Carlile's shopmen were not tolerable. Such attacks, it was stressed by prosecutors, were intended to sway the unprotected poor who had to be shielded from "contumelious abuse."

Sometimes shopmen continued to gain publicity after their incarceration. With the financial and tutelary support of Carlile, the "Newgate martyrs" (those imprisoned during the series of coordinated prosecutions in 1824) issued a journal, the *Newgate*

Monthly Magazine, which sold for a shilling and remained in circulation from September 1824 to August 1826. Intended to dramatize the case for "freedom of opinion both in theory and practice," it gave space to a potpourri of radical enthusiasms, including birth control, phrenology, temperance, and legal divorce. Richard Hassell, a farm laborer from Dorset who became one of Carlile's leading disciples, wrote articles on mathematics and chemistry for the *Newgate Monthly Magazine,* in which he analyzed "the fundamental principles on which the different sciences are built." Likewise, William Campion, a militant atheist, attacked the traditional accounts of Christianity. Adhering closely to the interpretations of Carlile, Campion, in a series of articles, rejected the history of Jesus as "a heap of folly, fraud, fable, and fiction" and characterized all human and "divine" actions as a product of the "operations and revolutions of nature." The *Newgate Monthly Magazine* also printed lengthy excerpts from the writings of freethinkers such as Shelley, Diderot, Voltaire, and Peter Annet, including some of Annet's controversial opinions about marriage and divorce. By its ties to Carlile and the views it espoused, the journal earned a respected niche in the literature of self-improving, radical workingmen.[49]

Several shopmen wrote essays for the *Republican* and other radical papers and published tracts under their own imprints. Humphrey Boyle, the first volunteer from Leeds to join Carlile, penned analyses of religion for the *Republican* and the *Leeds Patriot.* Like Carlile, he attacked "priestcraft" and superstition, emphasizing their incompatibility with science. In an article written in the Giltspur Street Compter in February 1823, which Carlile described as a "masterpiece," he refuted traditional arguments for the existence of an "immaterial being."[50] William Holmes, who carried on an extensive correspondence with Carlile for many years, was another contributor to freethought literature. Although he renounced his "infidel" convictions in the late 1830s and became a propagandist for evangelical Christianity, Holmes wrote a large quantity of atheistic verse from his eyrie in the Compter where he was imprisoned for two years. After his release in March 1824, he contributed to radical journalism for several more years, working as a tractseller in Sheffield and publishing articles in the *Sheffield Independent* and other provincial journals.[51]

Several volunteers moved permanently into radical politics as a result of their involvement with the "war of the shopmen." James Watson, who worked in Carlile's Water Lane shop from September 1822 to February 1823 and in another shop from the summer of 1824 to November 1825, was the best known. In the late 1820s he became an advocate of economic cooperation and in the following decade an important participant in the struggle for an unstamped press and an influential publisher of freethought literature.[52] Thomas Ryley Perry, the "itinerant comedian," augmented his position in radical circles after his ties with Carlile ended. An "avowed infidel" throughout his life, Perry supported himself by selling pamphlets after being released from prison in 1827, first in Wellingborough and then in Leicester. In the 1830s he, like Watson, was imprisoned for selling unstamped newspapers.[53] Similarly, Humphrey Boyle remained active in Leeds politics for many years after his initiation into radical agitation by Carlile.

The legal and political problems faced by Carlile's volunteers became especially pressing in 1821-1822. Then, as a result of stock seizures and interference with distribution, several publications had to be suspended. With the *Republican* itself in abeyance during 1821, a "siege mentality" prevailed at 55 Fleet Street and in the smaller Water Lane shop. Placards were displayed prominently in the shop windows, which avowed the determination of Carlile and his followers to continue their struggle. The broadside that best encapsulated this mood of defiance stated: "Two shopmen [were] arrested this afternoon . . . by the Bridge-Street Gang. The same obnoxious pamphlets shall be sold in spite of them: 'tis a right noble cause; they shall not, with all their combined powers, shut up the 'Temple of Reason.' O! base gang! You will do no harm to the cause; but good. This is the mart for sedition and blasphemy."[54] Carlile entreated "brave fellows from the North" to join him. "I would go on to do all that I may find power to do," he wrote in March 1822, "and I think I can answer for the brave few who have gathered around me."[55] He badly needed funds because his profits were depleted, and a subscription campaign that he commenced in August 1821 yielded only a few hundred pounds. But he survived, largely it seemed, with the help of his usual intangible assets: undiminished enthusiasm, perseverance, an application to the task at hand, and, most important, an ability to inspire loyalty, less from a general conviction that what he said was right than from a respect for the integrity and resoluteness with which he said it.

In January 1822, he resumed publication of the *Republican* after a suspension of a year, and in the following months he issued several freethought pamphlets that had not been sold since 1819, including Palmer's *Principles of Nature.* During the next two years, stock seizures and legal difficulties forced him to transfer his business from shop to shop. But he never accepted defeat as a realistic possibility. He continued to wage "war" against the advocates of conservative political and religious ideas. By the spring of 1822, after more than a year of frenzied activity, the Constitutional Association began to break up. It initiated its final prosecution in May. Then, after additional pronouncements, it disappeared into the recesses of history, a testament to the failure of clergymen and politicians to eliminate those "poor wretches" who, in the words of a leader writer on the *Glasgow Argus,* were spreading "the poison of deism and jacobinism over the land."

The Vice Society, however, continued to prosecute Carlile's shopmen, as did the Liverpool ministry. In the final months of 1822 the attorney-general commenced scattered actions against the volunteers, mostly based on the publication and sale of the *Principles of Nature.* These led to a number of prison sentences but did not impede significantly the distribution of freethought tracts. The only tangible outcome of the prosecutions was an unintended one: some reformers, hitherto silent, were prodded into criticism of the government. John Stuart Mill, for example, wrote three letters to the *Morning Chronicle* in January and February 1823 under the pseudonym "Wickliff," in which, with the attacks on the shopmen in mind, he apotheosized the virtues of press freedom. "Reviling or abusing what is not sentient, as a degradation of the individual who has recourse to it," observed Mill, "ought at most to be punished as an offence against decency."[56] Francis Place, Joseph Hume, and other moderate reformers echoed these sentiments.

The situation was quiet for a time after 1822, so much so that Carlile took it upon himself to issue a miniature edition of Paine's *Theological Works* in May 1823. He sold 5000 copies of the volume. Although many shopmen were still in prison, he had, it seemed, established the right to publish and distribute "blasphemous and seditious" literature. Neither the attorney-general nor the Vice Society appeared eager to resume warfare with him.

The calm was shattered in May 1824 when summary indictments brought by the attorney-general and the solicitor to the Treasury against eight shopmen were followed by stock seizures. These attacks represented a final effort by the government to destroy Carlile's publishing business. Beleaguered once more, he and his supporters fought back determinedly and gained the support of many reformers who had stood apart up to now. Carlile asserted that "the battle of IGNORANCE against KNOWLEDGE, SUPERSTITION against REASON, BRUTE FORCE against MORAL POWER, VICE against VIRTUE, DISHONESTY against HONESTY, TYRANNY against LIBERTY, is again raging." He issued a "Proclamation" of resistance, which called for subscriptions to aid those under attack.[57]

Nerves were stretched tightly during the spring and early summer of 1824, and Carlile's shopmen became imbued with a sense of political mission. Their resistance took on millennialist overtones. At her trial in 1822, Susannah Wright had affirmed a belief that "as the blood of the Christian martyrs became the seed of the Christian Church, so shall our sufferings become the seed of free discussion, and in those very sufferings we will triumph over you."[58] Her call to arms was now taken up by other shopmen. William Campion remonstrated in apocalyptic terms that "the blood of the martyrs is the seed of every church," while John Clarke, a "humble mechanic" who published an "eccentric" (Carlile's adjective) *Critical Review of the Life, Character, Miracles and Resurrection of Jesus Christ in a Series of Letters to Dr. Adam Clarke,* declared his readiness to join the "noble army of martyrs" in the battle to remove "mental darkness" from the minds of the working classes.[59] Even Francis Place, a reformer whose atheism was held discreetly in check and who looked askance at the "street" agitation of Carlile and his followers, waxed enthusiastic. In a pamphlet entitled *St. Paul the Apostle, and William Campion,* he compared the plight of Campion with that of Paul of Tarsus. Both men, Place contended, had been prosecuted wrongfully for political reasons. If the proceedings against Campion and other "Newgate Martyrs" were "not as unjust as they are infamous," he commented, "then no such thing as injustice ever existed on the face of the earth."[60]

The 1824 prosecutions were bitterly resisted, and while the government secured convictions against every one of the "Little Honourable House of Blasphemers"—with prison terms ranging from six months to three years—it did so at a political cost. The publicity was so adverse that charges of blasphemous or seditious libel were less easily employed after 1824 as weapons to suppress dissent. No further attempts were made during the nineteenth century to interfere with the publication of Paine or Palmer. The statement by the editor of the *Newgate Monthly Magazine* that these prosecutions were "the last grand struggle of dying priest-craft . . . [and] the last effort to chain the freedom of the press," was overdrawn and lacking in perspective.[61] But it was not entirely fictitious. The freedom of the working classes to familiarize themselves with radical ideas had been extended, and Carlile's claim to have affected the history of his time may be said to have been validated for the first time.

Notes

1. *Republican,* 8 December 1820; Carlile, *Observations on . . . Olinthus Gregory,* p. 33; Thompson, *Making of the English Working Class,* p. 720. A detailed study of this episode is in Wickwar, *Struggle for the Freedom of the Press,* especially pp. 180-245.

2. *Republican,* 21 January 1820.

3. See the legal opinion by "Mr. Christian" and related correspondence in T.S. 11, Box 945, Bundle 3465, P.R.O.

4. In November 1819 Lord Grenville, a member of the Liverpool government, tried unsuccessfully to persuade Lord Liverpool to include a provision in the blasphemous and seditious libels bill, giving magistrates the power "to ban the continual publication of blasphemous and seditious papers . . . both in the interval between indictment and trial and also after conviction." Memorandum from Lord Grenville to Lord Liverpool, 12 November 1819, cited in Charles D. Yonge, *The Life and Administration of Robert Banks, Second Earl of Liverpool, K.G.* (London: Macmillan, 1868), vol. 2, p. 426.

5. Carlile claimed that the Gaol Act of 1824 gave him the legal right to carry on his trade in prison. *Durham Chronicle,* 25 July 1840.

6. T.S. 11, Box 43, vol. 10, P.R.O.

7. There are scattered reports of prosecutions in the *Republican* and in T.S. 11, Box 43. For the case of James Ridgeway, a Manchester vendor prosecuted by the Constitutional Association, see Archibald Prentice, *Historical Sketches and Personal Recollections of Manchester* (London: Charles Gilpin, 1851), pp. 237-38.

8. The Exeter case was that of James Tucker. *Republican,* 17 September 1819.

9. There is a description of such a device in Carlile's shop in the *Reasoner*, 5 June 1859. See also *Republican*, 11 November, 19 April 1822; *A Report of the Proceedings, in the Mock Trial of an Information Exhibited Ex-officio by the King's Attorney General Against William Tunbridge* (London: Richard Carlile, 1823), pp. 9-10. Samuel Waddington, a bookseller in the Strand, was prosecuted for selling Palmer's *Principles of Nature* in his shop by means of a book and a ring in the ceiling. *Drakard's Stamford News*, 1 November 1822.

10. Constitutional Association, *Address* (1821), p. 1. See the famous tract by William Hone and George Cruikshank entitled *A Slap at Slop, and the Bridge-Street Gang* (1821). A cut by Cruikshank showing members of the association destroying a printing press is subtitled "An Interior View of the Den in Bridge Street, with the Gang at Work."

11. For a hostile account, see Francis Place's *On the Law of Libel; with Strictures on the Self-Styled "Constitutional Association"* (London: John Hunt, 1823), p. 52. See also Place Newspaper Collection, vol. 40, part 1, f.3, B.M.

12. Constitutional Association, *Address*, p. 2.

13. The phrase "Genuine Loyalty Company" is by Matthew Davenport Hill. *The Trial of John Barkley . . . Prosecuted by the Constitutional Association for Publishing a Seditious and Blasphemous Libel* (London: Effingham Wilson, 1822), p. 8. In 1826, Henry Brougham presented a petition against the continued imprisonment of several of Carlile's shopmen (*Newgate Monthly Magazine*, 1 April 1826), but he also characterized Carlile's views as "ridiculous and seditious" (*Traveller*, 24 December 1822).

14. He wanted his sons to risk prosecution when they reached the age of twelve and so he began to engage them in "atheistic" debates at an early age. *Republican*, 1 April, 27 May 1825.

15. Ibid., 4 January 1822.

16. Carlile to William Holmes, 1 January 1824, C.P.

17. *Deist*, vol. 2, p. vi; *Republican*, 3 November 1820.

18. *Republican*, 4 January 1822.

19. *To the Reformers of Great Britain*, 13 October 1821.

20. *Vice Versus Reason: A Copy of the Information Found Against Mrs. Carlile, for Publishing Mr. Carlile's Trial, and Defence Against the Prosecution for the Age of Reason* (London: Richard Carlile, 1819), p. 4. The *Mock Trials* covered only the first day of the trials but they were issued in pamphlet form in 1822.

21. On the Vice Society informations, see *Republican*, 12 May 1820. Thomas Davison and three Birmingham vendors were also prosecuted for selling copies of the articles by J. B. Smith, a Peterborough schoolmaster. *Republican*, 4 April 1823.

22. There is a brief account of the trial in *Wooler's British Gazette,* 29 October 1820. On the faulty drafting of the indictment, see Great Britain, Parliamentary Papers, 1823, 15 (562), pp. 14-15.

23. The indictment against her is printed in the *Republican,* 1 December 1820. There are references to an "official consultation" between the attorney-general and the solicitor general concerning the indictment. T.S. 11, Box 1067, Bundle 4938, P.R.O.

24. See *Report of the Trial of Mrs. Carlile on the Attorney General's Ex-Officio Information for the Protection of Tyrants: with the Information and Defence at Large before Mr. Justice Abbott* (London: Jane Carlile, 1821).

25. *Republican,* 3 November 1820.

26. *To the Reformers of Great Britain,* 24 June 1821. Other vendors were arrested for selling the Paine *Appendix.* See *Black Dwarf,* 28 March 1821. For Carlile's comparison between the Spanish Revolution and conditions in Britain, see *New Year's Address to the Reformers,* 1 January 1821.

27. *Bridge Street Banditti, v. the Press: Report of the Trial of Mary-Anne Carlile, for Publishing a New Year's Address to the Reformers of Great Britain, Written by Richard Carlile; at the Instance of the Constitutional Association* (London: Richard Carlile, 1821), pp. 90, 133.

28. Carlile's comments appear in the dedication to *Bridge Street Banditti.* Cooper died in 1824 after having received acclaim for his handling of the Mary-Anne Carlile case. William Cooper, *A Sketch of the Late Henry Cooper, Barrister at Law, of the Norfolk Circuit* (London: W. & H.S. Warr, 1856), p. 21.

29. *Suppressed Defence: The Defence of Mary-Anne Carlile, to the Vice Society's Indictment Against the Appendix to the Theological Works of Thomas Paine; which Defence was Suppressed by Mr. Justice Best, Almost at its Commencement* (London: Richard Carlile, 1821), pp. 18-19.

30. *Republican,* 4 January 1822. John Cam Hobhouse was one of the few reformers who refused to present a petition on the case. He told Carlile that "had I presented the petition I should have felt myself called upon to say that I think you have, however conscientiously, done much harm to the cause of liberty." Hobhouse to Carlile, 16 March 1822, Hobhouse Papers, Add. Ms. 36,459, f. 232, B.M.

31. *The Debate in the House of Commons on Wednesday, March 26, 1823; on Mr. Hume's Presenting a Petition from Mary-Anne Carlile, a Prisoner in Dorchester Gaol* (London: T. Moses, 1823), p. 27. During her imprisonment, David Ricardo and other reformers who did not usually engage themselves on the side of working-class agitators like the Carliles pressed for her release. Ricardo urged that "prosecutions ought never to be instituted for religious opinions," while Joseph Hume lambasted the Vice and Constitutional societies for being "little better than conspiracies against

the subject whose aims were to abridge the parameters of free discussion."
Ibid., pp. 3, 16.

32. Carlile to William Holmes, 25 March 1822, C.P.

33. *Republican*, 10 May 1822.

34. Carlile to Thomas Turton, 18 December 1837, C.P. His sister
married twice, the second time to a retired army captain, but in May 1837
she was living in extreme poverty in Devon. Carlile to Turton, 22 June
1837, C.P.

35. E. P. Thompson has described the "War of the Shopmen" as "a
contest for the rights of the press . . . sharp, emphatically victorious,
and . . . peculiarly identified with the cause of the artisans and labourers."
Making of the English Working Class, p. 720.

36. *To the Reformers of Great Britain*, 13 October 1821.

37. John Jones, as quoted in the *Republican*, 1 February 1822.

38. An example to the contrary was the trial in March 1822 of John
Barkley, who was defended unsuccessfully by Matthew Davenport Hill.
See Rosamund and Florence Davenport-Hill, *The Recorder of Birmingham:
A Memoir of Matthew Davenport Hill* (London: Macmillan, 1878), p. 55.

39. *Report of the Trial of Humphrey Boyle, Indicted at the Instance of
the Constitutional Association, as "A Man with Name Unknown," for
Publishing an Alleged Blasphemous and Seditious Libel, as One of the
Shopmen of Mr. Carlile* (London: Richard Carlile, 1822), p. 12. See also
"Letter from Susannah Wright to the Birmingham Union and Patriots'
Friends Society," *Black Dwarf*, 2 April 1823.

40. *Republican*, 23 July 1824.

41. There is a detailed exposé of the special jury system in Place, *On the
Law of Libel*, pp. 37-50.

42. *Speech of Mrs. Susannah Wright, Before the Court of King's Bench,
on the 14th of November, 1822* (London: Richard Carlile, 1822), p. 5.

43. Thomas Davison, an associate though not a shopman of Carlile, was
fined repeatedly for contempt during his blasphemy trial in 1820 when he
refused to delete portions of his defense.

44. *Report of . . . the Mock Trial of . . . William Tunbridge*, p. 19;
*Report of the Trial of William Vamplew Holmes, (One of Mr. Carlile's
Shopmen) on a Charge of Sedition and Blasphemy* (London: Richard
Carlile, 1824), p. 8.

45. *Republican*, 18 June 1824; *The Trials with the Defences at Large
of . . . the Persons Who Were Prosecuted for Selling the Publications of
Richard Carlile in His Various Shops* (London: Richard Carlile, 1825), p.
20.

46. See *Republican*, 9 May 1823, 14 May, 23 July 1824.

47. *Report of the Trial of Humphrey Boyle*, p. 15; Sir Joseph
Arnould, *Life of Thomas, First Lord Denman: Formerly Lord Chief Justice*

of England (Boston: Estes and Lauriat, 1874), vol. 1, pp. 199-201.

48. *Republican,* 9 May 1823; *A Report of the Trial of James Watson, for Having Sold a Copy of Palmer's Principles of Nature at the Shop of Mr. Carlile* (London: Richard Carlile, 1825), p. 8.

49. The most interesting of its excerpts was a lengthy abstract of Peter Annet's *Social Bliss Considered,* an eighteenth-century book that urged the legality of divorce. Richard Hassell also contributed articles to the *Mechanics' Magazine* on topics such as "On Garden Walls" and "The Law of Mechanics."

50. *Republican,* 28 February 1823.

51. On Holmes's renunciation of infidelity, see his two tracts: *An Old Infidel's Reasons for Renouncing Infidelity, and for Advocating the Faith He Once Laboured to Destroy* (London: Milton Press, 1846) and *The "Old Infidel's" Progress to Christianity* (London: James Paul, 1850).

52. There is an interesting autobiographical account by Watson in the *Reasoner,* 5 February 1854, Supplement. See also W. J. Linton, *James Watson: A Memoir* (Hamden, Conn.: Appledore Private Press, 1879), pp. 16-18, 57-58.

53. *Lion,* 17 October 1828. For information about Perry, see Joel H. Wiener, "Thomas Ryley Perry" in Baylen and Gossman, *Biographical Dictionary,* vol. 1, pp. 372 73.

54. *Trial of W. V. Holmes,* p. 6. Carlile maintained that the final sentence was not his own. *Republican,* 4 January 1822.

55. *Republican,* 8 March 1822.

56. J. S. Mill ("Wickliff"), *Morning Chronicle,* 8 February 1823.

57. *Republican,* 21 June 1824.

58. *Report of the Trial of Mrs. Susannah Wright,* p. 22.

59. *Republican,* 18 June 1824.

60. Place's *St. Paul the Apostle, and William Campion: Parallel between the Cases of St. Paul the Apostle, and William Campion,* was published in the *Republican,* 25 June 1824, and then reprinted in tract form.

61. *Newgate Monthly Magazine,* 1 August 1826. A recent postscript to these events occurred in December 1976 when the publishers of *Gay News* were convicted of blasphemous libel for printing James Kirkup's homosexual poem, "The Love That Dares to Speak Its Name." This private prosecution was initiated by Mary Whitehouse.

6

REPUBLICANS AND ATHEISTS

While a prisoner, Carlile attracted several thousand supporters from all sections of the country. They were mostly poor artisans, weavers, and laborers who regarded him and his shopmen as symbols of opposition to corruption and privilege. By their pennies and political enthusiasms they underscored the battle for a free press. They also read his publications regularly, met frequently to pass resolutions endorsing radical reform, and engaged in a wide spectrum of self-help activities. In a limited way, these supporters formed a cohesive "republican and infidel" movement, the first of its kind in nineteenth-century Britain.

Carlile's radicalism, as it developed from the pressure of events in the early 1820s, was essentially preindustrial. It was not directed against the inequalities of the new economic system with its long hours of work in factories and many urban problems; nor did it consciously appeal to the class feelings of poor people. Instead, it was based on a social paradigm of "producers" and "nonproducers," with rewards apportioned to output and individual "rights of nature" respected. Carlile hated social injustice. But he blamed the "traditional" enemies of the poor for it: kings, lords, taxgatherers, fundholders, magistrates, and, above all, clergymen. They were the appropriators of the soil and of common property, and those who profited from privileged institutions. It was the task of reformers, he believed, to destroy such parasites and to bring about fundamental social and political changes.[1]

Carlile's political aspirations were shaped by his early contacts with Sherwin and Hunt and by the writings of Paine, whom he described as his "universal political preceptor."[2] Paine's egalitarianism, his advocacy of a renewable political contract, which was to take the form of annual elections, and his bold assertion that revolutions were a necessary part of historical development became constituent elements of Carlile's radicalism. To these Carlile added "extreme" views, whetted by his experiences in London and Manchester in 1819. The Peterloo Massacre was "one of the greatest violations of moral decency ever placed on record," he wrote; if similar outrages were to be prevented, the people must resort to force, "to annihilate the existing order of things and to begin de novo." "Nothing but a revolution," he observed in 1820, "can remove a deep-rooted corruption, hence, revolutions are much to be desired when necessary."[3] As he informed readers of the *Republican*: "An unnecessary shedding of blood is at all times to be deprecated, but circumstances will occur when it is found to be indispensable. . . . Show me a state of oppression and of despotism, that was ever overthrown by the weapons of reason alone, and I for one will be forced to acquiesce in your pacific reasoning."[4]

Such attitudes (reflecting Carlile's shifting private moods as well as his general assessments of events) were given added piquancy by the initial successes of revolutionaries in Spain, Portugal, and Naples in the early 1820s. Immense changes were likely to ensue from these upheavals, he believed: "The embers of revolution are scattered throughout the continent, and a total extinction of them cannot take place."[5] Spain in particular was experiencing one of "the most brilliant and most fortunate revolutions that has been recorded in the annals of history." It had begun as a struggle by soldiers for better wages and living conditions and had acquired anticlerical dimensions, which Carlile found emboldening. "So strong is my hope in the cause of the Spaniards," he told readers of the *Republican* in 1823, at a time when the revolutionaries seemed likely to prevail, "so strong is my hope in the cause of justice, knowledge and moral right."[6]

He was optimistic about the possibilities for reform in Britain because of the public enthusiasm aroused by these continental upheavals and additionally because of the outpouring of support for Queen Caroline in 1820. Reformers rallied in unprecedented numbers around the queen, identifying her plight with that of the nation at large; and Carlile, from his room in Dorchester prison, outdid himself in rhetorical enthusiasm. "The blackest part of history has not yet displayed anything of this kind," he commented, while attacking a proposed Bill of Pains and Penalties, which would strip her of her title and all claims to the throne. He asserted that "we could willingly risk our lives in the attempt to reinstate her Majesty in her justly claimed authority."[7]

By expressing such extravagant political views in the *Republican* and his other publications, Carlile emerged as the leading advocate of "republicanism" in the early 1820s, and this, as much as anything else, branded him as a "wild radical" in the eyes of conservatives. From the outset of his collaboration with Sherwin in 1817, he had characterized himself as a republican, and he clung tenaciously to this cachet for the remainder of his life, at least partly as a means of differentiating himself and his supporters from the universal suffrage followers of Henry Hunt. Monarchy, he asserted again and again, was a "useless and expensive" bauble: "Any thing short of an elective legislature, and an elective magistracy, upon the widest possible system of suffrage and representation, cannot be considered a freedom from abuse and tyranny."[8] He reminded his readers that "the Americans do not pour oil on the head of their President, and he makes a much more respectable king than any we have in Europe." And he condemned the "tyrannical" rule of British monarchs, especially George III, whom he described as having '"a great thirst for blood" and an "intellect scarcely human."

Yet if Carlile and many of his followers identified themselves as republicans, the precise contours of their beliefs remained vague. In general, their advocacy of republicanism was less a concrete expression of antimonarchism of the kind championed subsequently by George Julian Harney, Charles Bradlaugh, and Sir Charles Dilke than it was an endorsement of ideas about popular sovereignty to be found in Paine's writings. Carlile, in fact, was "quite indifferent by what title the chief magistracy shall exist." So long as a ruler (whatever his title) did not restrict popular freedom or dilute the "full, fair, and free" representation of the people, he was willing to accept him as a political embellishment.[9]

Like other working-class radical reformers of the early nineteenth century, Carlile's evolving political views are a conflation of abstract and empirical attitudes. He favored appeals to "natural justice" of the kind to be found in the *Rights of Man*. To overcome the entrenched power of privileged groups, reformers, he affirmed, must support "truth," irrespective of the historical configurations or immediate political realities.[10] But influenced as he was by Cartwright, Cobbett, and other "pragmatic" advocates of reform, he gave much attention to specific historical incidents. Like Cartwright, who regarded the eleventh-century Norman conquest as the basis of social injustice, and Cobbett, who attacked the Protestant Reformation as a similar wrong turning in British history, Carlile developed a theory of oppression that was based on the Whig "Glorious Revolution" of 1688. This event in his opinion had fastened a Dutch "usurper," William of Orange, on the throne in place of the rightful James II, and had produced an "accumulation of misery, distress and degradation." Such an interpretation of history partly explains his inveterate hatred for the Whigs, whom to the end of his life he continued to regard as more persecuting than the Tories. It also illuminates a tension endemic to nineteenth-century working-class thought: between an analysis of history as abstract justice (à la Paine) and a more complex understanding of the nature of change.[11]

On economic and social issues, Carlile espoused traditional radical remedies. His aim—as professed in the *Republican* and elsewhere—was to eradicate "unnatural" inequalities. Thus, he subscribed to a code of social justice that placed a premium on individual advancement, an end to exploitive relationships, and the triumph of producers over "parasites." Such a framework for human behavior, he maintained, would insure that there would be "no jealousies, no quarrels, no distractions, no bloodsheds, no violation of laws, and . . . no barbarous punishments." Or, as he phrased it on another occasion: "Property holding tempered by the elective principle" would be allowed to flourish.

Paine's *Decline and Fall of the English System of Finance* and Cobbett's *Paper Against Gold* (a virtual paraphrase of Paine) provided the basic constituents of Carlile's economic analysis. Drawing heavily upon their attacks on paper money and fundholding, he affirmed that the national debt—based as it was on an artificial edifice of private interests—had brought about an unjust transfer of wealth from "the wretched and miserable artisan and agriculturist" to "idle and vicious parasites." At least 50 percent of the productive wealth of the country was siphoned off annually in this way.[12] Paper money was a "state juggle" (this was one of Cobbett's popular phrases) that strengthened the position of avaricious middlemen and distorted true exchanges of wealth. "The blessed effects of the paper system," observed Carlile facetiously at a time of economic downturn in the early 1820s, "are coming on thick and threefold, and happy will be those who, like the wise virgins of old, keep in their lamps, *alias*, metal instead of paper."[13]

Heavy taxation, he emphasized, was the abuse that above all wasted human resources and produced social and political injustice. The objective of government, he stated, must be to eliminate "profligacy and extravagant expenditure" and "poverty in the midst of plenty." The tax gatherer was the enemy of the poor, "preying upon [their] very vitals and keeping millions of stomachs in a state of starvation"; unless he was eliminated, "cheap, simple, and honest government" could not become part of the fabric of the nation.[14] An end to taxation would lead to a revamping of social relationships, with producers receiving just rewards and parasites being made to pay for their exploitive relationships to the community.

Carlile, like other radical reformers of the time, found only one form of taxation acceptable: a tax on land.[15] In the terminology of Paine, he conceived of such an impost as a "rental payment," which would indemnify the poor for their loss of original ownership in the soil. The property holdings of "nonproducers"—kings, lords, and priests—resulted from "robberies legitimized by corrupt powers." Therefore, without such a land tax, the propertyless masses had the right to take action against their superiors. "I would violate every species of property," he told readers of the *Republican*, "that deprives the industrious man of the means of his labour, or the produce of his labour, whatever it be called."[16]

Notwithstanding purple passages in his writings, Carlile was, in the spectrum of early nineteenth-century working-class radicalism, a comparative moderate on social and economic questions. His point of view was essentially that of the discontented artisan. He eschewed class conflict, rejecting every proposal that smacked even tangentially of "enforced" equality. Such unacceptable proposals included a form of land nationalization advocated by Thomas Spence and endorsed by many radical reformers, and the "community building" nostrums of Robert Owen that were beginning to attract substantial numbers of sympathizers. Carlile described Owen's cooperative theories—worse in his view than Spence's ideas—as likely to create a "milk-sop, effeminate life, through which a man has nothing to call his own, and in which the noble spirit of independence is molten down by the tyranny of rules and regulations." Personal advancement was for Carlile the "summum bonum" of life. He believed in rewards for "honesty, industry, courage, talent, fortitude, patience, perseverance, or virtue of any kind." As he told his readers: "I am a leveller of all distinctions among men save those which virtue, talent, and industry can get up." Even his proposals for prison reform were based on individualist premises: that the reprobate prisoner should be made to work his way back into society by producing as much wealth as he had destroyed.[17]

But although Carlile consistently acclaimed the virtues of economic individualism, it is misleading to regard him as a spokesman for "petty bourgeois" or small capitalist interests. He resented all forms of injustice and felt anger whenever he contemplated the sufferings of the poor. "When shall misery cease, humanity reign, and innocence walk unmolested?" he asked his followers. His answer was: "When he that has food can feel for him that has none—when man shall learn to prefer death to a life in misery".[18] His social and economic attitudes embodied, therefore, a strong plebeian coloration, as is made clear in the following encapsulation of his aims: "More equality of social condition; still leaving voluntary virtue, industry, and ingenuity, room and means to rise above that to which it is of superior worth; mutual check, equal and mutual reward for well-doing; equal and mutual punishment for wrong doing."[19]

If Carlile's political and economic views gave ballast to his reputation as a reformer and reflected many of the prevailing currents of working-class discontent, it was his emergence as a radical freethinker in the early 1820s that distinguished him from other reformers. More than anything else he believed that the overriding reform necessary as a prelude to all others was the destruction of Christianity in its traditional form. The shape of his antichristian views changed several times in his lifetime, but he never wavered in this central belief. "Other reforms will prove abortive," he wrote in 1821, "unless [they] be accompanied with an instruction that shall abolish superstition in the minds of the people."[20]:

Between 1819 and 1822, Carlile's views on religion may be characterized as deist, though in a militant sense. He rejected the belief in an "omnipotent and efficient" First Cause, which was the central tenet of deism as expounded by Paine, Palmer, and other writers. "The whole substance of my creed," Carlile stated in 1820, "is, that I BELIEVE IN NOTHING SUPERNATURAL." "I am bold to say," he told readers of the *Republican*, "that every account that exists about the appearance of a God or Gods, angel or angels, spirit or spirits, to any man or men, woman or women, is a fabricated and false account, [since] no such beings did exist, nor ever will exist."[21] On the contrary, he maintained, "the chief of the animal and vegetable world was immured in the solidity of nonintelligent matter." And as if to enhance his rejection of "genteel" deism, he deprecated the "philosophical theorists" who had preceded Paine, especially Peter Annet, David Hume, and Anthony Collins. They were mere triflers who had leavened their attacks on orthodox religion with preposterous notions of "deity" and "nature."[22]

Yet if Carlile cannot be described as a conventional deist in the sense of Paine or Palmer—except, perhaps, at the very outset of his career—he nonetheless believed that an "incomprehensible power" held the universe together. A "God of Nature" existed, he felt, "because there must be a power as a cause sufficient to all existing effects"; such a "God" imparted motion to inanimate matter and reconciled natural law with human reason. "*Nature is my God;* I own no other," he affirmed from his room in Dorchester prison in the early 1820s, while emphasizing the need to meditate upon this power and analyze its precise form.[23]

Politically, Carlile's attacks upon Christianity took the form of anticlericalism, an important facet of working-class reform in the early nineteenth century. In coruscating terms, he attacked the "Jew Books" and the gospels and depicted Christianity as a religion of "vice, cruelty, and inhumanity" that, in 2000 years, had produced unsurpassed "human misery, human torture and humanicide."[24] According to him, the Scriptures had been devised by conjuring priests as a means of reinforcing social inequalities; so long as the masses of poor people remained duped by them, they would be exploited by a clergy opposed to their best interests. "Witchcraft, priestcraft, kingcraft, and devilcraft," asserted Carlile, "have been one and all built on the ignorance, fear, and credulity of mankind." Only when the people took the bit between their teeth and attacked the "superstitious" foundations of organized religion (linked as these were to political and economic oppression) would genuine reform take place. "Oh, horrible religion," he wrote, "what havoc hast thou made of the earth! Thou are a pestilence, more destructive of life, happiness, and peace, than all other pestilences combined."[25] It was a theme to which he was to turn frequently in his journals and pamphlets.

Like Paine but more vehemently, he adjudged it a certainty that the Old Testament (excluding the Books of Job and Proverbs) was a "fabrication," or as he expressed it, "brutalized fantasy." It had been composed by unlettered tribesmen during the sixth century B.C. and bore no relationship to the events it described. Contrary to belief, the biblical Jews were a "savage and uncultivated" race whose true history remained uncharted. They had never resided in Egypt, had not occupied Judaea prior to the founding of a colony there by Cyrus, and, as Carlile conjectured on several occasions, were possibly of African origin.[26]

Christianity, too, lacked a verified account of its beginnings, he maintained. Like Paine and other freethinkers, he rejected all of the evidence for its existence that dated from the first century A.D., including frequently cited passages by Josephus and Philo Judaeus. He insisted that these were based on interpolations inserted long after the events in question in order to fabricate the myth of a divine Jesus. The truth, he claimed, was much different. The early Christians had carried out "the grossest forgeries to support the books on which their religion was founded," and he for one was prepared to unmask them.[27]

In the *Republican* and other freethought publications of the 1820s, Carlile singled out for derision those Judaeo-Christian practices sanctioned by a "carnal, brutal, and sensual" God: animal and human sacrifice; clerical privilege; religious intolerance; the "lusts of the flesh"; even masturbation, which he characterized in nineteenth-century parlance as a "horrid vice." He never ceased to regale his readers with accounts of biblical "debauchery, cruelty, and wickedness," contrasting these (in considerable detail) with the "pure morality" of nature. The Bible was, he stated, an "obscene, voluptuous, false, scandalous, malicious, and seditious" book that "presents nothing to our view, but a series of lives of persons, who have distinguished themselves from their fellows by their vices and wickedness." Those who published and sold it (Carlile was being only somewhat facetious when he made this suggestion) should be prosecuted.

Political hostility toward the Church of England and dissenting clergymen was a part of the fabric of working-class radical culture in the early nineteenth century, and Carlile took full advantage of this in seeking support for his views. In his writings he frequently cited anticlerical books such as William Benbow's *Crimes of the Clergy* (1823), which described clergymen as "sevenfold more the children of the Devil than they who make no profession of having been called," and John Wade's *Black Book* (1820), which blamed them for "fomenting war, strengthening the iron hand of tyranny, exciting to murderous violence, [and] stimulating one party of Christians to cut the throats of another."[28] Priests were "black slugs," maintained Carlile, "enemies of mankind" who stole from the poor and denied them the right to subsistence. Drastic action was needed to remedy this, including the abolition of tithes and church rates, the disestablishment of the Church of England, the application of church property to educational and social objectives, and an end to all forms of "compulsory" religious worship. "While religion is made the engine of the state to forge fresh fetters," Carlile asserted, "and whilst the established priesthood who are supported out of the taxes, are the supple tools of every existing authority; I for one shall live and die its foe."[29]

Increasingly he began to shift his attacks upon religion away from institutions toward a more general emphasis on "moral" and theological change. Man possessed a "limitless capacity for virtue and self-improvement," he affirmed, and "superstition" prevented him from "reaching that summit of happiness, which of all other animals, it is the peculiar blessing of man to enjoy." Carlile told his readers that "the mind that is untainted with religion, has more scope, and a better opportunity" for improvement than any other.[30] If superstition were superseded by reason—that is, if error and prejudice were replaced by knowledge—then all forms of injustice would disappear.

By the spring of 1822 Carlile had abandoned deism in favor of a more extreme view, "atheism and infidelity."[31] He began to asseverate that matter occupied every inch of space in the universe and that there was no possibility of a preexisting intelligence in the universe. Matter was puissant, indestructible, all pervasive; it was "the first cause of all things, [which] acts from its own inherent properties, without the aid, or possibility of aid, from any external impulse." Mind, a product of sensation, was a "mere pulsatory feeling that cannot exist without the animal frame"; while "God" was nothing but a fantastic projection of human needs.[32]

Other radical freethinkers, including the French writers Baron d'Holbach and Volney, had said much the same thing before Carlile and their views were well known. But Carlile was the first British reformer of the nineteenth century to give popular expression to such "infidel" views and to link them specifically to political change. He claimed (wildly inaccurately) to be the first person "in this Island, I may add the whole earth, who has openly defied the religious world upon this ground, that there is no such a God as the advocates of religion preach." He was prepared to dedicate his life to eradicating Christianity. "When a man becomes an atheist," he told his supporters, "he may be truly said to have waded through the quagmire of superstition and idolatry and to begin to live as a reasonable being." His objective, clearly defined for the first time, was "to root out this grievous, useless, ingenious tax [religion], to destroy this source of disunion and quarrel, to leave the human mind free to self-government, and to teach mankind every where to seek and to value truth."[33]

Carlile's "infidel challenge" was conditioned to a great extent by his reading of Baron d'Holbach, whose writings were available in cheap English editions by the early 1820s. Although Carlile reprinted several of d'Holbach's tracts in translation in the *Deist*, it was his careful perusal of the *System of Nature, or the Laws of the Moral and Physical World*, which was published in a three-volume edition by Thomas Davison in 1820, that had the deepest influence on him. In the *System of Nature*, first published in 1770, d'Holbach gave full support to atheism, proclaiming that every object in the universe was reducible to matter and that every "spiritual" concept, including the belief in god, was illusory. Whatever happens to man, he stated, derives from "the development of the first impulse given him by nature"; therefore, "to exist is to experience the motion peculiar to a determinate essence [and] to conserve this existence, is to give and receive that motion." In reformulating these ideas in the *Republican* and pamphlets such as *Observations . . . by Olinthus Gregory* and *Every Man's Book; or, What Is God?* (1826), Carlile became a transmitter of d'Holbach's theories to British working-class reformers in much the same way that he had performed this service for Paine.[34]

Other writers who impelled Carlile in the direction of atheism were Sir William Lawrence, who lectured on anatomy and surgery at the Royal College of Surgeons, John "Walking" Stewart, a travel writer, and Francis Place, the Benthamite reformer who became a regular correspondent in 1822. In 1817, Lawrence delivered an important series of lectures in London that challenged the prevailing biological orthodoxy of a "life force," offering in its place an analysis of mental phenomena couched in materialistic terms. He described mind as "the functions of the organic apparatus contained in the head" and (in terminology that Carlile subsequently paraphrased) maintained that "the distinguishing character of living bodies will be found in their texture or organization; in their component elements; in their form; in their peculiar manifestations or phenomena; and . . . in the origin and termination of their vital existence."[35] Stewart's writings on materialism, including the *Conquest of the Moral World* (1806) and the *Philosophy of Sense* (1816), were less incisive than those of Lawrence, but they too gave flesh to Carlile's atheism, based as it was on a belief in the all-encompassing reality of matter. More central were the contributions of Place. In March 1822 he wrote an article for the *Republican* entitled "On the Progress of Reason" (discreetly signed "Regulator"), in which he drew an analogy between "mental action" and the physical act of holding a pen. "The better the hand is taught to hold the pen," observed Place, "the better it will write, the better the head is taught, or learned, the better the man is said to be instructed." Reinforcing and expanding these views in their private correspondence, Place so impressed Carlile that the latter subsequently praised him for having "made atheism a point of honour."[36]

A faith in the regenerative powers of science was a further central aspect of Carlile's atheism. Enthusiasm for science constituted an important facet of working-class culture in the nineteenth century. Lecturers carried the latest scientific ideas to eager audiences of artisans and mechanics, while popular journals gave these ideas detailed coverage. All embracing in its symbolism, the imagery of science colored the vernacular of Carlile's movement. "There are no mysteries in nature," he told his followers, "but what man, by the aid and progress of science, might ultimately apprehend."[37] In his tract, *An Address to Men of Science*, he propounded the case for atheism based upon an understanding of science. "Superstition corrupts and deteriorates all the human passions," he asserted, while science alone is "qualified to amend and moralize them." With a mastery of scientific ideas, man, according to Carlile, could control the universe, which he described as "a great chemical apparatus, in which a chemical analysis, and a chemical composition is continually and constantly going on." Without such knowledge, priests and other vested interest groups would continue to work their ways undisturbed.[38]

Ironically, Carlile's zealous espousal of atheism from 1822 on came unstuck precisely when he attempted to give matter a scientific formulation. In his analysis of matter, he rejected the "life force" theory that Lawrence had refuted since this, in his opinion, was nothing but a variation on the theological doctrine of soul or spirit. Likewise he refuted atomic and electrical explanations of matter, both common at the time. "The idea of an *atom*," he wrote, "is, to my mind, always associated with the idea of a small visible solid body; nor can I consent to speak of atoms beyond microscopic reach."[39]

What he did propound (foolishly as it turned out) was an interpretation of matter popularized by Sir Richard Phillips, for many years the proprietor of the *Monthly Magazine*. Much more of a quack than a scientist, Phillips discarded Newtonian theories of life as "metaphysical," his idée fixe being that matter was comprised of a gaseous substance—oxygen and ozone combined—and that motion was generated by independent electric charges. He explained his "rational mechanical" theory in the following terms: "All cases of electrical excitement consist merely of the decomposition or separation of the acid and alkaline principles natural to the substance and decomposition of the body, or electric plate."[40] Carlile scorned some of Phillips's ideas as "unintelligible" (a view endorsed by most other reformers), but he stuck closely to the bulk of them for many years as he attempted almost obsessively to merge science with infidelity.

The several thousand men and women who comprised Carlile's "republican and infidel" movement resided in many sections of the country and consisted of a variety of workingmen. They included cotton spinners from Manchester and its hinterland; weavers from Halifax, Leeds, and other Lancashire and West Riding towns and villages; woolcombers from Bradford; and, in large numbers, tailors, masons, printers, shoemakers, carpenters, and other craftsmen from traditional artisan centers like Birmingham and London. In London, where Carlile had a large following, his backers included Spitalfields silk weavers, Shadwell ropemakers, and numerous artisans resident in districts like Soho, Hammersmith, and Camden Town.[41]

However, he was not uniformly successful in gaining a footing in urban centers, at least partly because of the rival claims of suffrage agitators. He had, for example, little success in Sheffield, which he described as an "abominably bleak and torpid town"; and in Newcastle, Manchester, and Leeds, Henry Hunt's Great Northern Radical Union, founded in 1821 to spread the claims of universal suffrage and, specifically, to weaken the appeal of "republicanism and atheism," competed successfully for the allegiance of working-class reformers.[42] Elsewhere, the reasons for Carlile's success or lack of success are not always clear. Suppressive tactics by Methodist clergymen in Huddersfield, a town where he had many supporters, had the effect of strengthening the resolve of his followers to organize themselves more effectively. But in Norwich, Edinburgh, and other cities, the use of political power by clergymen and magistrates drastically reduced support for him.

Nor can Carlile's supporters be characterized as ideologically homogeneous. In the 1820s, the line separating "moderate" from "extreme" reform was often blurred, and code words like *science* or *free discussion* betokened differing emphases, depending upon the circumstances in which they were uttered. As well, therefore, as working-class freethinkers and republicans (who usually described themselves as "deists," "materialists," or "infidels"), Carlile's followers included political activists, advocates of popular education, enthusiasts for science, and many "non-ideological" workingmen who, as was true of Carlile himself in 1817, identified their personal grievances with the broader campaign for reform. What bound the majority of Carlile's supporters together was a belief in free expression and a hatred for organized religion. And, also, feelings of plebeian solidarity. For although Carlile never appealed openly to the class feelings of the poor (he considered this to be demagogic when practiced by others), he was himself a poor man who wrote and sounded like one, and whose ability to communicate ideas effectively and simply derived from this fact. When he described himself as a spokesman for "the injured, the oppressed, the weak, and for outraged humanity," or used a phrase like "justice to the labouring people," he was drawing upon feelings of class consciousness that lay just below the political surface. More than anything else, this accounts for the cohesiveness and strength of his following, notwithstanding its heterogeneous composition.[43]

Republicanism and "infidelity" were the catchwords of Carlile's supporters, as they gave effect to their enthusiasms in a variety of ways. They established reading rooms and mutual improvement societies; set up groups with florid-sounding titles like the "Society for the Promotion of Truth" and the "Friends of Rational Liberty"; and attended "chapels" where antichristian sermons were preached on Sunday evenings and the evils of religion and "superstition" excoriated.[44] In Manchester, the Miles Platting Reading Society met regularly for several years. Led by Elijah Ridings, a well known weaver-poet, and John Harper, a laborer, it sponsored educational and political activities whose diversity illustrates the miscellaneous interests of Carlile's followers. It built an "infidel library" and exchanged scientific ideas by means of lectures and demonstrations. Its members regularly discussed the writings of freethinkers such as Paine, Volney, and, especially, Carlile, whom they described as "a giant in intellect, whose energies were directed towards the immediate improvement of the human race."[45] Likewise, members of a Paine society in Birmingham organized "Republican Funds" to aid Carlile and to pursue a host of political and educational activities.

The most significant organizations of Carlile supporters were, however, the zetetic societies. Established in several cities, these quintessential infidel groups were devoted to "seeking after truth" and pursuing "an analytical mode of argument and demonstration."[46] They engaged in a potpourri of scientific and antichristian activities. In Edinburgh, where the first zetetic society was founded in December 1821 (it was known as the "Edinburgh Freethinkers' Zetetick Society"), the tradesmen who led it undertook a vigorous program of Sunday evening discussions of theological and scientific ideas in an atmosphere which one of them described as conducive to "free discussion and philosophical pursuit." The Edinburgh zetetics also purchased scientific equipment and established a free-thinking library that was disbanded in November 1821 by local magistrates who prosecuted its leaders for blasphemy.[47] Similar programs were undertaken by zetetic societies in London, Salford, Glasgow, Ashton-under-Lyne, and Stalybridge. These groups collected subscriptions for Carlile and made a major effort to circulate his tracts and journals. They did everything in their power (in the words of a member of one zetetic association) to dispel "the

mist that at present envelopes the minds of our fellow countrymen."[48]

To Carlile's followers, "infidelity" meant atheism, but also a
more general belief in the need for a moral reordering of society. It
was political and self-improving as well as antireligious. The
political impulse of infidelity can be discerned in those Manchester
supporters of Carlile who pledged themselves to "regain their lost
rights and liberties before which kings and priests, crown and
mitres, thrones and monasteries, will be swept away"; its self-
improving side is to be found in the "rational discussion (of) moral,
theological, and political subjects" carried on by members of the
reading and zetetic societies.[49] But the several strands of infidelity
complemented each other. The same reformers who participated in
scientific activities often attended political meetings and celebrated
the birthdays of Paine and Carlile at local public houses, where
they toasted a free press or an end to religion and sang political
songs such as "In Liberty's Cause I Could Yield Up My Life." One
proud disciple, for example, as if to highlight the confusion,
boasted that he was a "Deist, Materialist, Reformer, and Revolu-
tionist."[50]

Although a gifted and resourceful combatant and a journalist
who possessed the ability to communicate ideas to ordinary people,
Carlile was in no sense an effective political leader. He had little
understanding of how to resolve the confusions intrinsic to
working-class radicalism and was, all too frequently, long on
rhetoric and short on concrete proposals. Increasingly, as his
prison term lengthened and personal contacts with reformers
diminished, he became less able to stanch defections among his
followers: by deists who were alienated as a result of his espousal of
atheist views and, more important, by working-class activists who
found political reform more congenial than freethought and who
defected to the side of Hunt and other suffrage leaders.

As early as 1820 Hunt had begun to attack Carlile. After he and
his "Radical Christian" followers founded the Great Northern
Radical Union in 1821, a struggle ensued in Leeds, Manchester,
Stockport, and other cities between the followers of Carlile and
Hunt with bitter charges and countercharges being exchanged.[51]
Hunt, who had a more precise grasp of his political objectives,
almost invariably got the upper hand. In Bolton, his followers

ejected Carlile's supporters from the Union rooms, and in Leeds many "republicans and infidels" publicly defected to the universal suffrage campaign. "Alehouse politics" prevailed also in Manchester where, according to Carlile, Hunt's faction "combined to exclude me, and those who act like me, from all connection with, or support from the great body of the Reformers."[52] Neither republicanism nor antichristianity could—or so it seemed—hold its own against franchise reform. By the beginning of 1823, Hunt's followers began to quarrel among themselves, and in that year the Great Northern Radical Union broke up, much to Carlile's satisfaction. But considerable financial and political support had been lost to him in the interim. A subscription campaign that Carlile initiated in 1821 faltered, and while the circulation of the *Republican* remained fairly constant during these years, there were districts in the north of England and in the Midlands where, in the early 1820s, Carlile lost many of his followers to Hunt.

Notes

1. There is a useful analysis of this "old radicalism" in Hollis, *Pauper Press*, pp. 203-19.

2. *Prompter*, 27 November 1830.

3. *Republican*, 11 February 1820.

4. Ibid., 3 September 1819, 21 April 1820.

5. Ibid., 11 April 1823, 15 September 1820. The best study of the impact of these continental revolutions on British radicalism is Henry Weisser, *British Working-Class Movements and Europe, 1815-48* (Manchester: Manchester University Press, 1975), pp. 7-31. See also William St. Clair, *That Greece Might Still Be Free: The Philhellenes in the War of Independence* (London: Oxford University Press, 1972).

6. *Republican*, 24 March 1820, 18 April 1823.

7. Ibid., 16, 23 June, 29 September 1820. John Stevenson describes this incident as "the last of the old-style metropolitan agitations in which London gave a lead to the rest of the country." "The Queen Caroline Affair," in J. Stevenson (ed.), *London in the Age of Reform* (Oxford: Basil Blackwell, 1977), p. 117.

8. Richard Carlile, *An Effort to Set at Rest Some Little Disputes and Misunderstandings between the Reformers of Leeds* (London: Richard Carlile, 1821), p. 5.

9. *Republican*, 24 March 1820; *Lion*, 13 February 1829.

10. *Republican*, 26 May 1820. See also Carlile, *Effort to Set at Rest*, pp. 5-6.

11. See John Cartwright, *The English Constitution Produced and*

Illustrated (1823), and William Cobbett, *A History of the Protestant "Reformation" in England and Ireland* (1824). Christopher Hill, "The Norman Yoke," in John Saville (ed.), *Democracy and the Labour Movement* (London: Lawrence & Wishart, 1954), pp. 11-66, is an analysis of the "Norman Yoke" concept in radical thought. For Carlile's own use of the "Norman Yoke" theory, see *Republican*, 21 January 1820, 17 May 1822; *Cosmopolite*, 16 May 1833.

12. *Republican*, 23 June 1820. As a result of Peel's Currency Act of 1819, fundholders were being repaid in dearer currency, he maintained.

13. In his *Paper Against Gold*, 9th ed. (1820), p. 84, Cobbett wrote: "Real money is the *representative* of MONEY'S WORTH OF THINGS: promissory notes are the *representatives* of DEBT."

14. *Republican*, 5 May 1820; *Gauntlet*, 31 March 1833; *Prompter*, 8 October 1831.

15. A leading advocate of the land tax was Harrison Wilkinson whose book, *Property Against Taxation* (1821), Carlile commented upon favorably.

16. *Republican*, 24 May 1822. Paine's statement is from *Agrarian Justice*, in Hayden Clark (ed.), *Thomas Paine—Key Writings* (New York: Hill & Wang, 1961), p. 337.

17. These views are expressed in many of his journals, but see, especially, *Prompter*, 4 June, 17 September 1831. In the *Republican*, 1 October 1824, he described capital as "an accumulation of the produce of industry."

18. *Republican*, 26 May 1820.

19. Carlile, *New View of Insanity*, p. 29.

20. *To the Reformers of Great Britain*, 24 June 1821.

21. *Republican*, 24 March, 5 May 1820.

22. Analyses of the "genteel deism" of the eighteenth century are to be found in Leslie Stephen, *History of English Thought in the Eighteenth Century* (New York: Harbinger Books, 1962, reprint), vol. 1, chs. 2-4; John M. Robertson, *A Short History of Freethought: Ancient and Modern* (London: Watts & Co., 1915), vol. 2, pp. 147-212; Edward Royle, *Victorian Infidels: The Origins of the British Secularist Movement, 1791-1866* (Manchester: Manchester University Press, 1974), pp. 9-23.

23. Carlile, *Observations on . . . Olinthus Gregory*, pp. 6, 20.

24. *Republican*, 5 July 1822.

25. Ibid., 11 August, 16 June 1820.

26. Carlile, *Observations on . . . Olinthus Gregory*, pp. 23-26; *Republican*, 18 March, 11 November 1825.

27. *Republican*, 18 August, 8 September 1820.

28. The quotations are from William Benbow, *The Crimes of the Clergy, or the Pillars of Priest-craft Shaken* (1823), p. 2, and John Wade, *The Black*

Book; or, Corruption Unmasked!!! (1820), vol. 1, p. 273. Two popular anticlerical works of the 1830s were: *A Slap at the Church* (1832), an unstamped journal edited by William Carpenter and John Cleave, and William Howitt's *A Popular History of Priestcraft* (1833).

29. See *Republican,* 13 October 1820, and *Lion,* 24 October 1828. Carlile had a particular hatred for Methodists, whom he accused of engaging in "devil-worship," "rapture," and infanticide.

30. *Republican,* 7 April 1820, 19 July 1822.

31. Ibid., 16 April 1824. G. D. H. Cole, though imprecise, dates Carlile's shift to atheism from 1821. Cole, *Richard Carlile 1790-1843,* reprinted in Michael Katanka (ed.), *Writers and Rebels* (London: Charles Knight, 1976), p. 76.

32. An excellent summary of Carlile's atheism is in his *Every Man's Book: or What is God?* (London: Richard Carlile, 1826), as well as in the *Republican,* 1822-24.

33. *Republican,* 12 March, 12 August 1824.

34. The quotes by d'Holbach are from James Watson's 1834 edition of the *System of Nature,* vol. 1, pp. 11, 44. J. M. Robertson states that the appearance of the book "significantly marks the era of modern free-thought." *Short History of Freethought,* vol. 2, p. 273.

35. William Lawrence, *Lectures on Physiology, Zoology, and the Natural History of Man* (London: William Benbow, 1819), pp. 80, 164. On Lawrence, see Charles W. Brook, *Carlile and the Surgeons* (Glasgow: Strickland Press, 1943); Daniel T. Stinson, *The Role of Sir William Law-rence in Nineteenth Century English Surgery* (Zurich: Juris Druck, 1969); and the biographies of Lawrence in the *Dictionary of Scientific Biography* and the *DNB.*

36. In his *Philosophy of Science or Book of Nature* (1816?), Stewart theorized that "universal matter, modifying into powers, must be the cause of all modifications or existence" (p. xxv). For Carlile's comment on Place's atheism, see *Christian Warrior,* 14 January 1843.

37. Carlile compared science to a phoenix that would "rise gloriously upon the decay of Superstition and Priesthood." *Observations on . . . Olinthus Gregory,* p. 67.

38. Carlile, *Address to Men of Science,* pp. 8, 16.

39. *Lion,* 2 May 1828. There is an analysis of the "life force" theory in June Goodfield-Todmin, "Some Aspects of English Physiology: 1780-1840," *Journal of the History of Biology,* 2 (1969), pp. 283-320. John Clarke, one of Carlile's more wayward Newgate disciples, held to a theory of matter that emphasized "the indestructibility of its atomical parts." Clarke, *A Critical Review, of the Life, Character, Miracles, and Resurrection . . . of Jesus Christ* (London: J. Clarke, 1825), p. 192.

40. Richard Phillips, *Essays on the Proximate Mechanical Causes of the General Phenomena of the Universe* (London, 1818), p. 8; "Electricity and Galvanism," *Monthly Magazine,* 50 (1820), p. 31.

41. Many of Carlile's readers acknowledged their debt to him for having "converted" them to freethought: for example, a Manchester supporter who described himself as "A True Christian before he heard of Richard Carlile, but now a Deist and Republican" (*Republican,* 10 May 1822), and an "Old Methodist of Forty Years Standing" who "arrived at the positive facts promulgated by Mr. Carlile; [and] is now satisfied, that all religion is a cheat, and finds himself far happier as a Materialist aged sixty" (*Newgate Monthly Magazine,* 1 February 1825).

42. The description of Sheffield is in *Republican,* 2 July 1824.

43. The hyperbolic enthusiasm of his supporters almost leaps out at the reader from the printed page, as in the characterizations of Carlile as "the Thermopylae of Free Discussion" (Squire Farrar of Bradford, *Republican* 15 August 1823) and "the bravest man in Europe" (Birmingham Paine Club, *Drakard's Stamford News,* 7 February 1823).

44. Sometimes a single reformer made all the running for Carlile as, for example, Robert Armstrong, a clockmaker from Stokesley, Yorkshire, who established a radical library and issued a short-lived newspaper, *The Missionary: or Stokesley and Cleveland Illuminator* (1823-24). Armstrong claimed to have distributed over 100 copies of the *Age of Reason* in Stokesley.

45. *Republican,* 10 May, 11 October 1822.

46. The Greek word *zetetic* ("to seek for") has stuck. In 1977, an American magazine, the *Zetetic,* was launched by a "Committee for the Scientific Investigation of Claims by the Paranormal."

47. The brothers James and Robert Affleck, who organized the Edinburgh society, were imprisoned after being prosecuted for blasphemy in 1823. They wrote articles for the *Republican,* including *Critical Remarks on the Truth and Harmony of the Four Gospels,* which was published by Carlile in tract form in 1827.

48. The statement is by the "London Philosophical Zetetic Society." *Republican,* 13 December 1822.

49. *To the Reformers of Great Britain,* 3 March 1821; *Lion,* 21 November 1828.

50. The supporter is Robert Armstrong of Stokesley, already mentioned. *Republican,* 11 April 1823.

51. Carlile described the Great Northern Radical Union as "that pickpocket thing" and "that useless, corrupt thing." *Republican,* 29 March, 7 June 1822.

52. *Republican,* 21 February 1823, 26 July 1822. The bitterness of the split is documented in Carlile's 1821 tract, *An Effort to Set at Rest Some Little Disputes and Misunderstandings between the Reformers of Leeds.* At a public dinner in Birmingham, T. J. Wooler refused to allow Carlile to be toasted because of his attacks on Hunt. *Republican,* 30 August 1822.

7

BIRTH CONTROL AND OTHER MATTERS

On November 18, 1825, six years after his imprisonment began and without any advance warning, Carlile was freed from Dorchester Gaol by order of Robert Peel, the home secretary. Many efforts had been made in the previous years to secure his release. Petitions had been forwarded to Parliament and the Home Office, and an intensive lobbying campaign carried on by Francis Place and other reformers.[1] All to no avail. Both conservatives and reformers were therefore taken by surprise at Carlile's sudden release. For not only had he continued to refuse to pay the required fine, but at the very moment of his release his associates were displaying a provocative print in his Fleet Street shop window: a visual rendering of the "God of the Scriptures" accompanied by lines such as "There went up Smoke out of his Nostrils, and Fire out of his mouth." To the consternation of the authorities in London, unruly crowds were gathering nightly to gape at this print.[2]

What to do after six years of prison? How to translate freedom into a positive contribution to reform and to cope with renewed political pressures now that he was ready once more to enter the orbit of radical agitation? These and similar questions confronted Carlile as he walked through the prison gates into the town of Dorchester on the morning of November 18, affirming to a small group of supporters his determination "to go forth to preach . . . to people and to nations."[3] He was disappointed that he did not receive an outpouring of support such as that awaiting Hunt when he was released from Ilchester Gaol in 1822 after a much shorter prison term. But Carlile knew that there were many working-class supporters in the country who continued to look to him for leadership, and to them he sent a jubilant message, proclaiming: "My new birth, my regeneration, my salvation, my being born again with fire and water and inspired with the spirit of the logos."[4]

For several weeks he experienced feelings of exhilaration. Having family business to transact in Devon, he took a "triumphant" coach journey there before making his way back to London. He rode atop the vehicle so as to inhale the country air and for part of the time carried on an "agreeable" conversation with a clergyman to whom he proffered the claims of "rationality." He also partook of sinful pleasures along the way. There was a sumptuous repast of goose and rabbit at a Bridport inn, buoyant encounters with knots of supporters in public houses, and, as a climax, three comfortable evenings spent at Congdon's Hotel, Exeter, a plush hostelry whose well-fitted public rooms were intended for the "Nobility, Gentry, [and] Public at Large," not a working-class blasphemer recently released from prison.[5] Whether Carlile gave way to curiosity and attended services in Exeter Cathedral can only be guessed at. But it would have required a feat of restraint quite out of character with his expansive mood during these days for him to have averted his eyes entirely from the magnificent statuary of the west front of the cathedral.

When he returned to London in January 1826, he still felt elated. "Pleasant, horrid London" had much to offer after six years, including reprobate activities previously disdained. He attended a pantomime, a Punch and Judy show, and a fair, and went to see a production of *Macbeth*, which elicited from him the crabbed observation that "it should never be performed." Within a few weeks, however, his conscience had begun to get the better of him. Pleasure became less attractive to him, and he began once again to pronounce a lamentation on the sins of urban life. He bewailed the superstition and immorality on display in London. "The punch of the puppet show, the clown of the pantomime, and the gingerbread figure of the confectioner," he asserted, "are each an instrument wherewith to operate upon the weakness of the human animal."[6] He declared himself in favor of suppressing "debasing" amusements such as public fairs. Freedom, a tonic only a short time before, was becoming a moral burden that could not easily be borne.

The immediate problem facing Carlile was how to reestablish his position as a leading spokesman for reform. His two most active rivals, Hunt and Cobbett, were engaging in bouts of speechmaking

with which he could not compete. Six years' "want of social intercourse" had increased his lack of self-confidence, making it difficult for him to adjust to a political environment that gave pride of
place to platform oratory. His dress was unfashionable and his
bearing awkward. Worst of all, his journalistic talents, his strongest
suit, were being called into question. The *Republican,* one of the
most vigorous working-class journals of the period, was suffering
from political neurasthenia. Its editorials were pallid (notwithstanding an energetic attack on Cobbett in April that was
"ghosted" by Francis Place), and its circulation was, for the first
time since 1820, beginning to decline.[7]

Even so, Carlile made an effective return to political life during
the early months of 1826. He cultivated the support of London
reformers by attending political meetings, including a celebration
in his honor at which he did not play an active part.[8] He also
worked closely with three of his shopmen who were still in Newgate
prison—Thomas Ryley Perry, Richard Hassell, and William
Campion—helping them to prepare a bevy of articles for the press
and to bring out the *Newgate Monthly Magazine.* Hassell was, in
particular, being groomed for a major role in working-class
politics, perhaps as the next editor of the *Republican.*

During the spring of 1826 much of Carlile's time was taken up by
a search for new publishing quarters. His shop at 84 Fleet Street
had been destroyed by the fires of November 1824, and since July
1825 he had conducted most of his business from leased premises at
135 Fleet Street. But in his judgment, if he was to maintain his
standing as a radical journalist, a new "Temple of Reason" was
needed. Respectability was the touchstone of political leadership,
he believed, and "public" embarrassments, such as those entailed
in working in unsuitable premises, had to be avoided at all costs.
"Such a reform as I am advocating," he wrote, "should not be
worked in a hole or corner, but it should be carried on in the most
open and in the most respectable manner."[9]

With the assistance of Place, negotiations for a shop at 62 Fleet
Street were begun in April. Place put Carlile in contact with several
businessmen who extended loans to him and helped him to negoti-
ate a ten-year lease on the property. The expenses were considerable: a down payment of £1000 and annual carrying charges of
more than £500. Yet, Carlile took on the obligations without

demur. The shop, centrally located and fitted out with commodious rooms, was precisely what he wanted. In June he moved into his new quarters, taking ambitious journalistic plans along with him.[10]

Publishing was, however, a much more precarious business than he ever understood. In the months prior to his release he had devised a scheme for a Joint Stock Book Company that was to revolutionize cheap publishing by printing complete editions of "standard" radical works not readily available to workingmen. Capital for the company was to be raised by £100 shares, with subscribers guaranteed an annual return of 5 percent on their investments. Carlile declared himself ready to accept full responsibility for publishing and printing liabilities and to protect the anonymity of investors.[11]

The Joint Stock Book Company was commenced in the summer of 1826 without, as it turned out, any real prospects for success. The actual capital subscribed—slightly more than £500—was much less than Carlile had hoped for, and the publications issued during the two years of the company's life made no significant impact on radical politics. They included a pocket edition of Shelley's *Queen Mab*; a reprint of the *Free Enquirer*, an eighteenth-century deist periodical for which the editor, Peter Annet, had been imprisoned and pilloried; *Janus on Sion, or Past and to Come* (probably written by George Ensor), an antiscriptural tract of impressive scholarship dating from 1816; three works by d'Holbach (*Letter from Thrasybule to Leucippe*, the *System of Nature*, and *Bons Sens*); and an edition of Volney's *Ruins of Empires* that was never sold to the public.[12] The losses incurred by Carlile in issuing these publications were substantial. To underscore the company's respectability, he sold its works at prices higher than he need have done taking into account only market factors. This hurt him badly. *Queen Mab*, for example, sold only about 250 copies at a price of two shillings, six pence, while d'Holbach's *Bons Sens*, overpriced at five shillings, did even less well. Several investors in the company, including Julian Hibbert, a wealthy atheist who was beginning to give regular financial support to Carlile, and John Grattan, a Chesterfield farmer who assisted him with translations, disengaged themselves from the scheme. Although the Joint Stock Book Company survived until the end of 1828, it was a failure, the first of many that Carlile was to experience in the years after his release from prison.[13]

While involved with publishing problems and seeking to extend his political position against the determined opposition of Cobbett, Hunt, and other reformers, Carlile commenced an activity that substantially affected his career as a radical reformer. This was as a propagandist for birth control, a subject too controversial for most reformers to touch but one that, when once persuaded of its merits, he identified with closely. *Every Woman's Book*, a pamphlet he wrote and published in March 1826, was the most specific endorsement of birth control to be published in Britain up to that time. He hawked it energetically for several years, popularizing its arguments and making himself the best-known advocate of birth control prior to the exploits of Charles Bradlaugh and Annie Besant in the 1870s.[14]

Birth control was an unlikely subject for Carlile to champion. He was "respectable," strait-laced, and temperamentally punctilious (though not averse to the charms of women). He made it a point to shun all sexual "indecencies," including Christian "fanaticism and ribaldry," particularly the "corporal sensuality" of Methodism. The Bible was in his opinion a compilation of erotic tales of onanism, pederasty, and "love-feasts." "Moral and philosophical" men and women (his supporters) were abjured to shun its desolating influences and instead to seek "rational" outlets for their needs.[15]

To his wife and children, Carlile was a paterfamilias who demanded total obedience. He had a quintessentially Victorian attitude toward women. They were, he maintained, "the best portion of the human race," creatures of virtue who had to be educated delicately and treated with veneration. The "unsusceptible and sensitive" minds of women were, he wrote, potentially "the most important channel through which virtue can be propagated and the social state be rendered peaceable, prosperous, and happy"; if tutored properly in the domestic graces, they were capable of attenuating the "combative principle" of the male and reducing discord in the world. However, their place was self-evidently in the home, or , if their radical husbands were involved in the struggle for political freedom, in the publishing office.[16]

There is nothing in this litany of conventional artisan attitudes to identify Carlile with feminism, and, indeed, before 1825 he showed no tendency at all in this direction. But in the early 1820s two factors supervened to modify his outlook. The less important of the two was the parlous state of his own marriage. His relationship with Jane Carlile had deteriorated from the time of their enforced joint incarceration in Dorchester prison, and shortly after his release he began to chafe openly at the constraints of marriage. No formal steps toward a legal separation were taken, but, seemingly, he began to attach himself to issues that promised somehow to "liberate" him from his conjugal ties. Thus, he was temperamentally receptive to birth control, with its implicit challenge to the permanence of family ties.

A more significant factor in Carlile's advocacy of birth control (and of women's rights) was the influence of Francis Place. A close relationship between the two men began in 1822, when Place began his efforts to secure Carlile's release from prison and became, at the same time, a regular correspondent. Disagreeing with Carlile's propensity for "extreme" radical views, Place sought to win him over to classical political economy, of which he was a leading spokesman. He impressed upon him the importance of the population doctrines of Thomas Malthus, which in his view provided the best antidote to economic distress by reducing the competition for jobs. But whereas Malthus urged population checks by means of "moral restraint" (delayed marriage), Place and James Mill, a close associate, proffered a much more radical solution: birth control. In *Illustrations and Proofs of the Principles of Population,* which he published anonymously in 1822, Place affirmed that "it was not disreputable for married persons to avail themselves of such precautionary means as would, without being injurious to health, or destructive of female delicacy, prevent contraception"; and in the *Elements of Political Economy* (1821), Mill took a similar position.[17] But because of the controversial nature of the subject, neither man spoke with as clear a voice as he would have liked, and it remained for Carlile to make birth control part of the vocabulary of working-class dissent.

Place's efforts to win Carlile over to birth control began with several articles that he contributed to the *Republican* (1822-23). Initially Carlile rejected Place's arguments while accepting some of the tenets of political economy. To Place's advocacy of "such means as while they do no injury to health, shall prevent conception," he replied that he favored "natural" intercourse, not the "French method" (a reference to the widespread, though erroneous, belief that contraception was freely practiced in France and that it had been introduced into Britain by Robert Owen).[18] "Unnatural" sexual activity would, Carlile stated, lead inevitably to "the deterioration of the character of mankind." He took the view— based on a combination of conventional moralizing and some familiarity with current medical thinking—that women "have an almost constant desire for copulation [and] . . . if the means to prevent copulation were publicly taught," it would "lead to a general gratification of this common desire, and to a breaking up of all individual attachments."[19]

While these exchanges were taking place, Place took a decisive step. In the summer of 1823, he privately printed three birth control pamphlets known as the *Diabolical Handbills,* to which he did not append his name. These epistolary essays were addressed to the "Married of Both Sexes," to the "Married of Both Sexes of the Working People," and to the "Married of Both Sexes in Genteel Life." Their aim was "to destroy vice, and put an end to debauch- ery" by persuading married couples to practice birth control. Procreation, insisted Place, had to be held in artificial check if competition for jobs was to be reduced. He suggested a specific method for accomplishing this: a sponge attached to a ball of ribbon that could be inserted by a woman into her vagina prior to sexual intercourse and then withdrawn immediately afterward.[20] Less enthusiastically, he also advocated coitus interruptus, a technique of birth control that was championed subsequently by Robert Dale Owen and other Victorian reformers.[21]

Carlile rejected the views expressed in the *Diabolical Handbills.* But he helped Place to distribute them and allowed his Water Lane shop to be used as a publishing "drop." Several times previously he had popularized issues that he did not entirely support, and birth control seemed no worse a subject than any other with which to arouse public feeling. Unforeseen by Carlile, however, was the opposition that the handbills generated among reformers. They made him an object of considerable hostility. But he did not back down. Confronted by criticism he regarded as unfair, his obduracy increased, and he worked to the limits of his ability to ensure the success of Place's tracts.[22]

Within a year of the appearance of the *Diabolical Handbills,* Carlile began to alter his own views. He was not yet willing to make a public avowal of his support for birth control. But angered by the adverse reaction of reformers, he was becoming increasingly sympathetic to its claims. In the autumn of 1824 he went so far as to describe love, in the pages of the *Republican*, as "the very source of human happiness, and essential alike to health, beauty and sweetness of temper." Why, he asked rhetorically, were "old maids generally ugly and of wretched tempers?" His answer was: "Solely from the want of a natural intercourse with the other sex."[23] Yet he continued to resist Place's importunities. "I have been bored into the mention of [population control]," he told Place in a letter. "I am altogether a prude and a modest young man." The merits of the sponge were clear, he conceded, but sexual intercourse was a personal matter that should not be elevated into a "great political principle." For Carlile, the gut issues remained as before: high taxation, political inequality, and, above all, the desiccating, ruinous effects of religion. "I prefer to attack known, real, and visible evils," he told readers of the *Republican*, "rather than to waste my fire upon a shadow, or a question as abstract as the *one* immaculate conception!"[24]

By January 1825 Place, the determined lobbyist, had worked his political magic. Carlile was now an unrepentant enthusiast for birth control who believed it to be an integral part of radical reform.[25] "In no shape whatever, as a simple act of mutual consent, can I conceive it to be disgusting or obscene," he wrote; on the contrary, it was the only "practicable scheme that can be associated with sexual intercourse." In "What Is Love?", an article he wrote and printed in the *Republican* in May 1825, he asserted that his aim was "to strip off all disguise and secrecy from this new and secretly promulgated plan to prevent contraception," partly to diminish "the horrid influence of Malthus, that the superfluous numbers of mankind should be legislatively left to a natural destruction for want of food." (This attack on Malthus placed him considerably out of step with the opinions of Place and Mill.) What was needed was a "wholesome check upon an excess of population," not by means of abortion, "a little-thought-of-matter of course," but by the vaginal sponge or "any other absorbing substance [that] would answer the same end."[26]

"What Is Love?" generated much controversy, especially its third reprinting, which was accompanied by a frontispiece engraving of a naked Adam and Eve. It was, however, the fourth edition of the tract, published at one shilling, six pence under the alluring title of *Every Woman's Book; or What Is Love?* that established Carlile as the foremost advocate of birth control in Britain.[27] In this revised version he stated that human life should be conceived only when it is "conducive to the improvement of the state" and that a primary aim of reformers must be to diminish "self-excitements and un-natural gratifications . . . for the accomplishments of seminal excretions in the male, and the appeasings of lascivious excitement in the female by artificial means." He claimed that "if love were made a matter of sedate and philosophical conversation, the pleasures arising from it would be greatly heightened, desire would never be tyrannically suppressed, and much misery and ill-health would be avoided."[28]

But there was more to *Every Woman's Book* than this brief summary (largely a rephrasing of Place) would indicate. For, in addition to the economic and social case for birth control, Carlile included a strongly "feminist" line of argument. Specifically, he attacked the moral and religious sanctions that constrained female desires and defined love as a "natural . . . and necessary propensity for intercourse" and religion as "a mental disease, that turns love into a fancied sin, and commits dreadful revenge, in excluding due sexual intercourse."[29] His conclusion was as follows: that although premarital chastity was desirable, women must be as free as men to make sexual choices and to satisfy their sexual needs. He was more insistent about this than any other reformer of the early nineteenth century. "Every healthy woman, after the age of puberty, feels the passion of love," he observed. "It is a part of her health, and as natural a consequence as hunger and thirst. Even very few unhealthy women are without the passion. Their disorder, in nine cases out of ten, is caused either by the absence of the passion or the want of its gratifications." More poetically, he put the question thus: "Why should Hymen be the tyrant of love anywhere?"[30]

Carlile's conviction that women were not "mere breeding machines" and that "equality between the sexes" was a proper objective for reformers gave a special flavor to his advocacy of birth control. He prefigured later themes of repressed sexuality and of a double standard in morality, and for this reason, *Every Woman's Book* became a powerful contribution to the literature of birth control written from the perspective of women. (In an amended version of *Every Woman's Book*, appearing in 1828 and reflecting the influence of Place, the "feminist" component was softened—a case of more Malthus and less sex.) Notwithstanding the publication of other birth control pamphlets in succeeding years—including Robert Dale Owen's *Moral Physiology* (1831), Charles Knowlton's *Fruits of Philosophy* (1832), and George Drysdale's *Elements of Social Science* (1854)—it remained a staple item on working-class publishing lists throughout the nineteenth century.

But in the short term, birth control did Carlile more harm than good. Sales of his tract were relatively poor, even accepting the dubious claim that 10,000 copies of it were sold between 1826 and 1838. And it aroused considerable animus against him from reformers, particularly Cobbett. From as early as 1820, the two men had been at odds with each other. The latter was an opponent of republicanism and atheism, while Carlile was a vigorous critic of "priestcraft," as evinced in Cobbett's *History of the Protestant Reformation,* which was published in 1824.[31] Not surprisingly, Cobbett attacked *Every Woman's Book* harshly. Describing the work as "so filthy, so disgusting, so beastly, as to shock the mind of even the lewdest of men and women," he stated that he would never sit in the same room with the "madman" who wrote it. (This vow was conveniently ignored when the two men patched up their quarrel in 1830.) Several of Carlile's supporters retorted that "for his indiscriminate abuse, his bad moral principle, and his insufferable dogmatism, we consider [Cobbett] fair game for satire or ridicule," and during the ensuing altercation, Carlile gave as much abuse as he got.[32] But Cobbett had a much larger readership, and some of Carlile's followers were weaned permanently away from him as a result of this dispute.

Many reformers other than Cobbett were disconcerted by Carlile's indelicate foray into sexual controversy. During a tour of Lancashire in 1827, Carlile was accused by some Irish reformers of immorality and of seeking to destroy the sanctity of the family. Subsequent peregrinations in London and the provinces elicited hostile responses from many of Henry Hunt's supporters. Conservatives and reformers alike rejected Carlile's views on birth control, even when for tactical reasons he began to play down his enthusiasm for it in the 1830s. Retrospectively he characterized *Every Woman's Book* as "the most useful book I have ever printed"; privately he admitted that it had cost him dearly in public support.[33]

Carlile's opinions on other aspects of the "woman question" are not as central to his career, but they illustrate his bent for controversy and willingness to champion unpopular causes. For example, although he did not support Shelley's attacks on marriage or those of James Lawrence in his influential book *The Empire of the Nairs* (which Carlile excerpted in the *Lion* in 1828), he took the position that "marriage should cease when affection between the parties has ceased," a point of view that was reinforced self-evidently by his own marital problems.[34] Divorce, he contended, should be obtainable by either party at law, not, as was the case, by the cumbersome, expensive procedure of a private act of Parliament. In 1826, he helped Richard Hassell abridge for the *Newgate Monthly Magazine* portions of Peter Annet's *Social Bliss Considered*, a book that advocated civil divorce and rights of cohabitation and separation. More pregnant with political significance was Carlile's belief, expressed tactfully, that women should have the right to vote and be elected to Parliament. He espoused these radical positions, which were not supported by the bulk of reformers, with the observation that a "constitution cannot be founded on equal rights that excludes the women from all share of power and influence."[35] Subsequently these views were put forth strongly by his disciple, Elizabeth Sharples, in a famous series of freethought lectures at the Rotunda in 1832.

Despite Carlile's fascination with sexual matters, his primary interest was in theological reform and, shortly after his release from prison, he found himself once again at a crossroads in this area. Between 1819 and 1826 he had championed deism and then atheism and had come to be regarded as the most militant advocate of working-class freethought. From his prison room he had launched a full-fledged attack against Christianity: by publishing the works of leading freethinkers and by reiterating that religion was a source of many of the world's evils. With the support of several thousand workingmen, he appeared to be on the verge of organizing a successful "infidel" movement. Yet once again he began to shift his views, this time in tandem with the Reverend Robert Taylor, a controversial freethinker who did much to weaken Carlile's credibility as a radical reformer.

Born in 1784, Taylor was an eccentric Cambridge graduate who took orders in the Church of England and held minor church offices in Sussex and Birmingham. He had been forced to give up these positions because of his deist opinions, which were an unorthodox mixture of astrology and etymological analysis. In the early 1820s

Taylor settled in Dublin where he founded a "Society of Universal Benevolence" (described by one opponent as a "temple of infidelity") and a monthly journal, the *Clerical Review*, in which he popularized his views. He moved to London in 1824, becoming secretary and chaplain of the "Christian Evidence Society," an organization of deists that met weekly at the Globe Tavern in Fleet Street and, subsequently, at Salter's Hall, Cannon Street. It was at about this time that he began to correspond with Carlile, who reprinted articles from the *Clerical Review* in the *Republican* and made a number of favorable references to Taylor's work.[36]

Dubbed the "Devil's Chaplain" by Henry Hunt, Taylor was vastly dissimilar to Carlile in temperament. He was a witty, ebullient man, a vendor of freethought ideas rather than a serious critic of religion. His magniloquent speaking style overshadowed the substance of his message. When he spoke he wore baroque clerical attire that often shocked his audiences. And his "Holy Liturgy," written for the Christian Evidence Society, was an exuberant lampoon of Church of England ceremonial.[37] Whatever Taylor did, he did with a sense of occasion.

Though his theological views were a mélange of unsubstantiated generalizations, they attracted Carlile and other working-class reformers because of their breadth and the scholarly trappings in which they were presented. Temperamentally, Carlile was incapable of remaining on one intellectual perch for too long. He was asking new questions constantly and pursuing new avenues of thought. While not ready to abandon atheism in 1826, he had become aware of the limitations of a philosophy that was couched entirely in terms of physical growth and decay. He was seeking a more sweeping interpretation of religion, to arouse the enthusiasm of his supporters and win over new converts. Taylor, whose ideas paralleled those he was beginning to develop independently, appeared to offer such nostrums.

The keystone of Taylor's "moral deism," which drew heavily on Charles Dupuis's as yet untranslated *Origines des tous les Cultes* (1795), was his belief that religion originated in sun worship and personified astrological relationships.[38] According to Taylor, "the only difference between Paganism and Christianity . . . was the difference between the allegorical fictions in which the one or the other couched the same physical theorems." He maintained that the "principle of harking back to the teaching of the ancient priests,

Christian, Jewish, or Pagan, was nothing more than allegorized astronomy, a personification of the planetary, physical, and mental phenomena, having no true relation to human history."[39] Ancient pagan religion was, he insisted, superior to Judaism and Christianity. Its communicants were less intolerant than modern religionists and, in contrast especially to the Jews of the Old Testament ("a melancholic and misanthropic horde of exclusively superstitious barbarians"), they favored "harmonious universalism." Christianity and Judaism were effete vestiges of earlier religions that had strayed far from their original purposes.[40]

Taylor also propounded a universalist typology of Christ. The latter was an "emblematical personification of the SUN," he wrote, "one of many to be discovered throughout history. The term CHRIST: CHRIST OUR SAVIOUR: OUR LORD: OUR BLESSED LORD AND SAVIOUR are epithets that have no identification in them. They were of familiar application, and in continual recurrence as applied to the SUN, to Jupiter, to Bacchus, Apollo, Adonis." As a result of his reading of Sir William Jones's *Asiatic Researches*, a work of considerable scholarship published in the late eighteenth century, he emphasized particularly the similarity between Jesus and the Hindu god, Krishna. Everything followed from this: that the Christian Gospels were identical with Hindu mythology and that numerous Christ figures throughout history, including the Phoenician Adonis, the Druidical Estre, and the Greek Prometheus, were allegorical variations of "Jesus."[41]

Even before his contacts with Taylor began in 1824, Carlile had begun to prefigure some of these ideas in his own writings. Influenced by Volney's *Ruins of Empires* and Sir William Drummond's *Oedipus Judaica*, an allegorical interpretation of religion which appeared in 1811, he began to make connections between paganism and the Judeo-Christian tradition: for example, between Christmas and the Roman Saturnalia, the Sacraments and the Eleusinian mysteries of ancient Greece, and the "miraculous" births of Jesus and of Krishna. The writings of Samson Arnold Mackey, a "fellow workman" in the cause of reform from Norwich, pushed Carlile further in this direction. In his *Mythological Astronomy of the Ancients Demonstrated* (1822), Mackey used allegory ("the master key to the ancient mysteries") and a "sphinxiad" (illustrating solar and astronomical relationships) to investigate religion. His conclusions, similar to those of Taylor, were that mythological names had "natural" roots and that solar worship was basic to an under-standing of the origins of religion.[42]

Significantly, Carlile's analysis of the Scriptures also drew him toward an allegorical interpretation of religion. From 1821 on, he began in weekly numbers of the *Republican* to ransack the Scriptures systematically: laying bare their "superstitions" and exposing them as "an idolatry founded upon fable and a corrupt institution."[43] His technique of "negative assertion" was to deny the possibility of an event's having occurred if it could not be verified positively. This led him in 1822 to reject the authenticity of all surviving contemporary accounts of Christianity. He believed that the existence of Christianity before the second century A.D. could not be documented factually and that it originated not in Judea but in Antioch, where it was sculpted out of Greek and Asian mythol-ogies by priests in order to consolidate their influence over a credulous populace.[44] The earliest reference to Christianity that he accepted was that of Pliny the Younger, a proconsul in Bythinia from 106 to 112 A.D., whose knowledge of events was limited to the province of Antioch.

Carlile likewise challenged the accepted historical account of Jesus, before his first contact with Taylor and many years before other freethinkers were willing to do so. (D. F. Strauss's important *Life of Jesus* was not published until 1835, while Charles Hennell's *Inquiry Concerning the Origin of Christianity* did not appear until 1838.) He rejected not only the existence of a "divine" Jesus—a common deist theme—but of a human Jesus. An Aberdeen manu-script entitled "New Trial of the Witnesses," which reached him in Dorchester in 1823 and which he published subsequently, provided "conclusive" evidence for him that the story of Jesus was entirely allegorical. In a leader in the *Republican* in January 1824, he told his followers: "I challenge Christendom to show, that any one book or person called Christian existed before the reign of Trajan: or within what is now called the first century."[45] An allegorical account of Jesus was fully consonant with atheism, Carlile main-tained, and he urged his followers, many of them skeptical, to adopt this position in petitions to Parliament.

From a reading of Jesus as allegory, it was but a short step—taken haltingly until his views began to converge with those of Taylor—to the more generalized perception of all religion as allegory. After conversations with a Unitarian preacher named Treleaven in

March 1824 at Dorchester, Carlile described Christianity as symbolical. The scriptural characters were "personifications of astronomical and other physical occurrences," he stated, the very word *Christ* being nothing more than a transposition of the Greek word for "anointed." He now explicated a statement that he had made in 1822: "Prometheus, Hercules, Bacchus, Moses, Joshua, Elijah, Osiris, Apollo, Thamus, Chrishna and Jesus Christ, with fifty other names, are but so many astronomical names of our solar planet, and the motions of the earth in relation to it, with their effects, allegorically personified."[46]

Carlile's ideas about religion merged increasingly with those of Taylor and, from the spring of 1826 on, the two men were in almost daily personal contact in London. Yet they disagreed in some important ways. Whereas Taylor preached a "physical allegory" of religion based on primeval sun worship, Carlile characterized his own ideas as constituting a "moral allegory" of religion, "the most grand, the most important . . . that was ever presented to the study of mankind." At the urging of Julian Hibbert, who was supporting him financially, he read Plato and was impressed by "the Grecian tale of reason, or the logos, persecuted by FORCE and STRENGTH." He conceived of a universal "principle of reason" at war throughout history with the forces of evil. In its present manifestation this principle was part of the struggle for reform. It was, he asserted, "the GOD OF REPUBLI-CANISM, the GOD OF LIBERTY, OF KNOWLEDGE, OF POPULAR opposed to *individual* Power; the GOD OF THE MANY *against the wickedness and tyranny of the few.*"[47]

Interweaving his own cosmic view of religion with that of Taylor, Carlile compared his situation to that of Jesus: "I am a real emblem of REASON prosecuted by FORCE and STRENGTH: of JESUS CHRIST crucified by or between TWO THIEVES. I am the *Jesus Christ* of this Island, and this age." He shared his insights with his readers, telling them: "I have stolen fire from the gods for the use of my fellow-countrymen; I have been persecuted by the gods of the day; and I have wearied the revenge, or have triumphed over these goals."[48] Some of his supporters were driven to distraction by such imagery, or, in more practical terms, into the arms of Cobbett and Hunt. But it was a line of thought that he continued to espouse.

An "exposure" of freemasonry in the *Republican*, which appeared from July to October 1825, further illustrates the shift in

Carlile's views. His initial goal in launching an investigation of freemasonry had been to eradicate still one more manifestation of superstition. But he soon began to reach conclusions markedly different from those he had anticipated. Freemasonry, he commented in September, was "allegorically . . . another version of the Christian Religion, substituting Hiram Abiff for Jesus Christ, or Prometheus, or Hercules, or Thamiz, or the SUN or ages below the horizon, gone down to Hell." The Temple of Solomon was the fabric of knowledge; the masonic sign represented pagan sun worship; and the Egyptian triple tau, or crux ansata, foreshadowed the cross. According to Carlile, freemasonry represented in its secret ceremonies "the persecution and destruction of brilliant reason and accomplishment by force, strength or thieves." It was a "beautiful science," though one that had languished for thousands of years. Now, by way of obstructing the machinations of ambitious clergymen, he was illuminating its original meaning for the enlightenment of mankind.[49]

To the chagrin of his followers, many of whom protested by writing letters to the *Republican*, Carlile began to describe himself as a "christian atheist." He urged his disciples to establish associations of "Zerotarian Catholic Christians," so as to bring "Atheists and Deists within the fold of a Church." They would then become a "genuine set of christians," able to trace religion through "all its mythological ramifications to its fountain, the sun."[50] These themes—fragments of Christian imagery blended with elements of radical freethought—became more insistent as Carlile came under Taylor's influence.

Still, such departures from "orthodox" atheism were tentative as yet. Toward the end of 1826, Carlile published *Every Man's Book: or, What Is God?*, a volume that espoused straightforward materialism. Launching an attack upon the Quakers, he averred that matter was the foundation of all life and that organic existence had no principle informing it other than "the order and regularity of mere mechanical power." He described mind as "nothing distinct from the body. It is the action to which experience and practice have trained the body."[51] He also criticized Taylor's "public profession" of deism. Such a doctrine was "trash" and "nonsense," according to Carlile. Though Taylor was a useful man, he was obsessed with "forms and ceremonies, little pomps and less fineries"; his "divine service," performed in the "chapel" of the

Christian Evidence Society on Sunday evenings, was "a liturgy positively more contemptible and more hypocritical than that of the Established Church."[52]

If Carlile's infidel convictions can be described as in a transitional stage during 1826, the same cannot be said of his personal attitudes, which were pessimistic. "The very best state of life," he commented earlier in the year, was "but an absence from pain; and nine tenths of animal life constitute a state of pain."[53] When his favorite shopman, Richard Hassell, died suddenly of a fever in November 1826 at the age of twenty-six, he was disconsolate. He felt jaded by the inclement London weather and by punishing financial and publishing burdens. He suffered from asthma and rheumatism, reminders of his six years in prison. In December, notwithstanding his daily use of medical "cures," which included frequent hot vapor baths, he was described by Francis Place, who was spending several hours a day with him, as "in a bad way."[54]

Worst of all for Carlile, the *Republican* had finally to be relinquished. By the end of 1826 its circulation had dropped to 2000 weekly (a loss of 60 percent since January), and the sums needed to keep it going exceeded the miniscule income that it brought in. The paper, as Carlile proudly affirmed in its final leader, had been a "monument of good and good example to future ages." It had presented "the most pithy and convincing arguments for philosophical atheism that are found in any books," had been the first journal to discuss openly the issue of "free trade in love," and had introduced numerous "useful" topics into its pages. When he bade farewell to its readers in December 1826—in the expectation that he would bring out another paper shortly—he did so with the belief that "had my ability been equal to my disposition to do good, more would have been done than has been done."[55] Needless to say, much more remained to be done.

Notes

1. Petition from Carlile to Dorset Quarter Sessions, 12 April 1825, Dorset C.R.O. In a letter to Peel he wrote: "Feel shame if your bosom be not impervious to it, at my six years of imprisonment." Carlile to Peel, 22 July 1825, Peel Papers, Add. Ms. 40,380, f.195, B.M. Henry Brougham, Joseph Hume, and Alderman Waithman presented petitions on his behalf, while John Cam Hobhouse, Sir Francis Burdett, and Daniel O'Connell refused to do so. Carlile thanked Brougham for the "handsome and ready

manner" in which he presented the petition. Carlile to Brougham, 10 June 1825, Brougham Papers, University College, London.

2. A colored version of this print, "God of the Jews and Christians," is in Home Office 44/15, P.R.O. It was also published as a frontispiece to volume 3 of the *Deist* (1826).

3. *Republican*, 4 November 1825.

4. Ibid., 2 December 1825.

5. This advertisement, taken from *Woolmer's Exeter and Plymouth Gazette*, 6 May 1820, is reproduced in the lobby of the present hotel, renamed the Royal Clarence Hotel.

6. *Republican*, 3 February, 8 September 1826. So strongly was Carlile aroused by fairs and fortune-telling that he called for the eradication of gypsies: "They are a class of thieves who deserve no sympathy: they are wild beasts, not social beings, who prey upon all, and for whose extermination the legislature should interfere." Ibid., 8 December 1826.

7. On the decline in circulation, see Carlile's letter to William Holmes, 9 July 1840, C.P. The *Bull Dog*, a scurrilous journal, dubbed the *Republican* "the Wash Tub Gazette and Old Woman's Chronicle" and claimed that its circulation had fallen to 350. *Bull Dog*, 2 September 1826.

8. There is an account of the dinner in the *Morning Herald*, 31 January 1826.

9. *Lion*, 19 September 1828.

10. For detailed information about Place's assistance, see Place Diary, Add. Ms. 35,146, B.M. A paper manufacturer named Dutton and a reformer named Dr. Gilchrist were involved in the negotiations. S.S. report, 10 November 1827, H.O. 64/11; *Christian Warrior*, 14 January 1843.

11. There are details in the *Republican*, 26 August 1824, 2 December 1825.

12. In the opening number of the *Free Enquirer* Peter Annet wrote: "We wage war against ecclesiastic fraud, priestly avarice, spiritual tyranny, obstinate bigotry, wild superstition, and presumptuous enthusiasm; and fight under the banners of truth." *Free Enquirer* (1826), p. 5. George Ensor, the author of *Janus on Sion*, used the pseudonym "Christian Emanuel," but in 1835 he published a reprint of the Carlile edition under his own name entitled *A Review of the Miracles, Prophecies, and Mysteries of the Old and New Testaments, and of the Morality and Consolation of the Christian Religion.*

13. See the *Prospectus of the Joint Stock Book Company, Established January 1, 1826, Under the Direction of Richard Carlile* (1826); Accounts of the Company, April-October 1826, C.P.; *Republican*, 29 December 1826. In a letter to James Watson in 1838, a reformer described the company as "a vile moneymaking concern, and the books shamefully dear." 'E.B." to James Watson, 12 October 1838, John Burns Papers, Add. Ms. 46,345, f. 28, B.M.

14. For a discussion of Carlile's place in the birth control movement, see Norman E. Himes, *Medical History of Contraception* (New York: Schocken Books, 1970 reprint) pp. 220-22, and Peter Fryer, *The Birth Controllers* (London: Secker & Warburg, 1956), esp. ch. 7. Marie Stopes erroneously attributes the authorship of *Every Woman's Book* to Francis Place. Stopes, *Contraception (Birth Control): Its Theory, History and Practice* (London: Putnam, 1935), pp. 284-89.

15. *Republican*, 19 July 1822, 14 January 1825. After he began to champion birth control, Carlile inverted his cultural symbols. Christianity then came to be described as a religion of "eunuchs, hermaphrodites, and impotent men and women."

16. *Deist*, dedication to volume 2 (1820); *Scourge for the Littleness of "Great" Men*, 7 February 1835.

17. [Francis Place], *Illustrations and Proofs of the Principle of Population: Including an Examination of the Proposed Remedies of Mr. Malthus, and a Reply to the Objections of Mr. Godwin and Others* (London: George Allen & Unwin, 1967 reprint), p. 165. In addition to his *Elements of Political Economy*, Mill's views are expressed in "Colony," an article that he wrote for the 1818 edition of the *Encyclopaedia Britannica*.

18. Place originated the story that Owen introduced the sheath from France, by planting a "third party" letter in the *Black Dwarf* in 1823. James A. Field, "The Early Propagandist Movement in English Population Theory," *American Economic Review* 1, 4th ser. (1911), pp. 7-9.

19. Carlile to Place, 8 August 1822, Place Newspaper Collection, 68, B.M.

20. The quote is from "To the Married of Both Sexes," p. 1. On the *Diabolical Handbills*, see Norman E. Himes, "The Birth Control Handbills of 1823," *Lancet*, 6 August 1927.

21. Robert Dale Owen advocated coitus interruptus in his *Moral Physiology; or, Brief and Plain Treatise on the Population Question* (New York: Skidmore and Jacobus, 1831). On coitus interruptus as a method of birth control in the early nineteenth century, see Stopes, *Contraception*, pp. 282-92.

22. For a vicious attack on the pamphlets by a supporter of Hunt, see the letter from Mary Fildes to Place, 7 September 1823, Place Newspaper Collection, 68, B.M. John Stuart Mill (using the pseudonym "A.M.") wrote two letters to the *Black Dwarf* defending the handbills. 27 September 1823, 10 October 1823.

23. *Republican*, 19 November 1824.

24. Carlile to William Holmes, 7 January 1824, C.P.; *Republican*, 12 November, 22 October 1824.

25. Carlile to William Holmes, 12 January 1825, C.P.; *Republican*, 18 March 1825.

26. "What Is Love?" *Republican*, 6 May 1825.

27. An abridged edition of *Every Woman's Book* was published by Godfrey Higgins of Yorkshire in 1826. Subsequent editions of the tract, all slightly altered, appeared in 1828, 1834, 1838, and 1880. The title of an 1892 edition was *The Philosophy of the Sexes: or, Every Woman's Book* (written by "Dr. Waters" and published by Robert Forder).

28. Richard Carlile, *Every Woman's Book: or, What is Love?: Containing Most Important Instructions for the Prudent Regulation of the Principle of Love, and the Number of a Family* (London: Alfred Carlile, 1838), pp. 36, 38.

29. Carlile, *Every Woman's Book* (1838 ed.), pp. 22, 27.

30. Carlile, *Every Woman's Book* (London: Richard Carlile, 1826), pp. 7-8; Carlile, *A New View of Insanity; in Which Is Set Forth the Present Mismanagement of Public and Private Madhouses, All the Late and Existing Defects of New Bethlem: with Some Suggestions Towards a New Remedy for that Almost-universal Disorder of the Human Race* (London: Richard Carlile, 1831), p. 68.

31. *Republican*, 4 March 1825. Carlile's hostile *Life of William Cobbett*, appearing in the *Republican* in April 1826, was reprinted and sold as a six-penny tact. There is a copy in the Cole Collection, Nuffield College, Oxford.

32. The attack by Cobbett is in his *Political Register*, 15 April 1826, and the reply from the shopmen is in *Newgate Monthly Magazine*, 1 July 1826.

33. Letter from Carlile to Lord Chief Justice Denman, 26 November 1833, C.P. In 1842, Carlile urged that families be limited to three children. Carlile to George Jacob Holyoake, 25 October 1842, Holyoake Papers, Co-operative Union Library.

34. Carlile, *Church Reform*, pp. 2-3. Shelley's *Queen Mab* contains the following statement: "A husband and wife ought to continue so long united as they love each other: any law which should bind them to cohabitation for one moment after the decay of their affection, would be a most intolerable tyranny, and the most unworthy of toleration."

35. *Prompter*, 9 April 1831. In 1826, Carlile contemplated reprinting Mary Wollstonecraft's *A Vindication of the Rights of Woman* but then abandoned the idea.

36. For biographical material on Taylor, see Guy Aldred, *The Devil's Chaplain* (Glasgow: Strickland Press, 1942); *The Philalethean* (1833); H. Cutner, *Robert Taylor* (San Diego, California: The Truth Seeker, n.d.); Introductions to volumes 1 and 2 of *The Devil's Pulpit; Containing Twenty-Three Astronomico-Theological Discourses by the Rev. Robert Taylor, B.A.* (London: Richard Carlile, 1831-1832). The *Glasgow Free Press* (6 April 1824) described Taylor as the "Archbishop of Pandemonium."

37. See Robert Taylor, *The Holy Liturgy, or Divine Service on the Principles of Pure Deism, as Performed Every Sunday in the Chapel of the Society of Universal Benevolence, 86, Cannon Street, City* (London: John Brooks, 1827).

38. The British Museum catalog lists no English translation of Dupuis's book other than two abridgements published by freethinkers: *Was Christ a Person or the Sun?* (1857) and *Christianity a Form of the Great Solar Myth* (1873).

39. Robert Taylor, *The Diegesis: Being a Discourse of the Origin, Evidences, and Early History of Christianity, Never Yet Before or Elsewhere so Fully and Faithfully Set Forth* (London: Richard Carlile, 1829), p. 303; *Prompter*, 25 December 1830.

40. His comment on the Jews is in *Diegesis*, pp. 18-20. Unlike Carlile, Taylor felt a dislike of Jews that is manifested in his writings.

41. On this theme, see Taylor, *Diegesis*, p. 174, and Robert Taylor, *Syntagma of the Evidences of the Christian Religion, Being a Vindication of the Manifesto of the Christian Evidence Society* (London: Richard Carlile, 1828), especially pp. 94-95.

42. Mackey was a self-educated shoemaker. In ascribing importance to sun worship and pagan mythology ("the master key to the ancient mysteries"), he anticipated many of Taylor's ideas. Sampson A. Mackey, *The Mythological Astronomy of the Ancients Demonstrated, by Restoring to Their Fables and Symbols Their Original Meaning* (Norwich, 1822), pp. 37-42.

43. *Republican*, 12 July 1822.

44. Carlile's views are summarized in the *Gospel According to Richard Carlile*, pp. 9-11; *Republican*, 29 October 1824; *Observations on . . . Olinthus Gregory*, pp. 40-42; *Church Reform*, pp. 91-94. Taylor claimed that all of the Christian manuscripts extant before the sixth century were forgeries. *Syntagma*, p. 56.

45. *Republican*, 2 January 1824. The complete title of the Aberdeen manuscript is *The New Trial of the Witnesses; or, the Resurrection of Jesus Considered, on Principles Understood and Acknowledged Equally by Jews and Christians. In An Examination of the Passages in the New Testament*, Paine characterized Jesus as "merely an imaginary or allegorical character, as Apollo, Hercules, Jupiter, and all the dictates of antiquity were" (p. 115).

46. *Republican*, 29 October 1822, 19 March 1824.

47. Ibid., 25 February, 14 January 1825.

48. Ibid., 18 February 1825; *Lion*, 16 October 1829.

49. *Republican*, 9, 16 September 1825.

50. Ibid., 18 March, 23 September 1825.

51. Carlile, *Every Man's Book*, pp. 21, 31.

52. *Republican*, 11 August, 10 November 1826.

53. Carlile, *Every Man's Book*, p. 22.

54. Place Diary, 30 December 1826, Add. Ms. 35,146, B.M.

55. *Republican*, 8, 29 December 1826.

8

INFIDEL MISSIONARIES

After a decade of involvement with radical politics, Carlile had lost none of his robustness. He was still determined to surmount obstacles to "every kind of useful reform" and to leave behind "a record of the good that one bold, honest and persevering man can do." But the odds against his success were beginning to lengthen. His health was poor and his income badly depleted. His political support, too, had diminished as a result of his advocacy of birth control, an issue that antagonized many reformers and gave ammunition to conservatives for use against him. Even worse from the perspective of his political reputation were his forays into allegorical freethought. These appeared tactically unwise and inconsistent with the tenets of working-class infidelity.

Obstacles notwithstanding, Carlile took four extended trips into the provinces between 1827 and 1829. These usher in a new phase in his life and are a milestone in the history of popular freethought. Hitherto he had relied on his pen to rally his supporters into a cohesive movement; now he turned to lecturing and discussion. His trepidation about public oratory had by no means disappeared, but he accepted reluctantly that moral and political redemption could not be secured by means of print alone. Unable to launch an immediate successor to the *Republican* (the first number of the *Lion* did not appear until January 1828) or to sell a quantity of tracts large enough to make a profit, he had no alternative but to initiate a series of lectures in the hope of turning events in his favor.[1]

The Carlile who left London in the spring of 1827, bound for Somerset on the first of his provincial journeys, was little changed physically from the reformer who had burst on to the political scene a decade earlier. His mien was still unprepossessing. He still lacked a sense of self-assurance. But he was more "moderate" in his views, more determined to cultivate an image of "sobriety, easy carriage, mild and inoffensive manners," qualities that he described as "the constituent parts of all that can ever be perfection in the human character."[2] He spoke in measured tones, rarely attempting to manipulate the feelings of his audiences by rhetorical devices. Opponents, however, persisted in seeing the "wild radical" of old. Six years of prison had etched lines into the upper ridges of his face, making him look older than his thirty-seven years; and his shoulder-length hair and unorthodox attire (he wore a high shirt collar fastened with a brass clasp that was a token of "smart" fashion in the West Country) merely reconfirmed their prejudices.[3]

The first tour, beginning in March 1827, lasted two months. Carlile concentrated his movements on Bath, Bristol, and the environs of Southampton and Portsmouth, the latter towns being well known to him from his days as an itinerant tinplateman. Despite vigorous efforts, he did not engender much enthusiasm. The number of working-class infidels in Gosport, Ramsey, and Southampton were fewer than twenty, he reported; and in Portsea, where about one hundred supporters gathered to meet him, the prospects were scarcely better. Emotionally the highlight of his journey took place in Bristol, where he engaged in a "blistering" confrontation with the Reverend William Wait, a nemesis from his Dorchester days. He and Wait traded intemperate barbs about Christianity and atheism, with each accusing the other of disturbing social harmony and threatening the well-being of the poor. Nothing conclusive resulted, but Carlile felt emboldened by the dispute to carry the fight more directly into the enemy's camp.[4]

When he returned to London at the end of April, his position was worse than it had been. He was heavily in debt. And in August, because of his failure to pay the taxes due on his shop, the authorities of the City of London placed an execution on his furniture and sold some of it at public auction. At about the same time the Joint Stock Book Company collapsed. Carlile, unable to recoup its initial expenses, sold off its remaining tracts as cheaply as he could. To the end booksellers were unwilling to handle the company's publications, and without income to purchase advertising space in newspapers or (in some cases) permission from proprietors to buy such space, the sales of its pamphlets rarely exceeded a few hundred copies each.[5]

A small income barely enabled Carlile to withstand the continuing financial pressures. An annuity left to him in 1827 by a Chelsea surgeon whom he had never met (in memory, read Thomas Morrison's will, "of my abhorrence of persecution for opinion, so contrary to the tolerant spirit of a free constitution") provided him with £50 per year. Likewise, Julian Hibbert and a few well-connected London friends gave him steady private support.[6] But notwithstanding such help and the pennies and sixpences of poor workmen, his position was becoming desperate, so much so that he considered terminating his lease on the shop and giving up his publishing business.

Marital difficulties continued to plague him. He and Jane Carlile berated each other constantly, and the death of their only daughter, Hypatia, in February 1825, quickened their mutual enmity. Jane supported most of his political and religious views publicly while privately scorning his allegorical interpretations and his advocacy of birth control. They bickered constantly, as is clear from a reading of the *Republican*. "Mrs. Carlile," the editor told the paper's readers on one occasion, "is annoying me with her tongue, while I want quietness to consider and not to hear the motions of matter."[7] An informer who was privy to the conversations of husband and wife reported that when Carlile left London in the spring of 1827, he did so with the intention of ending the marriage as soon as possible.

In July 1827, the second provincial tour began. It was to last six months, but though eventful, was not any more successful than the previous one. This time Carlile traveled to the north of England, where he spent a month in Liverpool and most of his remaining time in Manchester, frequently visiting nearby textile districts to lecture to artisans and weavers. Lancashire was terra incognita to him, since he had been there only once before for several hours on the morning of Peterloo. He was dismayed by the "deterioration" that he observed: the intemperateness of workingmen, their excessive poverty, and the "sheer animal propensity" that they displayed, which, he concluded, led to overbreeding and numerous abortions. Work in the cotton mills, with its discipline and appalling physical conditions, was in his view, "the very worst slavery that has appeared among mankind." He told readers of the *Republican*: "For want of attention to the health of people who work in cotton mills, a very diminutive and degenerate race of people is growing up in Lancashire, that promises to degrade our national character."[8]

A cluster of reformers known to him through the columns of the *Republican* emerged to greet him: Samuel Mercer, a Hyde weaver and loyal follower since 1822; John Wroe, formerly the editor of the pro-Hunt *Manchester Observer*; Elijah Ridings, the weaver-poet; Joseph Lawton, a Salford Methodist who subsequently migrated to the United States and became a leading distributor of freethought literature. But despite a good deal of enthusiasm, the political portents were discouraging. Many reformers attacked him for his support of birth control, while others denounced his religious theories, which they regarded as confusing and politically unprofitable. Meeting places were barred to him as a result of pressure applied by local magistrates, and he had to conduct some of his speechmaking in public houses and inns. In Padiham, a weaving village located between Burnley and Blackburn, he addressed a large crowd of workers inside a factory. Elsewhere he spoke outdoors, once, near Middleton, addressing a group of workers on waste ground just outside the town boundaries.

There were moments of sheer sensual delight on this political journey, as when (in spite of self-imposed restraints on his conduct) he was toasted lavishly at a dinner in his honor at a Bolton public house, or entertained for a half day at Wigan by a freethinking parish schoolmaster. Mostly, however, he endured discomforts. By coach and on foot—with the aid of a walking stick to assuage the rheumatic pain in his legs—he traversed innumerable Lancashire villages and towns, meeting groups of infidels and republicans and engaging in debates with local clergymen. Frequently the weather was unsuitable for traveling, and his funds, insufficient from the outset, became rapidly depleted. From day to day he had to support himself by selling his tracts at low prices and by relying upon the goodwill of radical workingmen to give him food and lodging, as well as gifts.

In September 1827, he preached his "moral allegory" of religion for the first time outside London. The site was Mount Brinksway Church, near Stockport, a Bible Christian meeting place that had been leased to a group of deists led by Rowland Detrosier. Detrosier was a fustian cutter, who was later to become a famous lecturer in working-class circles. He opposed Carlile's atheism and his allegorical theories, his own beliefs centering on the concept of an "omnipotent, eternal and unchangeable Being . . . the Creator of all things visible and invisible."[9] Yet he willingly shared his pulpit with a reformer whom, more than any other, he believed to be advancing the cause of freedom of the press.

The Mount Brinksway sermon was reported extensively in the local press and elaborated on by Carlile in two pamphlets: the *Sermon upon the Subject of the Deity* and the *Gospel According to Richard Carlile*.[10] In these works he developed at length the ideas that, with Taylor's assistance, he had begun recently to expound. He defined the principle of reason, or logos, as "the sum of human knowledge, past, present, and to come"; and by means of etymological illustrations provided by Taylor attacked traditional accounts of Christianity.[11] The latter, according to Carlile, possessed about as much truth as "the story of Jack the Giant Killer, Don Quixote, Valentine and Orson." These accounts were not of Hebrew origin, he maintained, but were conceived "by Greeks and in Greece." (Subsequently he endorsed Taylor's opinion that they had originated in India.) Christianity was "a perversion of the mystery or allegory of Prometheus and the Logos under the name of Jesus Christ." The messianic peroration with which he concluded his *Gospel* conformed with the bulk of his message. He stated: "I have gone through the necessary preliminary, having taken my degree in the University of Heaven, or Dorchester Gaol, as the persecuted PRINCIPLE OF REASON, the only essential to make a crucified Christ, and a genuine Christian."[12]

As a result of his Stockport oration, Carlile became engulfed in controversy similar to what he had experienced in 1819. He was denounced by churchmen and magistrates who could not perceive any differences between his current vocabulary and his earlier atheism. Yet paradoxically, many working-class reformers concluded that he had abandoned freethought in favor of more conservative beliefs. Members of several of Lancashire's millennialist sects attacked him harshly, including disciples of the prophet Joanna Southcott from Ashton-under-Lyne and a coterie of Bible Christians from Salford whose beliefs were derived from the writings of the eighteenth-century Swedish theologian, Emanuel Swedenborg. The Bible Christians, who held the lease on Mount Brinksway chapel, evicted Detrosier and his deist followers because they had allowed Carlile to preach his sermon there. There also took place a three nights' debate in a Manchester public house between Carlile and a Unitarian minister who attacked his allegorical theories and defended Christianity as a benevolent religion that had brought about most of the benefits enjoyed by mankind. Hailed as a clash between "Christian and Anti-Christian viewpoints," this acrimonious encounter ended in deadlock.[13]

While Carlile's Lancashire tour proceeded amid conditions that can most charitably be described as unpropitious, an event occurred in London, in October, that revived his fortunes by generating favorable publicity for himself and his followers. This was the trial and conviction of Robert Taylor for blasphemous libel on the basis of sermons he had preached at meetings of the Christian Evidence Society.[14] For nearly three years Taylor had been delivering weekly sermons to his disciples that were antichristian in substance and, from an orthodox point of view, mockingly irreverent in tone. During that time he had not been prosecuted. When, however, on the occasion of his "Ninety-third Oration," in the spring of 1827, he described Jesus as a "Jewish Vampire" and used a string of equally choice epithets to characterize other scriptural personages, the lord mayor of the City of London and several aldermen commenced an action against him for blasphemy. The attorney-general, James Scarlett, supported the prosecution in what was termed his "private" capacity.

Taylor defended himself ably at his trial, surprisingly so considering his aversion to political combat. He told the packed courtroom in the Guildhall that his primary aim in speaking of "the Character of Christ" was "to undeceive and disabuse a priest-ridden people, to recover them from the insanity of a barbarous superstition; to reclaim their minds to reason, and their hearts to virtue." His prosecution was, therefore, "untenable on Christian grounds, untenable on moral grounds, untenable on legal grounds, untenable on any grounds whatever, but those of the ascendancy of might over right, of rampant hypocrisy over prostrate innocence."[25]

For his pains he was sentenced to one year of prison in Oakham Gaol, but his defiant words brought Carlile into action on his behalf and gave to the case a national dimension. Abruptly terminating his Lancashire tour, Carlile returned to London and for the next several months occupied himself with little other than Taylor. He did all that he could to arouse feelings of indignation and anger among reformers. With the aid of Hibbert, with whom he was now working closely, he raised subscriptions for Taylor, wrote petitions on his behalf, and kept up a vigorous protest against his treatment in prison, of the kind that he had sustained many times during the war of the shopmen. His shop at 62 Fleet Street became a focal point of political agitation. Its windows were festooned with bold placards describing conditions in Oakham Gaol, which was located in the tiny and somewhat inaccessible county of Rutland; its counters spilled over with reports of the trial and of Taylor's speech at his sentencing, both of which were published by Carlile in tract form.[16] Numerous letters from Taylor expatiating upon his sufferings in prison and elucidating his religious interpretations appeared in the *Lion*. Privately Carlile did all that he could to encourage Taylor, forwarding pamphlets and packets of books to him and constantly soliciting subscriptions on his behalf.

The relationship between the two men was not, however, a tranquil one. Taylor lacked intellectual grit and, as he disarmingly admitted, did not possess "the characteristic obstinacy of Christian martyrdom."[17] On aesthetic grounds alone he infinitely preferred his personal freedom to a lengthy stay in prison. (His gentlemanly proclivities induced him to expend the princely sum of fourteen shillings weekly for a parlor, bedroom, and private servant in Oakham.) This irritated Carlile who regarded the prison—small, quiet, off the political mainstream—as an ideal abode in which to work and write. Inasmuch as Taylor rejected this "long view," it often became necessary for Carlile to rewrite, censor, and even suppress some of the lugubrious adjectives that the former employed to describe his fate.

The early months of 1828 were exciting ones for Carlile. In January, with Hibbert's support, he launched the *Lion*, a six-penny weekly paper dedicated to popularizing "EVERY KIND OF USEFUL REFORM" and to conducting a "war against superstition."[18] Freethought—allegorical as well as atheist—was its chosen métier, and Taylor was a virtual guru to its largely working-class readership. But although it remained in existence until December 1829 and established itself as a major radical journal, the *Lion* failed to achieve anything like the earlier success of the *Republican*. Its weekly circulation rarely surpassed 1000, which mostly reflected Carlile's own loss of support. Some of the former readers of the *Republican* had been won over to Hunt's campaign for a democratic suffrage or to Owen's schemes for social cooperation; others were dismayed by the allegorical views of Taylor and Carlile. At best, therefore, the *Lion* solidified the loyalties of a dedicated group of republicans and freethinkers, while giving Carlile the opportunity to propound his program of religious and political reform.

In March 1828, Carlile founded at his Fleet Street shop a "School of Free Discussion," whose professed aim was to remove "the superstitious mischiefs which [scholars] learn in the common schools."[19] It represented a fusion of the deist conception of a "Temple of Reason" with the ideal of self-education, as nurtured in Dorchester prison by Carlile and given expression by those working-class reformers who were establishing pedagogical institutions in different sections of the country. Members of the school met on Sunday and Wednesday evenings to discuss subjects such as "Religion Is the Real Abomination of Desolation Set up in High Places" or "Want of Evidence for the Validity of the Christian Religion." A catechism followed every "lesson," with Carlile seeking to gain a consensus on basic principles. "[If] any one have a reason, a fair reason, substantially founded in the truth and correctness of things, all have, or should have, that same reason," he maintained. But unanimity proved a will-of-the-wisp. Dissenting points of view were encouraged by Carlile: from deists, "Freethinking Christians," Quakers, Jews, and defenders of orthodox Christianity. Yet, he observed discouragingly that "we are under the necessity of assuaging the character of wrangling philosophers."[20]

Any chance for success that the "School of Free Discussion" might have had was, ironically, dashed by Carlile's misguided efforts to assure respectability for it much as he had tried to do for the Joint Stock Book Company and his earlier publishing efforts. He charged an attendance fee of one shilling per meeting (subsequently lowered to six pence), in order to ensure the participation of prudent, "intelligent" workingmen. Better to have an honorable failure, he seemed to suggest, than inundation by the rabble, who neither cared for education nor were capable of profiting from it. Such a concern with respectability was mistaken, however, because Carlile's political success depended ultimately on the allegiances of poor people who could not afford to pay more than one or two pennies weekly. It was an error that he was to repeat on future occasions.

Attendances at the "School of Free Discussion" were often miniscule (an informer reported that the number of persons present at meetings was about ten), but it was not an abject failure.[21] The school enabled Carlile to open a reading room and library in his shop, where books and pamphlets by antichristian writers were put on display. It stimulated some working-class activists to additional efforts: for example, Peter Baume, the French-born "Reforming Optimist" of the school, who subsequently opened several "chapels" and became a publisher of cheap political literature.[22] Carlile, too, was helped in a personal way by the existence of the school because it gave him an opportunity to cultivate his abilities as a speaker. Although he continued by a wide margin to prefer writing to speaking, he learned how to present arguments effectively and to wear down his opponents by a skillful use of debating techniques.

During the years 1827 to 1829, Carlile became immersed in antichristian thought. He felt increasingly confident that this issue, rather than parliamentary reform, Catholic emancipation, birth control, or any other subject then preoccupying reformers, was the "moral power that is to subdue the earth and its elements, and to make of them a paradise." Infidelity, he declared in a "public letter" to the Duke of Wellington in January 1829, will become man's "highest boast, his great distinguishing supereminence, while the name of Christian or faithman shall sink into a bye-word of the most bitter reproach and the most deep disgrace."[23] He began to write a comprehensive history (never completed) of the idea of "god," which was intended to compress critical views of religion into a single volume.

He corresponded daily with Taylor, who remained immured in Oakham Gaol until February 1829, and spent many hours with Hibbert, making ample use of the latter's superb library of freethought literature in Kentish Town. And, not surprisingly, he became persuaded of the absolute rightness of his "moral allegory" and of the worthlessness of all other interpretations of religion.[24] Central to Carlile's evolution as a freethinker during these years were two books that he published by Taylor: *The Syntagma of the Evidences of the Christian Religion*, published in March 1828, and *The Diegesis: Being a Discovery of the Origin, Evidence and Early History of Christianity*, a much more substantial volume that appeared a year later. The *Syntagma* contained a brief exposition of Taylor's views. In a style that was three parts wit and one part substance, Taylor derided all existing "evidences" for the existence of Christianity. He maintained that Christianity was "the wildest romance that ever entered into a romantic brain's invention" and described Jesus as "an *ens* of conceit, a figment of delirium, proceeding from the heat-oppressed brain!" Of greater interest were typological connections that he delineated: between Apollo and Jesus, Bacchus and Moses, Krishna and Christ. Emphasizing the "almost exact conformities of the Christian and Pagan mythologies," Taylor attacked "the multifarious systems of Heliolatry and Idolatry that had for antecedent ages subjugated the abused reason of mankind."[25]

Delayed for several months because of difficulties faced by Carlile in procuring funds for it, the *Diegesis*, when it did appear, made a considerable impact on popular freethought. Although devoid of systematic analysis (Carlile and Hibbert reworked the first draft substantially), it was a detailed attempt to place the Western religious tradition within a universalist framework.[26] A pagan sensibility informed its pages, and its numerous etymological references were intended to show that sun worship was the basis of all religions. The *Diegesis* also proffered a claim for Alexandria as the transmission point between Eastern and Western religions. Previously Carlile had stated his belief that Antioch was the cradle of Christianity. Now Taylor presented a forceful case for Alexandria. (Neither man gave any credence to Judea, the correct site.) Taylor maintained that the Therapeuts, "the original fabricators of the writings contained in the New Testament," had lived in Alexandria, and that before the era conventionally assigned to the beginnings of Christianity, they had manufactured "the gospels and apostles of the New Testament." Christian scripture was, in Taylor's words, "therapeutic gospel plagiarized": it had been extracted from the tales of the Brahminical god, Krishna, and the Phoenician god, Bacchus. "The Egyptian Gospel," he wrote, "was the Diegesis, or first type, from which our four gospels are mere plagiarisms. . . . It contained the whole story of Jesus Christ, and the general rule of faith professed by a set of Egyptian monks . . . many years, probably ages, before the period assigned to the birth of Christ."[27]

The destruction of the Alexandrine library had, in Taylor's view, camouflaged this universalist foundation of religion. He was seeking to restore the original insight, to link paganism to Christianity. "The most mysterious and abstruse doctrines of the New Testament were but the realization of the emblematical types of the ancient Paganism," he observed. An example provided by him was the sacred letters "I.H.S.," which referred not to "Jesus Hominus Salvator" but to the sun god "RES." He declared that Christian priests had, by a change of names, "vamped up a patchwork of mythology and ethics, a mixture of the Oriental Gnosticism and the Greek Philosophy, into a system which they were for foisting upon the world as a matter of a divine revelation that had been especially revealed to themselves."[28]

Carlile was influenced strongly by the *Diegesis,* and although he continued to champion atheism along with his allegory of "the oppression and persecution and final triumph of the principle of reason among mankind," he began increasingly to present his readers with bits and pieces of Taylor's "physical allegory" of religion.[29] People have no known god but the sun, he stated on one occasion. Subsequently he paraphrased Taylor in this way: "The Chrishna of the Hindoos was united to the Prometheus and Logos of the Greeks, and these to the Jesus or Messiah of the Jews, and out of the union sprang the Christ, the Jesus Christ, the Logos, the son or word of God."[30] For much of its existence the *Lion* was a sounding board for Taylor's theology, with Carlile privately letting it be known that he had reached independently many of the same conclusions about religion which he and Taylor were jointly elucidating.

In July 1828, with Taylor still in prison, Carlile undertook his third trip to the provinces. It was a contentious, frustrating journey that added little to his reputation. First he traveled to Bristol and Bath, trying to give a stimulus to his publishing business by selling off cheaply old tracts and wax medallions of reformers manufactured for him by some Birmingham artisans. When that failed, he visited Oakham Gaol, where he spent several days with Taylor. This was the first meeting between the two men since Taylor's trial five months before, and, while not devoid of tension, it helped to solidify their relationship. Oakham, "a low building presenting nothing of the exterior of a gaol," was as attractive to Carlile as he had imagined it to be, while Taylor, it soon became evident, had lost none of his antipathy for prison. But the two men ignored their differences and made plans for the future. It was agreed that as soon as Taylor was released, they would undertake a joint "infidel mission" to the provinces. This would be a coping stone to Carlile's efforts. With their combined talents working in unison, the bastions of religion would fall, or, at the very least, their foundations would be weakened and allegorical ideas given an opportunity to develop.

In Nottingham, Carlile's first major stop after leaving Taylor, things quickly began to unravel. Intending to remain in the city for a week or two as a preliminary to visiting Hull and other areas of the northeast, he spent the better part of a month there, frustrated by an inability to win converts and denounced by local clergymen, one of whom characterized him as an "itinerant of infidelity."[31] He had few supporters in Nottingham, and his meetings in public houses and private rooms, where he maintained that Jesus was "the Saviour of mankind through the Principle of Reason," were poorly attended.[32] As elsewhere, some reformers who might otherwise have supported him were affronted by his support for birth control, while others rejected his allegorical theories on the ground that they were a diversion from more pressing political and social issues. Squabbles and disputes dogged him at every step. He was barred from meeting rooms, heckled intemperately, and pelted with gravel by cantankerous youngsters.[33]

Joseph Gilbert, a Wesleyan preacher with a reputation for baiting "infidels," was Carlile's most persistent opponent in the city. Although described by Carlile as "by far the most respectable public opponent that I have yet had for oral discussion," Gilbert attacked him in the local press, spreading innuendoes about his sexual immorality, which were based on a reading of *Every Woman's Book.* Carlile responded in warm terms and brought a libel suit against Gilbert that dragged on inconclusively for several years. The only tangible effect of this suit was to weaken further Carlile's financial position and to increase his hatred for the law. "Better to bear the ills we have than to fly to those we know not," he observed sardonically several years later while still embroiled in the complexities of the Gilbert case.[34]

Notwithstanding the turmoil that accompanied him in Nottingham and its environs, Carlile experienced some pleasant interludes. Once, after a lengthy coach ride with two atheists to whom he did not identify himself, he described the three of them as forming a "rational trinity in unity." He cultivated the company of "fine young women" whenever he could, a pastime which, seemingly, grew on him as his marriage deteriorated. After sharing a coach near Nottingham with five attractive women, he commented: "If the law allowed it, one might have very wisely fallen in love with the whole of them." But, as was generally true of his travels, physical discomfort far outweighed the modicum of satisfaction that he experienced while on the road. Aches and pains constantly wore him down. "Had I not been free from sin, the jolting of the coach, acting upon my rheumatic hip, would most assuredly have been, in the shape of punishment, satisfactory enough to god or devil," he remarked after a typically crowded, uncomfortable coach trip.[35]

With financial and personal problems in London beginning to mount up once more, Carlile gave up his plans to travel to Hull and the northeast. He returned to London in September in a chastened mood, with one newspaper observing delightedly that "the notorious Carlile has been driven out of Nottingham by the voice of the people."[36] On the contrary, he insisted: he had curtailed his trip "in deference to the illness of Mrs. Carlile," a statement as implausible to those knowledgeable about his family situation as it was specious. In fact, he had been beaten and had to fall back on self-delusion for consolation. He told readers of the *Lion*: "I really do feel that I am great, that I am a little man of very great importance, when I see, as I saw in Nottingham, the whole talent and learning of the town cowering and trembling before my presence and dreaded speech."[37] Bravado could not pay the bills or gain fresh converts, however. With his publishing business almost at a halt and the circulation of the *Lion* dropping below 1000, he reluctantly had to dismiss his only remaining shopman. There seemed few prospects for improvement.

If lecturing and journalism reached a low ebb during 1828, there were, nonetheless, some intellectual compensations. One was phrenology, the "scientific" analysis of mental traits by studying the conformity of the skull. Developed by a Viennese anatomist, Franz Joseph Gall, and his associate, Johann Spurzheim, in the late eighteenth century, phrenology became popular in Britain in the 1820s as a result of the efforts of George Combe, a Scottish educational reformer whose *Elements of Phrenology* and *Constitution of Man Considered in Relation to External Objects* both sold thousands of copies. In the writings of Gall, Spurzheim, Combe, and other advocates of phrenology, detailed craniological systems were discussed. These postulated a division of mental activity into faculties controlled by organs in the brain, the anterior of the brain being conceived of as rational and its posterior as passionate and "physical." More specific traits were then analyzed by investigating the shapes of individual skulls.[38]

For Carlile and other reformers the details of phrenology were less important than its broad claim to be able to explain mental and moral phenomena in physiological terms. As one radical journalist asserted: "[Phrenology] appears best calculated of any system of mental philosophy yet given to the world, to be the foundation of correct moral practice, in regenerating mankind from a state of ignorance to a state of intelligence and virtue."[39] According to Carlile, it was an "infidel science" of almost cosmic possibilities. Everything was reducible to phrenological study, he maintained, including mind, which was an extension of "bodily function and action" and had "no other than the animal original."[40] During these years he began to lecture on phrenology, devising an interpretation of the brain that was based on four areas rather than the usual thirty or more. His aim was to make "cranium geometry" a useful branch of knowledge, so that men and women could substantially improve their lives. Even when a leading London exhibitioner, J. D. Deville, read the "bumps" on his skull incognito and concluded that his organ of "veneration" was unusually large, he did not waver in his conviction that phrenology was the true "science of mind."[41]

There were problems with phrenology, however, one being the extent to which it appeared to dampen the effects of individual effort. If, as most phrenologists asserted, the conformity of the skull was fixed, there was little room for personal development. But if, as Carlile believed, self-education was able to alter circumstances decisively, then physical modifications to the skull would inevitably occur. He believed that the shape of his own skull had been changed because of his constant use of his rational faculties and that the same would happen to others. He told his followers that depending upon the interaction between mental and physical attributes, "a head may be made mathematical, musical, poetical, mechanical, philosophical, moral or religious, as may be desired."[42]

Under Francis Place's tutelage, Carlile also became an ardent supporter of political economy during these years. From the outset of his relationship with Place in 1822, he had been subjected to a heavy dosage of Bentham, David Ricardo, James Mill, and other propagandists for "social human welfare"; and the results of this indoctrinating process were beginning to be seen in the pages of the *Lion*. "The first principle of all matters of commerce," Carlile told the paper's readers, ". . . [is] the relation of the supply to the demand." Rhapsodizing about the virtues of free trade and unrestrained competition, he condemned the Speenhamland system of outdoor poor relief for its failure to distinguish between the "impotent" and the "vicious" poor (the latter not, in his view, being eligible for relief) and pleaded for the superiority of "natural" economic laws over interference by government or trade unions. "The great radical failure," he wrote, "is in the people themselves, who waste, by their bad habits, by drunkenness and religion, the means of consuming those more necessary comforts in diet, dress, and dwelling, which would give a high degree of activity to trade, and create a greater demand for labour."[43]

Carlile's support for laissez-faire economics represents a shift away from his earlier radicalism, based as it was on Paine, Cobbett, and Sherwin, but it does not indicate a total abandonment of it. Even during this period of maximum "conversion" to political economy, he continued to hark back to simpler preindustrial virtues and to favor some collectivist remedies for social and economic injustices. For example, at a time when he was giving full endorsement to supply and demand arguments, he made the following statement in the *Lion*: "We would be tyrants to enforce an equality of cleanliness, of industry, where the means of living depend upon it, of modes of dwelling that are conducive to health, and the prevention of disease, and of that species of order and manner which is offensive to none, but to all agreeable."[44] The contradiction in his thinking is more apparent than real. As a result of Place's importunities, Carlile adopted "extreme" individualist ideas, but his reactions to events continued to be affected to a considerable extent by a visceral identification with the poor. Unlike many political economists, he understood that economic thought had to reflect real situations. This meant a human face and a degree of personal warmth that belied excessive claims for capitalism.

In February 1829, Taylor was liberated from Oakham Gaol. The circumstances of his release were controversial. Although he had been restive during the final months of his incarceration, he had promised Carlile that he would engage in "no unworthy yielding, no truckling compromise" to secure his freedom. Yet recognizances for his good behavior had been paid by reformers with his agreement, a compromise that, in Carlile's view, made him a "prisoner" of the government for several years.[45] Still, Carlile was overjoyed at the prospect of working with Taylor. He spoke of the "high promise" and "brilliancy" of the future. Taylor, he believed, had the ability to win over to infidelity large numbers of reformers; his speeches were larded with wit and were invariably entertaining, a statement that could not possibly be made about his own orations. How could it be otherwise with a man whose platform attire was described as follows: "[Taylor] was arrayed in the flowing gown of a clergyman; his neat clerical hat was conspicuously borne in his hand, an eye-glass depended from his neck, and the little finger of either hand was ornamented with a sumptuous ring; his hair was arranged in the most fashionable style; and a pair of light kid gloves completed the elegant decorations of his person."[46] Despite its lack of dignity, hubris was a quality not to be discarded lightly by reformers.

In the expectation that their talents would mesh and that they would create a successful infidel agitation, Carlile and Taylor began to plan a tour that would take them to many sections of the country. "We are now as one man," observed Carlile euphorically. They would travel to the blackest lairs of clerical superstition, marching under the banner of antichristianity, "that noble, that glorious principle, on which hinge the future dignity and prosperity of mankind." "We are going to unfurl the standard of infidelity," averred Taylor, "we are going to overthrow and destroy the christian religion; we are going to battle." Their aim was to establish "areopaguses" (infidel chapels) in different areas, grouped around a central hall in London where Taylor would preside as "the avowedly infidel minister of the first congregation of rational men."[47] Funds were to be raised by means of an "Infidel Rent" (in emulation of Daniel O'Connell's "Catholic Rent" in Ireland) with, it was anticipated, more than £10,000 to be collected from working-men and wealthy reformers like Hibbert.

The imagery of this "atheist mission," which began in May 1829 with but a tiny fraction of the anticipated sum in hand, was that of Paul of Tarsus. Taylor and Carlile characterized themselves as bearers of an apostolic message to the "heathens." They carried with them a printed circular, which stated:

The Rev. Robert Taylor, A.B., of Carey-Street, Lincoln's Inn, and Mr. Richard Carlile of Fleet-Street, London, present their compliments as Infidel missionaries, to (as it may be) and most respectfully and earnestly invite discussion on the merits of the christian religion, which they argumentatively challenge, in the confidence of their competence to prove, that such a person as Jesus Christ, alleged to have been of Nazareth, never existed; and that the Christian religion had no such origin as has been pretended; neither is it in any way beneficial to mankind; but that it is nothing more than an emanation from the ancient pagan religion.[48]

Taylor also wrote two orations that were distributed gratis. These summarized in potted fashion the themes of the *Syntagma* and the *Diegesis*, and of Carlile's *Gospel*, and concluded that "the Christian religion is altogether fabulous and false" and that "the whole system of faith or morals in any way associated with that figment of priestcraft, is but the baseless fabric of a vision." "We proclaim our hostility to priests and priestesses," these orations stated. "We set up virtue on the throne of truth. Our banner bears the legend of our purpose, DELENDA EST CARTHAGO: Christianity shall be no more."[49]

Popular freethought, however, gained relatively few converts from this first "atheist mission" of the nineteenth century, which in structure and style was imitated by groups of freethinkers and secularists from the 1840s on.[50] In Cambridge, "the seat of science and citadel of theology," where the tour began, clergymen failed to take up the challenge, and few working-class reformers appeared. Local newspapers refused to accept paid advertisements announcing their meetings. A similar pattern occurred in other towns that they visited between May and September, including Manchester, Bradford, Nottingham, Stalybridge, Blackburn, Leeds, and Stockport. Except for some Primitive Methodists and other "cranks," clerics refused to debate with them, a circumstance that elicited the following tart observation from Taylor: "Reason has unfurled her banner, but thou hast been deaf to reason." He pleaded for rational discussion, not "scorn and contempt, reviling and detractions."[51] In Liverpool before a large audience, Taylor participated in a lengthy debate with a clergyman who propounded a theory of religion based on materialism. The outcome was inconclusive, though the pleasure of joining battle with such an opponent was enough to cause Taylor to use hyperbole of a kind more generally favored by Carlile: "What we have said and done in Liverpool will never be forgotten."[52]

While clergymen ignored their presence, Carlile and Taylor, to their dismay, were positively noticed by others. Some reformers, including Archibald Prentice, who owned and edited the *Manchester Times* and was to become a leader of the anti-corn-law movement in the 1840s, and John Finch, a Catholic disciple of Robert Owen, attacked them fiercely. Likewise, local magistrates exerted pressure on landlords to prevent them from making their rooms available for meetings. At Taylor's insistence, he and Carlile refrained from outdoor speaking and appearances in public houses, both of which he considered socially demeaning; the bulk of their meetings therefore had to be held in small private rooms where audiences were necessarily small.

It is difficult to assess the overall effects of this "atheist mission," partly because the bulk of working-class freethinkers who attended the meetings had been won over already. Yet there were some specific gains. Taylor's baroque presentations rarely disappointed his audiences. He was unfailingly amusing, a gifted actor if a shallow analyst of ideas. He employed showmanship and satire to get his points across. But once he had left the room (which he usually did as soon as his discourse ended), it was up to Carlile to make the points stick. Carlile conducted the discussions and defended their joint infidel views against all comers. If there were members of the audience to be won over—not always the case—Carlile did the winning.

Though small in number, these audiences were varied in composition. Stockport, one of the strongest bases of working-class freethought in the north of England, produced about 400 auditors on several occasions, while Bradford, Ashton-under-Lyne, and Huddersfield did almost as well. These were all centers of agitation in the 1820s where artisans and factory workers engaged in miscellaneous political and antichristian activities, including, in the case of Huddersfield, several attempts to establish a permanent infidel chapel. Elsewhere the situation was less encouraging. Many workingmen in Lancashire and Yorkshire clearly preferred political reform to infidelity; and in the industrial cities of Manchester and

Leeds, where supporters of Carlile and Hunt continued to do battle against one another, the reaction to the tour was noticeably tepid. There was, as Carlile stated, an insufficient "concentration of feeling" in these cities. The best thing that he would say about the small numbers of workingmen who responded to their entreaties was that they were "respectable" and eager to support the cause of reform.[53]

As the tour progressed, the relationship between Carlile and Taylor came under increasing strain. Carlile was serious, ascetic, compulsively driven by his particular vision of reform. Except for a penchant for female companionship and an occasional few hours spent in a public house, he was not willing to give up a single moment of time that might be used to more "instructive" effect. Almost all of his waking hours were spent at the slogging task of winning over disciples, as he rushed frantically from one village or town to the next, making advance arrangements for speeches and meetings, and attempting by every means at his disposal to make the "infidel mission" a success. For Taylor, on the other hand, comfort took precedence over conviction. He was "light and buoyant," devoted to the classics, gregarious and exuberant about everything that he did. In his waistcoat pocket he carried a copy of Shelley's *Queen Mab*, and whenever there was time, he rushed off to a local theater or concert hall. "I differ from you," he told Carlile, "as the nadir from the zenith in every view you take of theatrical entertainment." He was a political aesthete. "If we cannot make Infidelity pretty, elegant, attractive, and fashionable," he lamented, "we shall never make it succeed."[54] To concede that Carlile was the more serious reformer of the two is not to deride the validity of Taylor's judgment.

With their "infidel rent" exhausted, Taylor and Carlile returned to London, somewhat disconsolately, in September. The travails of their situation had begun to sink in on them. They lacked "pecuniary support" (only Hibbert remained a steady subscriber) and had not succeeded in opening any "aeropaguses," with the exception of a single doomed attempt in Huddersfield. Carlile's "School of Free Discussion" was recommenced for about two months in the autumn of 1829, but it proved a poor substitute for Taylor's anticipated "first congregation of rational men." A public offer by the two men to give antichristian tuition in exchange for payment was not taken up by any reformers. And as the London winter set in, Carlile's health, buoyed by the excitement of the preceding months, began to decline once more. "My face has swollen to an internal bursting so I cannot venture out," he told his readers in December.[55]

Expectation, however, breeds its own success (to some degree), and the paucity of concrete achievements during the tour in no way diminished a flood of luxuriant rhetoric. Taylor's assessment of the journey lacked for nothing in swagger. "We have produced great effects," he claimed, "greater than ever were produced in the world by means so small as ours."[56] Carlile also rose verbally to the occasion. He predicted the imminent demise of Christianity. "If so," he told his followers, "I shall live the greatest man that ever lived in the world." Such prophecies were decidedly premature, but as the events of the next two years were to show, attempts to give effect to them were only just beginning.

Notes

1. He was forced to give up the lease on a small printing shop in Water Lane and to sell some printing materials he had acquired. This placed him once more at the mercy of contract printers, especially William Cunningham who replaced Thomas Moses as his regular printer at the outset of 1827. See *Scourge for the Littleness of "Great" Men*, 8 November 1834.

2. *Lion*, 4 April 1828.

3. The description is taken from William Haley's *Bull Dog*, 26 August 1826. In a description of him in 1831, Carlile is depicted as wearing "foppish dress." Henry Vizetelly, *Glances Back through Seventy Years: Autobiographical and Other Reminiscences* (London: Kegan Paul, Trench, Trübner, 1893), vol. 1, pp. 69-70.

4. For information about this tour, see *Lion*, 4 January 1828.

5. On Carlile's financial difficulties, see ibid., 19 September 1828, 31 December 1834, 21 February 1835. The execution of his furniture is described in an informer's account dated 13 August 1827, H.O. 64/11, P.R.O.

6. Hibbert paid off most of his debts and supported him for many years. *Scourge for the Littleness of "Great" Men*, 8 November 1834. The best biographical sketch of Hibbert is Joel H. Wiener, "Julian Hibbert," in Baylen and Gossman, *Biographical Dictionary*, vol. 1, pp. 221-22.

7. *Republican*, 15 September 1826.

8. *Lion*, 10 July 1829, 30 May, 29 February 1828.

9. Gwyn A. Williams, *Rowland Detrosier: A Working-Class Infidel, 1800-34* (York: St. Anthony's Press, 1965), p. 13.

10. Carlile described the sermon as "the first instance in which in any one church or chapel, a preaching of the non-personality of deity and Jesus Christ had taken place." *Lion*, 9 May 1828.

11. Richard Carlile, *A Sermon upon the Subject of Deity, Preached on Sunday, Sept. 9 . . . from the Pulpit, before the Congregation, of the Church of Mount Brinksway, near Stockport* (London: Richard Carlile, 1827), pp. 5-16. The *Sermon* was reprinted several times without an acknowledgment of Carlile's authorship. For example: *The Law of Reason* (1831), pp. 23-38; *Should There Be a Law Against Blasphemy?* (1842).

12. *Gospel According to Carlile*, pp. 12, 30-32.

13. *Lion*, 9 May 1828. "Verax," an anonymous contributor to the *Stockport Advertiser*, 30 August 1827, stated of Carlile and Taylor: "They would surround us with all the horrors of reigning Atheism, keeping her quiet amidst conscription and plunder, established on the ruins of rank and property, crowned with the ravished diadems of fugitive and assassinated monarchs, petrifying all Europe with her dithering frown, and drunk with fury and with blood."

14. Carlile described the trial as "the salvation at a critical time of my present establishment." *Lion*, 31 January 1829.

15. *Trial of the Rev. Robert Taylor, A.B. & M.R.C.S. upon a Charge of Blasphemy, with His Defence, as Delivered by Himself, Before the Lord Chief Justice and a Special Jury, on Wednesday, October 24, 1827* (London: John Brooks, 1827), pp. 15, 28. Lord Justice Tenterdon, summing up, asserted that Taylor was guilty of blasphemy because he brought "the Christian religion into disbelief . . . in a tone of sarcasm and coarseness." *Trial*, p. 29. See also *The Judgment of the Court of King's Bench upon the Rev. Robert Taylor, A.B.M.C.R.S., on a Conviction of Blasphemy Towards the Christian Religion; with the Whole of the Speeches in this Case, on the 7th of February, 1828* (London: Richard Carlile, 1828).

16. The informers' reports in H.O. 64/11 tell a good deal about Carlile's activities in the aftermath of the Taylor trial.

17. *Lion*, 6 March 1829.

18. Ibid., 4 January 1828.

19. Ibid., 21 March 1828.

20. See ibid., 4, 18 April 1828, 20 February 1829.

21. S.S. report, 4 May 1828, H.O. 64/11. At one session at the school two informers were present and both filed reports with the Home Office.

22. There is a detailed undated report on Baume's activities in H.O. 64/16.

23. *Lion*, 9 January 1829.

24. He was influenced by Godfrey Higgins's *The Celtic Druids* (London: Rowland Hunt, 1829), a book that postulated a link between Greek and Christian lettering and emphasized the universalism of religion.

25. Taylor, *Syntagma*, pp. 82, 99, 112.

26. A reference to the editing of the *Diegesis* by Carlile and Hibbert is in *A Report of the Public Discussion between the Rev. John Green and the Rev. Richard Carlile, Held in Saint Andrew's Hall, Norwich, August 24th and 28th, 1837* (London: Alfred Carlile, 1837), p. 74.

27. Taylor, *Diegesis*, pp. 64, 127.

28. Ibid., pp. 156, 214-15, 254.

29. See, for example, *Lion*, 16 October 1829.

30. Ibid., 18 December 1829, 1 May 1829.

31. The derogatory reference is by "Homo" in the *Nottingham Mercury*, as cited in the *Lion*, 12 September 1828.

32. The quote is from the *Lion*, 12 September 1828.

33. A friend reported that had Carlile not "been well surrounded and guarded by so many able bodies and courageous friends, his life would have been in danger." William Smith to Carlile, c. September 1828, C.P.

34. A nonsuit was declared in the Gilbert case in 1832 as a result of a technical error. On this dispute, see *Nottingham Journal*, 13 September 1828; *A Biographical Sketch of the Rev. Joseph Gilbert by His Widow* (London: Jackson and Warford, 1853), pp. 72-73; *Lion*, 22, 29 August, 5 September 1828; the Carlile papers, including a handwritten petition to Lord Tenterden, 5 December 1831.

35. *Lion*, 1, 8 August 1828.

36. *Macclesfield Courier and Herald*, 20 September 1828.

37. *Lion*, 17 October 1828.

38. On phrenology, see particularly: J. C. Flugel, *A Hundred Years of Psychology, 1833-1933* (London: Gerald Duckworth, 1933); David DeGuistino, *Conquest of Mind: Phrenology and Victorian Social Thought* (London: Croom Helm, 1977); T. M. Parsinnen, "Popular Science and Society: The Phrenology Movement in Early Victorian Britain," *Journal of Social History*, 8 (1974), pp. 1-20; Arthur Wrobel, "Orthodoxy and Respectability in Nineteenth-Century Phrenology," *Journal of Popular Culture*, 9 (1975), pp. 38-50. There is an excellent article on Gall in the *Dictionary of Scientific Biography*.

39. *Freethinkers' Information for the People* (1842-1843), no. 15, p. 113.

40. See, especially, *Prompter*, 11 June 1831.

41. *Lion*, 5 July 1828; *Prompter*, 11 June 1831; *Republican*, 14 April 1826. James Jennings, *An Inquiry Concerning the Nature and Operations of the Human Mind* (London: Poole & Edwards, 1828), p. 143, reports that Deville had more than 1200 phrenological casts in his collection. In 1829, Carlile and Taylor examined Sir Isaac Newton's statue in the chapel of Trinity College, Cambridge, and concluded that "its phrenological indications are *numbers* and nothing eminent but number. He was a mathematician and nothing but a mathematician." *Lion*, 29 May 1829.

42. *Lion*, 20 June 1828, 8 May 1829.

43. Ibid., 20 November 1829; *Prompter*, 16 April 1831; *Cosmopolite*, 15 June 1833. The *Newgate Monthly Magazine* was also filled with political economy (including summaries of writings by James Mill), with Place being a regular visitor to Newgate prison during 1825-1826.

44. *Lion*, 4 January 1828. Carlile wrote in December 1829: "Though the land has been parcelled and monopolized by conquest, it is still the people's farm; and its advantages will ever remain a people's right, when they can be conquered back again. It is a part of their life, and should be held in administration of the best means for general subsistence." Ibid., 4 December 1829.

45. Ibid., 20 February 1829.

46. *Trial of the Rev. Robert Taylor*, p. 2.

47. *Lion*, 2 January, 6 March, 10, 17 April 1829.

48. Ibid., 29 May 1829.

49. Robert Taylor, *Second Missionary Oration, (Addressed Especially to Infidels,) as Delivered, or Intended to be Delivered, Before the Three Universities . . . in the Summer of the Year 1829* (London: Richard Carlile, 1829), pp. 4, 5, 23-24. See also Robert Taylor, *First Missionary Oration, as Delivered, or Intended to be Delivered, Before the Three Universities . . . in the Summer of the Year 1829* (London: Richard Carlile, 1829).

50. The concept of the "atheist mission" is analyzed by F. B. Smith, though he fails to indicate the significance of Carlile and Taylor. Smith, "The Atheist Mission, 1840-1900," in R. Robson (ed.), *Ideas and Institutions of Victorian Britain* (New York: Barnes and Noble, 1967), pp. 205-35. See Royle, *Victorian Infidels*, pp. 39-40.

51. *Lion*, 12 June 1829; *Leeds Mercury*, 11 April 1829. Taylor and Carlile described the tour in weekly "Infidel Bulletins" published in the *Lion*. There are also accounts of the tour in the *Leeds Mercury*, the *Leeds Patriot*, and the *Manchester Times*.

52. *Lion*, 4 September 1829. There are references to this debate in *Liverpool Mercury*, 28 August 1829; Carlile to George Jacob Holyoake, 16 October 1842, C.P.

53. *Bolton Chronicle*, 1 August 1829. The *Leeds Mercury*, 20 June 1829, described their audiences in Leeds as "wretchedly small." "Shepherd" Smith claimed that the tour gave an "ultra character" to the infidel movement and made it more difficult for moderates to join. "History of the Infidels and Their Antipodes for the Last Twenty-five Years," *London Phalanx*, 19 February, 12 March 1842, 19 March 1841.

54. *Lion*, 21, 28 March 1828, 19 June 1829. Taylor wrote: "The eye as well as the ear is a parcel to the mind, and toll must be paid there." Ibid., 10 July 1829.

55. Carlile to Turton, 7 November 1829, C.P.

56. *Lion*, 25 September 1829.

9

THE ROTUNDA

In May 1830, a new chapter in the history of working-class freethought began with the opening by Carlile of the Rotunda, in Blackfriars Road, London. It was intended to usher in a revolution and to be a "capitol of public virtue, the nucleus for a reformation of abuses . . . the birthplace of mind, and the focus of virtuous public excitement." Under its banner of religious and political radicalism, a war to the death was to be waged against "the aristocratical or clerical despotism, corruption, and ignorance of the whole country." In Carlile's words, the Rotunda would offer "a splendid and fortuned finish to his original, bold, brave, unbending, consistent, and undeviating career."[1]

The venture began in the early months of 1830 when Carlile acquired a lease on a building at 3 Blackfriars Road (then Great Surrey Street), on the south side of the Thames River. The cost was considerable: £400 annually for rates, taxes, gas heating, and miscellaneous items. It was greater by far than his combined income from the Morrison annuity and publishing activities. Even so, with the help of Hibbert and W. Devonshire Saull, a wine merchant and amateur scientist who worked on Taylor's behalf for several years, the plunge was taken. Several other reformers, discreetly anonymous, subscribed sums of money to extend the perimeters of "rational debate" and give a fillip to popular freethought.[2]

The Blackfriars Road building, erected in 1782, had been partly destroyed by fire in 1805 and then rebuilt. Having been used as a theater, a museum of natural history, and a literary and scientific institute, it was in a dilapidated state when Carlile took it over. In addition to its spacious living quarters, it contained two large public rooms: one built originally for equestrian purposes and the other a circular auditorium surrounded by a gallery that Carlile had painted over with astrological symbols to assist Taylor's lecturing. There was also a refreshment parlor, a library, and several smaller rooms, which were used for political and social intercourse. In all, about £1300 was spent in refurbishing the premises and preparing the building for public use.[3]

The Rotunda was opened to the public officially in May 1830, and from then until July 1831, it was the center of working-class radicalism in London. Taylor was the principal orator during most of this time, lecturing two or three times weekly on topics such as the "History of the Virgin Mary," the "Vindication of the Character of Saint Judas Iscariot," and the "Pagan Origin and Character of St. Paul's Cathedral." His abilities as a public speaker shone during these months. Not only did he pepper his discourses with deprecating witticisms, but—as on the 1829 tour—the rakish clerical garb that he wore was in itself a source of amusement. According to an informer's report (not the most extravagant to have survived), when he spoke he wore bishops' robes with a tricolored ribbon draped across his shoulders. It was also stated that he made prominent use of a decorative eyeglass.[4]

On Sunday evenings, Taylor and Carlile staged elaborate theatrical performances at the Rotunda, which sometimes were repeated on the following Tuesday or Friday. On these occasions, the circular auditorium was packed to overflowing with hundreds of artisans and mechanics who, having paid threepence or sixpence, reveled in Taylor's "physico-astronomical" demonstrations, particularly his stagings of "Sons of Thunder" and "Raising the Devil." He made considerable use of props—a communion table, orreries, a six-foot cruicifix—though probably not live animals as was rumored.[5] Funds did not allow him to gratify his thespian proclivities fully, but these infidel dramas are among the more interesting examples of radical theater in the early nineteenth century. They attempted to infuse antichristian propaganda with entertainment value, something that Carlile bridled at privately but encouraged publicly as a way of drawing large crowds to the Rotunda.[6]

Several of the dramas staged were political in content, including "Swing! or Who Are the Incendiaries?" which depicted in a favorable light the agricultural laborers in several southern counties who were then rioting for better conditions. Mostly, however, Taylor sought to undermine Christian theology and ritual. Thus, in his dramas and sermons from the "Devil's Pulpit" (as his podium at the Rotunda came popularly to be known) he attested to the central place of sun worship and ancient astronomy in the history of religion. "The whole story of the creation of the world, and the allegorical life, character, death, and resurrection of Christ," he told his audiences, was "acted as a play, or holy pantomime, in the ancient mysteries of Mithra and of Bacchus, from which every doctrine which we now called christian is entirely derived." He also elaborated on subsidiary themes: that Jesus was a "personified sun" passing through the twelve signs of the zodiac; that the Hebrew word *God* and the Coptic word *Sun* were identical; that astrological symbols represented the twelve patriarchs, the twelve apostles, and the twelve gates of the apocalyptic city; and that the Sun (translated by Taylor as "Jes" or "IES") was the "supreme Deity of the ancient fire-worshippers of Persia."[7]

In April 1831, he delivered at the Rotunda a series of discourses on freemasonry that marked a new departure for him. Beginning in 1825, Carlile had employed masonic symbolism to elucidate his "moral allegory," but Taylor had shied away from it. Now, at Carlile's urging, he began to employ "physico-astronomical" techniques to illuminate freemasonry. In his sermons he claimed that freemasonry was a product of Egyptian, Jewish, and Christian superstitions and that it was "absolutely identical with the celebrated Eleusinian mysteries of Greece, the Dionysian Mysteries, or Orgies of Bacchus, and the Christian Mysteries of the Sacrament of the Body and Blood of Christ." It comprehended the two key secrets of pagan religion: that Javes, the Grand Architect of the Universe, was Jupiter (that is, "God the Great Architect") and that Ammoc was Jesus, or a variant of Jupiter. The sun, according to Taylor, was "Jupiter, in Spring; Christ, in Summer; Jesus, in Autumn; and Amen, in Winter."[8] Though devoid of political content at a time when the revived agitation for parliamentary reform was beginning to play a central part in the development of a working-class consciousness, such pronouncements impressed his audiences because of the theatrical flair with which they were delivered. They gave an impetus to popular freethought.

During these months of histrionic activity by Taylor, Carlile played a quiet, though effective role at the Rotunda. He conducted "divine services" on Sunday mornings, at which he systematically lambasted the "monstrosities" of Christianity. He read "lessons" from Volney, Paine, d'Holbach, Gibbon, and other freethinkers, indispensable exercises, Carlile believed, if Christianity was to be purged of corruption and restored to its "original purity and lustre." He also delivered numerous lectures: some on political topics such as the need for an extension of voting rights to working-men or a reduction of taxation, but most, like those of Taylor, intended to accelerate the progress of infidelity. Acknowledging a "joint apostleship" with Taylor, Carlile emphasized the significance of the physical (Taylor) and moral (his own) allegories. Both insights, he maintained, rested on foundations of universal truth: that "all the religions of the earth have been alike in their essentials; that they have all worshiped one common source of divinity; that they have all been allegorically right and true; and that they have all been historically and literally wrong and untrue." Christianity, it followed, was a sectarian relic that faced imminent destruction.[9]

Lacking Taylor's charismatic qualities as a public performer, Carlile attracted audiences of one hundred to two hundred work-ingmen, whereas Taylor occasionally drew three or four times as many. Still, Carlile was a competent speaker, able to weave into an agreeable tapestry miscellaneous images and ideas and to convert an opponent's arguments into points gained for his own side. He felt himself making strides in winning over working-class reformers to antichristian agitation.

Yet the grandiloquent expectations of Carlile and Taylor were rapidly dissipated. For one thing, they had no success in inducing clergymen to participate in debates. Even the most self-confident spokesmen for orthodox Christianity were, understandably, reluctant to enter the den of infidelity on Blackfriars Road, given the hostility of many of the reformers who came there to all forms of religion. The few Christians who participated in debates came to flay infidelity, not to learn from it, assuredly not the purpose for which they were summoned by Taylor and Carlile. Sweden-borgians, Unitarians, and other representatives of "nonrespectable" sects were willing to plunge into the waters of public discussion at the Rotunda. But their positions were, in Carlile's opinion, "peculiar"; and rather than risk devaluing the reputation of the institution by encouraging them to participate, he sometimes made it difficult for them to attend.

Under Carlile's leadership, the Rotunda also became a center of political agitation. The early months of 1831 were important ones in the history of reform, taken up as they were with opposing views of the merits of the bill for extending the suffrage that was introduced into the House of Commons by the Whig government in March. To gain support for the Rotunda, Carlile had few scruples about allowing even his most inveterate opponents among reformers to make use of its facilities. Like a master of ceremonies at a pantomime, he understood that interest in popular agitation could best be sustained by sponsoring as many radical acts as possible. Freedom of expression was, in his view, "the only system of purification in society that abates wrong bias, and strengthens right and wrong." And he was determined at all costs to make the Rotunda "the first public building fairly appropriated to the whole principle of free discussion."[10]

Thus, advocates of universal suffrage, trade unionism, and economic cooperation were given an opportunity to plead their cases at Blackfriars Road during 1830 and 1831. Carlile disagreed with much of what they said and sometimes charged fees of two or three guineas nightly for their use of the public rooms. But he frequently bartered the halls away for a portion of the evening's receipts, or gave up a room gratis on condition that the sponsored activity did not compete directly with the infidel presentations by himself or by Taylor. Cobbett and Hunt spoke frequently at the Rotunda, and, in 1831-1832, the National Union of the Working Classes, a pro-Hunt organization of working-class radical reformers, held most of its weekly meetings there. It distributed copies of Henry Hetherington's *Poor Man's Guardian*, a popular unstamped paper whose democratic and Owenite views Carlile deprecated, and among its leading speakers were Hetherington, James Watson, a former shopman who was now critical of infidelity, and Julian Hibbert, who sought to bridge the gap between religious and political reform. Another frequent speaker was John Gale Jones, an acquaintance of Carlile for many years who was not affiliated with any of the radical associations then forming. Jones addressed small groups of workingmen and instilled many of them with enthusiasm for universal suffrage and political democracy.[11]

Informers and spies traversed the premises of the Rotunda

nightly, and critics, alluding to its subversive nature, unfairly described it as a center of violence.[12] Predictably, however, the result was an occasional minor incident of unrest, as in November 1830, at the time of the resignation of the Duke of Wellington as prime minister because of his opposition to parliamentary reform and his succession by Lord Grey at the head of a Whig government committed to an extension of voting rights. Tricolored flags were hoisted over the Rotunda and reports circulated that the government intended to close the building. On successive evenings thousands of workingmen massed there to "protect" it but only a few scuffles ensued.[13]

Superintending an enterprise as complex as the Rotunda required considerable skills, which Carlile, as he demonstrated, possessed in abundance. He attended almost every lecture given on the premises, and with the aid of his seventeen-year-old son Richard and several employees, he supervised the collecting of fees, the provision of refreshments, and the scheduling and arrangement of meetings. Tensions between freethinkers and political reformers sometimes erupted. Carlile, for example, clashed repeatedly with Hunt because of his own enthusiastic support for the limited measure of Whig parliamentary reform and the latter's uncompromising opposition to it on the ground that it did not significantly advance universal suffrage. On at least one occasion supporters of the two men exchanged blows inside the Rotunda, with Carlile describing Hunt as the "devil's viceregent on earth," and Hunt accusing him of being a government spy and of displaying physical cowardice at Peterloo. These charges and countercharges led to Hunt's exclusion from the Rotunda and, in 1832, to similar action being taken against the National Union of the Working Classes.

Of greater importance to Carlile than his quarrels with Hunt (which formed part of the backdrop of working-class radical politics for more than a decade) was the increasing enmity between himself and Taylor. Despite a facade of public agreement, the two men never developed a close personal relationship. They were temperamentally too far apart, and as Taylor's personal failings became more evident, his usefulness to Carlile diminished. By the spring of 1831 Taylor had developed a proclivity for brandy, or perhaps more accurately, as an informer recounted it, for cold gin and water.[14] Several of his "entertainments" had to be cancelled on short notice, while others were staged ineffectively. In the view of Carlile, Taylor compounded his sins by commencing a liaison with the housekeeper of the Rotunda, a woman of low birth whom he brusquely and unjustly described as a "prostitute."[15]

As a result of his success in making the Rotunda a center of radical agitation in London, Carlile's publishing prospects began to improve and by the middle of 1830 his weekly income approached £20. In November, he launched the *Prompter*, a three-penny unstamped weekly newspaper that ran for just over a year. "THE NATION NEEDS A PROMPTER," the journal's masthead proclaimed, and, as sketched in its first number, its object was to make war against "the bad part of every system, against bad measures, and against the general bad passions and ignorance of mankind." It was a successor to the *Lion*, which had been wound up at the end of 1829. (In January 1830, Carlile distributed specimen copies of a projected daily paper, *Carlile's Journal for 1830*, but plans to publish it foundered because of lack of funds.) Less comprehensive than the *Lion*, the *Prompter* gave considerable space to political as well as "infidel" news. It served as a journal of record for the Rotunda, publishing accounts of many of its events and offering lively comments on the speechmaking that was on display there.

While the Rotunda was increasing in importance, Carlile began to quarrel with many leading working-class reformers in addition to Hunt and Taylor. Differences of personality had much to do with this because the qualities of moral righteousness and self-help that Carlile so visibly displayed did not sit well with many of his contemporaries. But, equally, he disagreed with the political positions taken by the majority of working-class reformers in the early 1830s. For example, he denounced Owenite schemes for economic cooperation although these were a cohering facet of radical politics during the period, as groups of cooperators orga- nized bazaars and wholesale stores and attempted to implement theories of social harmony. Such "artificial" solutions to economic problems were, in Carlile's opinion, a distraction from more pressing issues. Thus, after attending the inaugural meeting, in May 1829, of the British Association for Promoting Co-operative

Knowledge, an Owenite organization led by Hetherington, Hibbert, and James Watson, he refused to have any dealings with it, though he allowed it to meet at the Rotunda.[16]

More controversial was his opposition to universal suffrage at a time when most working-class radicals were championing it. While still a prisoner in Dorchester, Carlile had begun to draw back from his commitment to "elective republicanism" (universal suffrage). In 1829, he was expelled from the Radical Reform Association, which was agitating for universal suffrage, annual parliaments, and the ballot. He attended several meetings of the organization but was barred after unsuccessfully urging the adoption of an infidel program. Disillusioned by the refusal of workingmen to give their attention to "meaningful reform," Carlile described the leaders of the Radical Reform Association (including Hunt) as "contemptibly devoid of intellectual and useful purpose."[17]

Subsequently, in March 1830, another working-class organization, the Metropolitan Political Union, was formed in London, "to obtain by every just, legal, constitutional, and peaceful means, an effectual and radical reform in the Commons House of Parliament." Carlile attended its first meeting together with Hunt, Henry Hetherington, and Daniel O'Connell, the Irish Catholic leader. Again he attacked publicly the working-class obsession with universal suffrage, urging instead that a popular antichristian movement be supported. He also proposed that William Cobbett, who had resigned from the Radical Reform Association after quarreling with Hunt, be elected to the Council of the Metropolitan Political Union. Amid hissing and shouts of "disunion," he was taunted by several speakers, including O'Connell, who described him as a "comical blade" and made cutting allusions to his Devon accent.[18] Carlile's contacts with the organization ceased at this point except for his continuing denunciations of its leaders. But the incident pushed him further away from the core of working-class radicalism in London, particularly from Hunt's supporters, who insisted that universal suffrage must take precedence over all other reforms. When, in May 1831, the National Union of the Working Classes was founded as a successor to the Radical Reform Association, which had been wound up in the preceding December, Carlile described it as an "abortion," while conceding that it was "the best effort at the formation of a political society that has yet been made." He denigrated its leadership, especially Hetherington whose *Poor Man's Guardian* had a much larger circulation than the *Prompter*. Finally, in January 1832, he evicted it from the Rotunda.[19]

All political societies, insisted Carlile during these tumultuous years in the history of radical reform, were harmful. They were "contemptible, frivolous, paltry nothings" that obstructed the consummation of rational reform and could not "turn out, among the whole of them, a single regiment of brave fighting men." Again and again he emphasized that political reform must take a back seat to theological change if real improvements were to take place. But as betweeen the universal suffrage nostrums advocated by "mob-meetings, mob-resolvings, and petitionings" and moderate parliamentary reform of the kind proposed by Lord John Russell and the Whigs there could be no question as to his preference. Thus, he endorsed strongly, as a step in the right direction, the £10 household franchise being pushed by the Whigs. "Let the people be but half represented in the House of Commons," he observed, "and I will be satisfied, and exhort others to be satisfied, and to wait the moral working of legislative events."[20] Little support was to be won for this position at the Rotunda, and Carlile was attacked by many reformers for his views.

Only during the "war of the unstamped press" in the early 1830s did he work harmoniously with other reformers, though much of his work was done covertly. The four-penny duty on journals and newspapers, imposed in 1819, was a major political issue because it drastically increased the price of newspapers and placed them beyond the reach of readers who were poor. In the autumn of 1830, an agitation against the "taxes on knowledge" began, led by the working-class journalists Hetherington, Watson, and John Cleave, all of whom supported universal suffrage. Numerous vendors were imprisoned and hundreds of unstamped journals were published and sold illegally during the ensuing six years, a situation that induced the Whig government headed by Lord Melbourne to reduce the duty to one penny in 1836.[21]

Carlile was not a leading participant in this struggle, but he made important contributions to it. Reaffirming his belief that the press must be as "free as the air," he described the agitation as a "rallying point of public spirit" and vowed to "see what I can do to carry it on."[22] He allowed William Carpenter and C. M. Riley to issue their unstamped *People's Press* from 1 Bouverie Street (a side entrance to 62 Fleet Street) in December 1830, which was an opening cannonade in the struggle for repeal. Subsequently he gave financial support to Henry Berthold, a journalist from Saxony whose short-lived unstamped cotton paper, *Berthold's Political Handkerchief*, attracted considerable publicity.[23] To buttress Berthold's legal challenge—which was based on the tenuous argument that the stamp tax did not apply to newspapers printed on materials other than paper—Carlile published several cotton almanacs and broadsheets, including *Cobbett's Spelling Book*, which attacked the use of fiction in schools, and the *Coronation Handkerchief*, which poked fun at the "earthly trinity" of kings, lords, and priests. One of his almanacs gained a circulation of 10,000 in December 1831, but he withdrew it after a prosecution was commenced against his son Richard. As he told his Manchester agent, Abel Heywood: "In complying with your request to send you six almanacks, I wish to be understood as not responsible, and not encouraging you to sell them. . . . I rely on your honour not to compromise us."[24]

Carlile also published and edited several unstamped newspapers, including the *Prompter*; the *Union* (1831-1832), a two-penny journal that attempted to foster unity between middle-class and working-class reformers; the *Gauntlet*, a freethinking and political journal that he commenced in February 1833; the *Political Soldier* (December 1833-January 1834), whose objective was to disseminate "sound republican principles" in the army; and *A Scourge for the Littleness of "Great" Men* (1834-1835), a paper specializing in vituperative attacks against other reformers.[25] Most readers of the unstamped press were unaware that Carlile also made significant contributions to the *Cosmopolite*, a one-and-a-half-penny journal published between June 1832 and November 1833 whose weekly circulation was about 5000. A succession of names graced the journal's pages, but it was Carlile who wrote most of its leaders and prepared it for distribution. His unsigned articles touched on many of his enthusiasms. He attacked lawyers, for example, as "enemies of the people," described the London police force established in 1829 as "vile lacqueys of despotism," and depicted the triumvirate of kings, lords, and priests as "a huge tapeworm ratifying itself throughout the stomach of the body politic." In a more restrained tone he advocated reduced public expenditure and an acceptance of the £10 franchise, which was finally enacted into law in June 1832. Occasionally, too, he made allusions to infidel themes. "The commencement of a British Millennium," he wrote in the *Cosmopolite*, would occur when "moral resistance" to the payment of church rates was undertaken; he also advocated the transformation of the Church of England into "a public school, a national school, and a rational school."[26]

Ironically, it was the *Prompter*, one of Carlile's most moderate journals, which got him into difficulty with the law once more after a hiatus of five years. In the paper's third number, appearing on November 27, 1830, he addressed a letter, "To the Insurgent Agricultural Labourers," that was tucked away on an inside page. His intention was to give solace to the rural poor who, provoked by starvation and harsh working conditions, were setting fires to ricks and engaging in other acts of property destruction. In his brief comments on these "Swing" disturbances, Carlile attempted to set the grievances of the rioters within a larger social context. "Much as every thoughtful man must lament the waste of property," he observed, "much as the country must suffer by the burnings of farm produce now going on, were you proved to be the incendiaries, we should defend you by saying, that you have more just and moral cause for it than any king or faction, that ever made war, had for making war." His advice to the laborers was as follows: "Go on as you have begun; and learn, not only in precept, but in your own example, that great political sentiment of Thomas Paine—the greatest political friend of the labouring man that ever put pen to paper for his instruction—that 'FOR A NATION TO BE FREE, IT IS SUFFICIENT THAT SHE WILLS IT.'"[27]

Rhetorical advice of this kind was, admittedly, more in character with the "wild" Carlile of a decade earlier than with the reformer of 1830 who had tempered many of his political sentiments and whose chief concern was to bring about religious change. But in no sense was the *Prompter* article intended as a call to arms. "Neither in deed, nor in word, nor in idea," he wrote, "did I ever encourage or wish to encourage, the agricultural labourers in acts of arson or machine-breaking."[28] Nor was there a scintilla of evidence to link his words with any actual disturbances. His writings were aimed primarily at artisans and factory workers, not at agricultural laborers, and no more than 5 percent of the 2000 copies of the *Prompter* that were published each week reached country districts.

Why then did the government of Lord Grey, newly installed in power and with an attorney-general, Thomas Denman, who had a reputation as a defender of press freedom, bring an ex officio indictment against Carlile, an action that took him and most other reformers by surprise?[29] Almost certainly, as Carlile surmised, it had to do with the government's determination to destroy the Rotunda. By November 1830, the latter had become a formidable base of working-class disaffection, with large numbers of political reformers and infidels attracted to it. Yet it could not be eliminated, short perhaps of the imprisonment of Carlile. As members of the government well understood, the fate of the Swing rioters was extrinsic to Carlile's concerns, but a successful prosecution of him might help them to secure their political aims.

Genuinely nonplussed by the circumstances of his prosecution— in the future, remarked Carlile, he would "not again make sure of anything in politics"—he fought hard to vindicate himself. He assured his readers that he would stand firm. "I have a just cause," he maintained. "I plead for the injured, the oppressed, the weak, and for outraged humanity."[30] Shortly after the launching of the prosecution he was, according to Francis Place, in a "mood of high exultation"; and when Place suggested that he attempt to have the proceedings squashed, Carlile vehemently rejected this advice. He told Place: "I shall not thank you if you put a stop to my trial. . . . Do what you can for me afterwards."[31]

In January 1831, Carlile was tried at the Old Bailey on four counts of seditious libel. Unlike his earlier judicial confrontations, however, the trial was not a cause célèbre in radical circles. Several meetings were convened hurriedly at the Rotunda to protest the prosecution, and at a "mock trial" conducted by his supporters, he was easily acquitted. But most reformers took little interest in his fate. Defense strategy was concerted with a handful of close associates, including Hibbert, Taylor, John Gale Jones, and several Rotunda loyalists.[32]

In his accustomed bulldog manner Carlile rejected all offers of legal aid. (This may have been a judicious decision since a solicitor with whom he briefly conferred filed a report with the Home Office on their conversations.) But he had not improved much on his meandering, bellicose courtroom style of eleven years before. Instead of concentrating on the central issue raised by the prosecution—whether he was guilty of seditious libel for having given support to the rural laborers—he made a discursive six-hour speech in which he succeeded only in scoring general political points at the expense of the Whig government. All prosecutions for seditious libel, he stated, were "neither more nor less than acts of tyranny," their purpose being to suppress freedom of opinion. The Swing rioters had, he maintained, been expressing "a wild kind of justice"; and his aim had been nothing more or less than to extend a "feeling heart" to them. Furthermore—and legally more relevant—he contended that a double standard of law made it almost impossible for a poor man to receive his due. The *Times* and other stamped newspapers constantly made inflammatory pronouncements about political events without incurring the risks of prosecution, he observed, while he, an impecunious journalist, suffered from "injustice."[33]

Newman Knowlys, the recorder of the City of London, who presided at the trial, interrupted Carlile repeatedly and then delivered a summation to the jury that all but guaranteed a guilty verdict. The only surprise was the jury's acquittal of Carlile on two of the four charges against him. Knowlys then meted out an exemplary sentence: two years' imprisonment in the Giltspur Street Compter, located in London; a fine of £200; and recognizances of £1000 to insure good behavior for a period of ten years. Carlile protested vigorously at the circumstances of the trial and the brutality of the sentence, accusing Knowlys of conduct "that can only be matched in the State Trials of the Tudors and the Stuarts." He told readers of the *Prompter*: "I cannot but think myself *the sacred ministerial and vicarial* scape-goat, sacrificed or driven out of the community, as an atonement for national sins, in which I had no share."[34]

Partly assisted by counsel provided by Francis Place, he launched an appeal against the verdict that dragged on for two years and only exacerbated his hatred for the legal system. He drafted numerous petitions on his case from prison without any success. Furthermore, the acquittal of his quondam rival Cobbett in July 1831, on charges of seditious libel stemming from similar comments about the Swing rioters, angered him (though he congratulated Cobbett) because it exemplified the vagaries of the law. In a petition to Thomas Denman, who was appointed lord chief justice in April 1833, Carlile wrote: "Judgment and justice have been denied me. . . . A similar case, by the accident of a difference in reason, place and judge, has placed Mr. Cobbett in the House of Commons."[35]

Carlile received little support from working-class reformers during his trial. "Infidelity boxes," placed in and near the Rotunda, yielded the less than munificent sum of several hundred pounds, insufficient to compensate him for his loss of publishing income or to meet the cost of his appeal. Most radical associations, including the National Union of the Working Classes, refused to collect subscriptions for him, although they worked hard to raise money to aid the vendors of unstamped newspapers. Only a few prominent reformers supported him, among them James Watson and the future Chartist leader, William Lovett, who was at the time an advocate of economic cooperation.[36] The nub of the problem, as Place noted, was Carlile's lack of political savvy. He had so distanced himself from the core of working-class discontent that few radical reformers were prepared to embrace him in his hour of need.

Carlile's term in the Compter, extended subsequently to thirty months because of his refusal to pay the fine and the securities for good behavior, began in January 1831. Prison once more proved to be a tonic to his "creativity." The self-help ethos that informed his earlier incarceration had given way to apocalyptic judgments about the likelihood of radical change. Yet he had lost none of his vigor and obstinacy, and he was determined at all costs to resist oppression and win his objectives. "It may seem strange," he told readers of the *Prompter*, "but whether from habit, or what else, it is no less true, that in the course of our great political struggle I like a gaol, and am more happy here than I can possibly be anywhere else, until the time of our final triumph."[37]

By comparison with other prisons, the Compter was comfortable. Its proximity to the Rotunda was advantageous, and
Carlile's room (overlooking a churchyard) was furnished with a
sofa, writing desk, fireplace, and books, tracts, and newspapers
supplied by his friends and associates. Visitors had easy access to
him, and Taylor, Hibbert, John Gale Jones, and his son Richard,
who supervised the Rotunda in his absence, met regularly with
him. "Temperance by example" was once again his actuating
principle. "It would be a really useful punishment to compel strict
cleanliness of person, and twelve hours a day, of close application,
to reading, writing, and arithmetic," he observed. He separated
himself from the "common" felons and criminals who were locked
up nightly in the Compter, maintaining this self-imposed "quarantine" throughout his confinement except during the cholera scare of
February 1832 when gaol regulations were suspended and prisoners
left to fend for themselves.[38]

The great advantage of the Compter was that Carlile could
continue to conduct his publishing ventures reasonably efficiently.
He edited the *Prompter* for ten months after his imprisonment
began and maintained a steady flow of radical tracts, including
another edition of his *Manual of Masonry*, based on his articles on
freemasonry in the *Republican* in 1825; *A New View of Insanity*,
which was a provocative analysis of "madness" containing caustic
statements about social and political issues; and the *Devil's Pulpit*,
a weekly compendium of Taylor's discourses at the Rotunda that
began to circulate in March 1831 and sold more than 2000 copies
weekly.[39] But managing the Rotunda from the Compter proved to
be a daunting task. For several months the building continued to
function smoothly in Carlile's absence, with Taylor attracting large
audiences to his weekly entertainments. In the spring of 1831, he
delivered an especially popular series of discourses on the "Star of
Bethlehem." He employed props to show that the gospel "is astronomical . . . is all to be seen, and is all exhibited in the visible
heavens"; and that "the SUN, who is the Jesus Christ, and the only
Jesus Christ that ever existed, as he passes respectively into each one
of the twelve signs of the zodiac, assumes the character of that
particular sign and is assimilated and entirely identical with it." He

also visually "demonstrated" that John the Baptist was an allegory of "death unto sin, and a new birth of righteousness."[40]

But although these presentations were successful, Taylor's lack of a consistent vision and, particularly, his intemperance, began to affect his entertainments. Complaints about the quality of his work were heard with increasing frequency. Richard Carlile, Jr., lacked the authority to discipline Taylor or to keep the peace between the warring factions of political reformers and freethinkers who occasionally confronted each other within the building. He kept his father informed about problems but was unable to master them. Thus attendances at the Rotunda declined during the spring and early summer of 1831, and income from miscellaneous radical activities fell off. By September, Carlile, according to an informant, was losing £5 weekly and rapidly going into debt.[41]

The most serious blow to the Rotunda occurred, however, in July 1831, when Taylor was tried and convicted of blasphemous libel. In April, an information was filed against him by the Vice Society for two provocative lectures that he had delivered. The first, a Good Friday sermon on the "Crucifixion of Christ," included the sardonic observation that Simon the Cyrenian or another "blaspheming infidel" had been crucified instead of Jesus and offered the following passage for the delectation of those present: "And what was to hinder [Jesus] from showing himself alive after his passion. A man may put himself into a passion, I hope, and put himself out of it again, without breaking a blood-vessel." The other sermon, preached by Taylor on Palm Sunday and entitled "The Cup of Salvation," was even more offensive to churchmen. "HOW COULD ANY MAN WALK WITH GOD?" he queried mockingly, "with their indefinite, indescript, and indescribable God, their incomprehensible and infinite space-filling God? WHEN [their] GOD CANNOT WALK HIMSELF. (Why, to be sure.) HE WOULD BE AT HIS JOURNEY'S END, BEFORE HE SET OUT. AND AS HE FILLS ALL SPACE, HE MUST SIT STILL IN ALL SPACE, LIKE A GOUTY OLD MAN IN HIS ARM-CHAIR, AND STAY AT HOME THROUGH ALL ETERN-ITY." After imbibing wine as part of the evening's "entertainment," he observed amid chuckling from the audience: "THE REASON WHY THE BLOOD OF CHRIST DOES INDUCE GOD TO FORGIVE US OUR SINS IS, THAT HE LIKES A DROP OF THE *crater*, AS WELL AS WE DO: THAT PUTS

HIM INTO A GOOD HUMOUR, AND THEN HE IS NOT SO PARTICULAR ABOUT US."[42] Taylor's wit was little appreciated by members of the Vice Society, who selected for prosecution those passages most informed by a scoffing tone. Irreverent laughter, in their view, was too potent a weapon to be allowed free rein.

The trial took place in July at the Surrey sessions. Taylor conducted his defense energetically but without a sufficient sense of gravity. His references to religion were delivered in his usual jocular tone (producing considerable laughter among the spectators), and he pleaded his innocence on the ground that he had not meant to "revile the Christian religion" or those who professed it. On the contrary, he affirmed, he had "as high a veneration for the beautiful and pathetic language of the Scripture as any man upon the face of the earth." Unamused by these antics, the jury found him guilty. He was sentenced to two years' imprisonment in Horsemonger-Lane Gaol in south London and to a heavy fine and the payment of recognizances.[43]

Taylor's incarceration destroyed the Rotunda as a center of theological and political radicalism. Both his oratorical exhibitionism and Carlile's dogged intellectualism were now missing, and adequate substitutes could not be found. Political reformers continued to use the Rotunda's premises for several months, but their interests diverged increasingly from those of Carlile and Taylor. Hibbert and John Gale Jones tried unsuccessfully to become surrogate infidel orators. Jones, a deist, spoke with more conviction about universal suffrage than he did about the physical and moral allegories of religion, while Hibbert, a brilliant scholar and a companionable man, lacked the quality of showmanship necessary for effective speechmaking. Efforts to restage several of Taylor's performances were unsuccessful. And although the young man who replaced Carlile as reader of the Sunday "lessons" was James "Shepherd" Smith, afterward to become a well-known millennialist preacher and newspaper editor, he lacked the maturity to sustain the interest of his audiences.[44]

Only in the early months of 1832 was the Rotunda briefly suffused with some of its old magic. The occasion was a series of "spiritual discourses" by Elizabeth Sharples, a Bolton disciple of Carlile who lectured under the nom de plume "Isis." Her Rotunda sermons (mostly written for her by Carlile) were delivered several times weekly to small, enthusiastic audiences of workingmen. "Isis" wore a "showy" dress for the occasions and stood on a floor strewn with white thorn and laurel. Her delivery, while not inspired, was decorous.[45]

The discourses dealt largely with the allegorical interpretations of Carlile and Taylor. Sharples reiterated that Jesus was a personification of the sun and "a definition of the principle of reason" and that the Gospels were "a personification of the Sun's twelve labours, its going down to hell, its crucifixion, death, burial, resurrection and ascension: its annual business, its daily and monthly task: a physical record of astronomical effects: an astrological almanac."[46] Even more interesting was the note of feminist commitment that occasionally crept into her speeches. In passages that she may have written herself, Sharples told her listeners that throughout history women were the victims of "religious, perpetual, undivorceable marriage," and that their "undue submission, which constitutes slavery, is honourable to none." They would "not be neglected, and subdued, and treated as captives, as they are now treated," she stated, if they became "wise in mental emulation and social distinction with their brother man." It was a theme that evoked memories of Carlile's birth control campaign and gave a stimulus to the forthcoming struggle by women to improve their lot.[47]

Sharples could not sustain the interest of her Rotunda audiences for more than a few months. She was diffident, politically inexperienced, and deficient in theological information. Having delivered a set oration, she would immediately retire from the public area, to the discomfit of those who wanted to prolong and extend the discussions. "I wait only for a little experience," she observed tentatively, "a little confidence, to trust myself to estimate the reality of my character."[48]

Time, however, was not on her side—nor that of Carlile. Audiences dwindled as political, social, and religious reformers went their separate ways: to universal suffrage "classes" held in different sections of London, to the flourishing Owenite "Institution of the Working Classes" that met weekly on Theobald's Road, and to small freethinking "chapels" where a medley of antireligious themes was sounded and a stream of propaganda against Christianity issued forth. Carlile's financial situation deteriorated in spite of support from Hibbert, and, bereft of an adequate income, he was forced to lease portions of the Rotunda to a circus and musical company. Even these steps proved insufficient, and in April 1832 the owner of the building terminated the lease. Thus, two significant years in the history of working-class radicalism in London came to an abrupt end, with some permanent accomplishments in the development of a political consciousness among the poor and the increased spread of infidel ideas. The subsequent history of the Rotunda—its conversion into a theater and, in the twentieth century, into an auction house (now destroyed)—provides an ironical commentary on the expectations it once aroused.

The collapse of the Rotunda further separated Carlile from the majority of working-class activists. Yet he continued to nourish aspirations for the future, including the ludicrous hope of winning a parliamentary seat. He had harbored this ambition for many years. And with Hunt having won a seat at Preston in 1830 and Cobbett about to do the same at Oldham in the forthcoming general election, he began to consider the possibility more seriously. Declaring himself to be "the best-supported politician in the country," he published an election address in June 1832, laying claim to a seat at Ashton-under-Lyne. He expressed confidence that reformers there would secure his election, although, as it turned out, only a handful supported him, most of whom did not even qualify for the franchise. It was left to their spokesman, Joshua Hobson, to render the political coup de grâce to Carlile. "The time is not come," Hobson informed him, "when such a constituency as we have in Ashton, will return such a sweeping reformer as Mr. Carlile."[49]

The rejection, though wounding, is of less interest than Carlile's election address, which included observations on many subjects that did not ordinarily fall within his purview. Calling for a reduction in taxation, he endorsed proposals for a property tax, "parochially assessed and gathered," and for "the most free and fair trade that can be imagined between the people of all countries."[50] He also offered the opinion that the new London police were more likely to violate the rights of workingmen than to protect them. In place of this force, he recommended the establishment of a citizen constabulary along the lines suggested in earlier years by Major Cartwright and other reformers.

As the ups and downs of prison life began to affect Carlile and the Rotunda fell apart, he became, as in his Dorchester years, crotchety and volatile. His *New View of Insanity*, issued in the spring of 1831 from the Compter, was the most contentious of his tracts. It gave voice to a mixture of unusual causes: phrenology, sexual liberation, "hygeism" (which was the belief that good health depended upon the unrestricted circulation of the blood), compassion for the insane, and, unexpectedly, musings on the subject of "madness."[51] For many years Carlile had employed the imagery of "madness" in his writings, especially in reference to religion.[52] But in *A New View of Insanity* he extended it into new areas, in the process anticipating some modern psychological and political insights. Insanity, he averred, was a political "crime" that was constantly being redefined to meet the needs of those in power. It was an effective way of suppressing dissent. The stigma of "madness" was attached to those who rejected orthodox opinions, he wrote, beginning with the early Christians and extending to recent critics of authority like himself. Furthermore, sexual repression, and specifically the refusal to allow women a knowledge of birth control, was a way of inducing "madness." As he observed in *A New View of Insanity*: "Love and religion, as these principles are now attended to in this island, are the two great sources of hypocrisy, mental deceit, mental lying, and social misery, as well as insanity."[53]

Only when the true causes of insanity were understood could meaningful reform be carried out, Carlile maintained. He recommended infidelity as the best remedy for madness, because it teaches "the disordered mind" to think of nothing "but what is known, [and] can be explained, and well accounted for."[54] Birth control was another remedy, as was bodily and intellectual temperance of the kind advocated by J. G. Spurzheim, who in his *Observations on the Deranged Manifestations of the Mind* (1817) wrote that "all that disturbs, excites, or weakens the organization, chiefly the nervous system, has an influence on the manifestations of the mind."[55] Several of Carlile's "cures" for insanity read like an enumeration of respectable virtues, including "useful labour," the absence of all "vitiating" activities, controlled mental exertion, and the "least possible restraint and annoyance." Animated by a combination of conventional moral attitudinizing and personal quirkiness, they reflect Carlile's enthusiasms at a time when his prospects as a reformer were, seemingly, approaching a low ebb. Not surprisingly, his proposal "to take up the case of a few religious-insane patients, upon the principle of no cure, no pay," did not produce a surfeit of takers.

As in the 1820s, Carlile's prison experiences accentuated his political and emotional isolation. The more he perceived himself to be distanced from events, the more he fell back on messianic expressions of self-righteousness. He became prey to fits of depression and exultation, a somber statement such as "I may truly say, that my time is not yet come, and that every future generation will be benefited by my labours, when my toil-worn body is prematurely shaken back to dust," being followed by a ringing affirmation of purpose. "I may not live to see its entire success," he observed in reference to his moral allegory of religion, but "if I do so live, I shall die with the satisfaction of having lived well, and to some good purpose."[56]

During the spring and summer of 1831 he continued to praise Taylor. He told readers of the *Prompter* that Taylor had demolished "all heresies, all sects, all contradictions and jarrings, all low fanaticism, and holy madness"; his *Devil's Pulpit* (which appeared in tract form in April) left "nothing unfinished, nothing unexplained." Somewhat uncharacteristically, he even endorsed Taylor's prediction that the Day of Judgment—to be indicated by the passing of the Great Comet—would occur on Christmas Day, 1833, exactly 1260 days from the beginning of the final apocalyptic period that had commenced on July 27, 1830.[57]

Yet while he was asserting in almost strident terms his theological agreement with Taylor, the relationship between the two men was nearing its end. Carlile was his former enthusiastic self immediately after Taylor's trial. "I politically rejoice that you are so treated," he told Taylor. "This little imprisonment of yours . . . has done more work in our way, than we could have done in a year without it." This did not console Taylor, who rued the absence of "social intercourse" in Horsemonger-Lane Gaol and, as he had done in

1827, complained endlessly about his plight. On one occasion he wrote privately to Lord Brougham as follows: "What I have suffered (and no language can describe it) may be considered—as enough." Carlile urged him to "be of good cheer" and to stand firm. "It is now with you no time for poetry, for hyperbole, for love, for rhapsody, or for jest," he advised with a slight touch of contempt. "You have, and we have for you, a serious game to play."[58]

At about the same time Carlile began to assert the claims of his own "moral allegory" in contrast to Taylor's interpretations. His edition of the *Manual of Masonry* in April 1831, with a new "Keystone of the Royal Arch of Freemasonry," diverged considerably from Taylor's views about freemasonry. Freemasonry, explained Carlile, was not only astronomical in meaning but had its "moral counterpart in human culture." "God" existed as physical and moral knowledge (the equivalent of the two keys of Peter), and the masonic tau and the Christian cross were both "symbols of science." "The advent of the Jewish Messiah, the advent of Christ, and the advent of a reasonable state of society, in which mystery and superstition shall yield to plain practical science, in the constitution of the human mind," are, he wrote, "one and the same reality, the moral of the mystery of Judaism, Christianity, and Masonry."[59]

A more decisive break with Taylor took place during the time of the "Isis" lectures at the Rotunda. Eliza Sharples became Carlile's "spiritual" partner in infidelity: a symbol of female redemption whom he named after the Egyptian goddess of reason. She was Woman idealized. And by means of her messianic discourses, he announced publicly his "conversion" to a moral allegory of religion, now bedecked in the imagery of Christianity though little different from the message he had proclaimed at Stockport in 1827. In a letter addressed to Sharples, which was printed in *Isis* in May 1832, he stated: "I DECLARE MYSELF A CONVERT TO THE TRUTH AS IT IS IN THE GOSPEL OF JESUS CHRIST. I DECLARE MYSELF A BELIEVER IN THE TRUTH OF THE CHRISTIAN RELIGION."[60] Subsequently, he claimed that "the astronomical interpretation [of Taylor] is still but a symbolical interpretation; while this moral interpretation defines God to be the highest moral power and principle known to man." The meaning of the "glorious moral resurrection" was expounded through the lips of "Isis": that the Bible was "an abstruse allegory of the creation of the thinking powers of man" and that religion was the saga of "the good man struggling to communicate knowledge to his fellow men."[61]

Thus, in the spring of 1832 Carlile and Taylor parted company intellectually. Carlile became a prophet of Christian rationalism, ready to confront "confusion and mystery and the forces of darkness." He described himself as the first man in history to disseminate "the true doctrine of Christ as God," or, as he put it: "That which is to come is to be the reign of reason in the human mind, after the overthrow of idolatry and superstition, religious dissent and sectarian churches." He advised his readers to learn how that Christ is risen, how that the Temple is rebuilt, and how the kingdom of heaven is at hand."[62] These views, strongly enunciated, alienated many of his followers, including Hibbert. But with Christ on his side, much could be endured, and he was determined to propound the virtues of the "republican Scriptures" as soon as he gained his release from prison.

Notes

1. *Prompter*, 13 November 1830, 7 May 1831.

2. The estimate of £400 is based on a Secret Service report, c. June 1831, H.O. 64/11. On the support of Hibbert and Saull for the Rotunda, see reports in H.O. 64/11, especially one dated 29 November 1831.

3. On the history of the Rotunda, see *Prompter*, 13 November 1830; Peter Cunningham, *A Handbook for London* (London: John Murray, 1849), vol. 2, p. 793. There is a detailed financial statement (May 1830-June 1831) in the *Prompter*, 2 July 1831.

4. This description is drawn from one of many of Taylor to be found in the informers' reports, H.O. 64/11. See also Vizetelly, *Glances Back Through Seventy Years*, vol. 1, pp. 98-99.

5. Carlile's denial that live animals were impaled is in *Cheltenham Free Press*, 29 February 1840.

6. One hostile writer commented on these entertainments as follows: "Never have we heard a discourse in so *astronomical-comical, frenetical-poetical, dogmatical-lunatical a manner.*" *A Letter to Henry Hunt, Esq. M.P. for Preston, on the Hous—Pous of the Necromancer-Theologer, R. Taylor, in his Pandemonial Sermon* (London: W. E. Andrews, 1831), p. 4.

7. *Devil's Pulpit*, vol. 2, p. 137, and vol. 1, p. 29. Carlile published the text of *Swing* as a three-penny tract in 1831 and described it as "the most popular of public political procedures and entertainment that has ever been provided." *Prompter*, 19 February 1831.

8. *Devil's Pulpit*, vol. 1, pp. 251, 277.

9. *Prompter*, 1 January 1831. See also ibid., 26 February 1831.

10. *Gauntlet*, 16 March 1834; *Devil's Pulpit*, vol. 2, p. 6.

11. Between August and October 1830, William Cobbett delivered lectures at the Rotunda on parliamentary reform that were reprinted in tract form. After failing as a conciliator, Hibbert withdrew from the NUWC in January 1832.

12. It was described by the *Weekly Free Press*, 13 November 1830, as a "bear-garden" where crime was rampant.

13. *Prompter*, 25 December 1830. The best account of these events is in an informer's report, 16 November 1830, H.O. 64/11. See also *Prompter*, 20 November 1830.

14. There are references to Taylor's drinking problem in informers' reports in H.O. 64/11.

15. Taylor's sexual ties are alluded to in private letters between him and Carlile in the Carlile papers. There are scurrilous references by Carlile to this relationship in *Scourge for the Littleness of "Great" Men*, 4 October, 11 October 1834.

16. There are accounts of meetings of the BAPCK in several radical journals including the *Magazine of Useful Knowledge*, the *British Co-operator*, and William Carpenter's *Political Letters and Pamphlets*.

17. See *Scourge for the Littleness of "Great" Men*, 10 October 1834, and the contradictory accounts in the *Poor Man's Guardian*, 11 November 1834, and *Carlile's Political Register*, 7 December 1839.

18. *Weekly Free Press*, 13 March 1830; Carlile to Daniel O'Connell, c. January 1843, C.P.; *Prompter*, 19 February 1831. On the history of the RRA and the MPU, see David Large, "William Lovett," in Patricia Hollis (ed.), *Pressure from Without in Early Victorian England* (London: Edward Arnold, 1974), p. 106.

19. Hetherington claimed that Carlile was expelled from the council of the MPU but Carlile denied it. *Poor Man's Guardian*, 1 November 1834; *Gauntlet*, 23 June, 4 August 1833.

20. *Prompter*, 12 March 1831, 3, 24 September, 26 February, 1833.

21. On the history of this agitation, see Wiener, *War of the Unstamped*, and Hollis, *Pauper Press*.

22. *Prompter*, 28 May, 20 August 1833.

23. Carlile afterward got into a dispute with Berthold who described him

as "insane." *Berthold's Political Handkerchief,* 17 September 1831.

24. Both cotton broadsides are in H.O. 64/11, and the incident involving his son is discussed in an informer's report, 26 December 1831, H.O. 64/11. The letter to Heywood, dated 30 December 1831, is reprinted in Abel Heywood, Jr., *English Almanacks During the First Third of the Century* (Manchester: Privately publ., 1904), pp. 18-19.

25. He also organized petitions against the taxes. Thomas Wakley to Carlile, c. April 1836, C.P.

26. *Cosmopolite,* 3 November, 11 August 1832, 16 March 1833, 13 October 1832.

27. *Prompter,* 27 November 1830.

28. Ibid., 14 May 1831.

29. Denman privately admitted that ex officio indictments were unusual in cases of this kind. Memorial from Thomas Denman, 24 May 1832, reprinted in Arnould, *Denman,* vol. 1, pp. 368-72.

30. *Prompter,* 5 February 1831, 25 December 1830. He told his readers: "I stand on a rock,—my principles are built on a rock,—and cannot be conquered." Ibid., 18 December 1830.

31. Francis Place to Leslie Grove Jones, 7 January 1831, Add. Ms. 35, 149, f. 12c, Place Papers, B.M.

32. There is a discussion of his pretrial strategy in an informer's report, c. December 1830, H.O. 64/11.

33. *Prompter,* 29 January 1831. There is a complete report of the trial in ibid., 22 January 1831; John MacDonell (ed.), *Reports of State Trials* (London, 1889), n.s., vol. 2, 1823 to 1831 (1889), pp. 459-627.

34. *Prompter,* 14 May 1831. Place described it as "the heaviest sentence ever inflicted on a libeller within one's memory." Place Diary, Add. Ms. 35,146, B.M.

35. Carlile to Denman, 26 April 1833, C.P. The basis for his appeal was that only one commissioner had been present in the courtroom when the verdict was announced. Carlile to J. Evans, 10 January 1831, and other documents in C.P.

36. Watson's *Working Man's Friend* (13 July 1833) and Carpenter's *Political Letters and Pamphlets* (13 January 1831) reprinted the offending *Prompter* article and a few working-class political unions assisted Carlile. See *Poor Man's Guardian,* 27 August 1831; *Isis,* 1 December 1832.

37. Quoted in Campbell, *Battle of the Press,* p. 127.

38. Carlile, *New View of Insanity,* p. 11. He hoped that the Whig ministers would receive "the blast of the cholera, as a just punishment for their hypocrisy, false pretence, and wickedness." *Isis,* 14 July 1832.

39. S.S. report, 17 May 1831, H.O. 64/11. Carlile described the *Devil's Pulpit* as "a volume of astronomical information, unequalled by any writer

on the subject in ancient or modern times." It was reprinted in 1881 by the Freethought Publishing Company.

40. *Devil's Pulpit*, vol. 1, pp. 6, 8, 60.

41. Carlile claimed that he was earning £20 weekly from the Rotunda before his prosecution. *Isis*, 7 July 1832.

42. *Devil's Pulpit*, vol. 1, pp. 216, 237, 230.

43. *Prompter*, 9 July 1831. There is an account of the trial in ibid., 23 July 1831.

44. On "Shepherd" Smith, see William A. Smith, *"Shepherd" Smith the Universalist* (London: Samson Low, 1892); and John Saville, "J. E. Smith and the Owenite Movement, 1833-34," in S. Pollard and J. Salt (eds.), *Robert Owen: Prophet of the Poor* (London: Macmillan, 1971), pp. 115-144.

45. The Rotunda sermons were reprinted in the *Isis*, which was published from February to December 1832. Descriptions of Sharples are taken from informers' reports in H.O. 64/12.

46. *Isis*, 31 March, 28 April 1832.

47. Ibid., 11 February, 14 April, 26 May 1832.

48. Ibid., 31 March 1832.

49. *Prompter*, 12 March 1831; *Isis*, 16 June 1832.

50. *Isis*, 9 June 1832; *Cosmopolite*, 9 June 1832.

51. Carlile described hygeism as "a species of moral physiology." There were interesting stereotypical judgments in *A New View of Insanity*. Examples are: Scotchmen are "slavish to superiors, dangerous to compeers, tyrannical to inferiors, and greedy of gain" (p. 31); "I am not aware that Wales has ever thrown up a brilliant man" (p. 64).

52. Examples of the imagery of religious insanity in his writings: The prophecies are the work of "mad men" (*Observations on . . . Olinthus Gregory*, p. 28); "There is no proof of sincerity in religious pretensions, but where it produces decisive marks of insanity" (*Republican*, 22 September 1826); "Every religious person is insane" (*Lion*, 6 March 1829). George Ensor wrote in *Janus on Sion* that one-eighth of Bedlam's cases between 1772 and 1787 "originated in Christian belief" (p. 102).

53. Carlile, *New View of Insanity*, p. 2.

54. Ibid., p. 36.

55. J. G. Spurzheim, *Observations on the Deranged Manifestations of the Mind* (London: Baldwin, Cradock and Joy, 1817), p. 107. One of Spurzheim's explanations for the purported high incidence of insanity among the English people was the gloomy weather.

56. *Isis*, 14 July 1832; *Prompter*, 25 June 1831. In February 1832, he wrote: "I despair not—*I persevere, and will persevere,* though *I am one of the forlorn hope.*" *Isis*, 25 February 1832.

57. *Prompter*, 28 May, 16 July 1831.

58. Carlile to Taylor, 16 July 1831, C.P.; Taylor to Lord Brougham, 15 June 1832, Brougham Papers, University College, London; Carlile to Taylor, 23 July 1831, C.P. Taylor wrote to Carlile: "You are in heaven. I am in Hell." Reprinted in *Prompter*, 16 July 1831.

59. Carlile, *Manual of Masonry* (1831), pp. xiv-xvii.

60. *Isis*, 5 May 1832.

61. Ibid., 30 June, 15 September, 28 July 1832.

62. Richard Carlile, *A Respectful Address to the Inhabitants of Newcastle upon Tyne and Its Vicinity* (Newcastle upon Tyne: William Kent, 1834), pp. 5, 16; *Prompter*, 9 July, 1 October 1831. See also *Cosmopolite*, 26 January 1833.

10

A "MORAL MARRIAGE"

Freedom was not to be Carlile's for more than another year, and before then there were practical tasks at hand. It was necessary to put Christ aside for the time being and to concentrate upon more mundane objectives. In November 1831, as a result of financial losses, Carlile was compelled to give up the *Prompter*, and he was not able to bring out a successor, the *Gauntlet*, until February 1833. Until then he made do with lesser products: the *Union*, which consisted mostly of reports of reform meetings; the *Cosmopolite*, for which he wrote unsigned articles; and the *Isis*, a compendium of Eliza Sharples's Rotunda discourses, together with a substantial number of his own articles and essays.

With the exception of the *Isis*, most of Carlile's writings while imprisoned in the Compter dealt with political subjects, a situation that reflected the realities of the moment rather than a shift of interest on his part. The radical enthusiasms of the early 1830s were basically political in nature: stimulated initially by the movement for parliamentary reform; then, after passage of the Reform Act, as an offshoot of measures being discussed in the reformed House of Commons. The complexities of allegorical rationalism held little attraction for many working-class reformers during these years. And Carlile made tactical adjustments to fit this situation. But religion alone fully absorbed his interests, and his analysis of municipal reform, poor relief, the evils of the factory system, and other political issues of the day were pallid by comparison.

Finances were a continuing source of concern to Carlile. He had lost heavily on the Rotunda, including assessed taxes still owed and in lieu of which some of his personal goods had been confiscated by the authorities of the parish of Saint Dunstan's in the West. With the help of Hibbert, whose generosity never wavered, he met the quarterly payments on his house and shop. But toward the end of 1831 he had to take a lodger into his premises and to sell many of his furnishings, and this necessitated moving Jane Carlile and his sons into a section of the house fronting on Bouverie Street. By the following spring his publishing business, with the exception of the *Isis,* had come to a halt. He had lost £60 on the *Union* and owed William Cunningham, his printer, considerable sums of money resulting from losses on the *Lion.* He was reduced once again to selling old copies of his tracts at low prices (usually by breaking up bound volumes into parts or numbers), a demeaning expedient that failed to bring about the desired results. In a letter to the readers of *Isis* in July 1832, he laid bare his plight: "My affairs at this moment present me with nothing but growing difficulties, unpaid labour, a sinking of capital, and increasing debt."[1]

Yet notwithstanding these unfavorable portents, Carlile made a temporary recovery in 1833, largely because of the success of the *Gauntlet: A Sound Republican London Weekly Paper,* a quarto-sized, three-penny unstamped weekly that appeared in February and circulated for a little over a year. The *Gauntlet* was to be his last major publication. Eschewing freethought for the most part (there are only incidental references to his religious allegory in its pages), it emulated the format of successful political newspapers by providing its readers with a large quantity of radical news. It printed reports of reform meetings and parliamentary debates, accounts of legal proceedings, mildly prurient summaries of the exploits of criminals, and an immense variety of articles on reform contributed by readers. In short, it exhibited the full regalia of a newspaper, a new formula for Carlile and, as it turned out, a successful one. For almost a year the *Gauntlet* maintained a circulation of 5000 to 10,000; then, as an interest in reform tapered off, its circulation began to fall. But for almost a year, it brought into 62 Fleet Street a reasonable income from publishing.

While editing the *Gauntlet,* Carlile began to champion political causes and, on the surface, seemed to be moving closer to the center of metropolitan working-class radicalism. For example, he strongly condemned economic and social inequalities in Ireland. "Justice for Ireland," he told his readers, "is the first principle of an Englishman's present political honesty." The largely Roman Catholic population of Ireland was pathetically ignorant and superstitious, he observed; even so, it deserved humane, rational treatment instead of the coercive policies that were applied by Whigs and Tories. "The people of Ireland should resist abuses to the death," commented Carlile, "and the people of England should aid and abet them in every possible way."[2] His militant stance—not in synchronization with his more moderate positions on other issues—helped win him some readers for the *Gauntlet*.

He also made great play with the Cold Bath Fields incident of May 1833, when a meeting called by the National Union of the Working Classes to petition for a national convention "as the only means of obtaining and securing the rights of the people," ended in the death of a police officer and a subsequent inquest verdict of "justifiable homicide" that was cheered by many radical reformers. This sequence of events placed Carlile in a quandary. On the one hand, he rejected the idea of a convention as dangerous (though he had supported such a proposal twelve years before); at the same time, he upheld the right of reformers to assemble peaceably. In attempting to suppress the meeting local magistrates had, he asserted, behaved tyrannically, much in the manner of the Tories at Peterloo. He therefore kept up an agitation in the *Gauntlet* on the "Calthorpe Street Affair" (as the incident came to be known), publishing the names of the jurymen in gold letters and affirming that they "shall be . . . ever sounded with civil gratitude, as honest names, and as citizens who shall be ranked among the saviours of their country."[3]

The most important political cause that Carlile championed in the *Gauntlet*, however, was the enrollment of "volunteers" in a crusade against the excise taxes, which, like other reformers, he believed were sapping the moral and productive powers of the nation. In March 1833, he commenced his interest in this subject. His plan was to apply pressure against the government by having volunteers enroll their names with him or one of his agents. Then, by a quantitative show of "moral power," he would bring about an 80 percent reduction in excise taxes. "With a hundred thousand names I will overthrow an administration," he averred confidently.[4] He insisted that his volunteers would not form political unions, which he distrusted, but "associations" of individual subscribers. And he asserted that genuine radical reformers were needed for the task, not those prepared to do little more than put their names to a piece of paper.

There was, as Carlile soon discovered, a market for this kind of instant activism. Several thousand reformers throughout the country—including many backers of Hunt and members of the National Union of the Working Classes—enrolled their names in the *Gauntlet* during the spring of 1833. In issue after issue, they announced themselves ready to work for repeal of the "unjust and arbitrary, and scandalously oppressive" excise taxes and signed petitions that inveighed against these taxes for allegedly "keeping millions of stomachs in a state of starvation."[5] Carlile appeared to be leading a political movement that commanded a genuine excitement of numbers, one considerably in excess of his "infidel" following. Yet short of the kind of overt political agitation that would undermine his interest in theological reform, what were his volunteers to do? He had not thought this out, and the answer, as it turned out, was nothing at all. Thus, as the prospect for his release from the Compter grew near, his agitation simply petered out. By the summer of 1833, it had nearly disappeared, with few obsequies being expressed for its demise.

The success of the *Gauntlet* fostered other publishing activities, notwithstanding disputes with agents about money and distribution. Carlile was determined to bring out an abundance of printed matter, and in competition with Watson, John Cleave, B. D. Cousins, and other publishers of cheap political and freethought tracts, he began to issue a large number of pamphlets in 1833-34. He reprinted the *Moralist*, which appeared originally in 1823; published still another edition of the *Manual of Masonry*, and brought out a volume of aphorisms culled from the writings of Paine. More controversially, he published Francis Macerone's *Defense of Householders: Book of Instructions for Popular Fighting*, a manual of revolutionary street tactics in which the author, a former aide-de-camp to the king of Naples, affirmed that "a time is at hand when military freemen will have to battle with military despots."[6] As he had done on previous occasions, Carlile supplemented these publications with brass crests and coats of arms inscribed with slogans such as "FREE DISCUSSION," "DOWN WITH PRIESTCRAFT," and "RIGHTS OF WOMAN." The crests sold reasonably well and inspired other radical publishers to do the same.

While still a prisoner, Carlile's personal life underwent a profound change. According to his version of events, which seems basically reliable, he and Jane Carlile had decided to separate in 1830.[7] In the absence of a financial agreement, they remained together at the outset of his imprisonment, with his family residing in a portion of the Fleet Street residence. However, the arrival of Elizabeth Sharples in January 1832 peremptorily ended this arrangement. She rapidly supplanted Jane in Carlile's eyes and, within a few months, became his "moral companion" and mistress.

Eliza came from a middle-class Bolton home. By rushing off to London to join a movement of radical freethinkers, she cut her ties to her family, and when she reached Fleet Street in the winter of 1831-1832, she was alone and penniless. Almost immediately she began to pay daily visits to Carlile in prison. Transformed into "Isis," she discoursed regularly at the Rotunda: an ineffectual speaker but, for a brief period, an admired cult figure. She expressed intense pleasure that "I who, six months ago, was absolutely without prospect, without purpose in life, should now be waving the magic wand of intellect over the darkness of this land, this real Egyptian darkness . . . and be successfully introducing new love, new light, new life into this people."[8] Eliza's affection for Carlile quickened under these circumstances, and in a letter written shortly after her arrival in London, she described him as "the first of those who are eminent in the world as teachers of truth and nature." She referred to his room in the Compter as the source of "more mental light, more sound moral and political knowledge, and theological knowledge, if it be asked for, than any other place of this earth." During the early months of 1832, she spent part of every day with him in prison, familiarizing herself with his moral allegory, preparing her Rotunda discourses, and planning a new life.[9] In March, she took over supervision of the Rotunda and of his publishing business, though it was evident that she lacked Jane Carlile's business acumen. And, from the spring of 1832 on, she and Carlile began to make physical love in the Compter.

This interlude in the life of a working-class infidel who continued openly to espouse "respectable" values was of considerable political significance. Eliza was warm-hearted and gregarious, a woman who gave body and soul to the man who had lifted her out of obscurity. She wrote impassioned love letters to him, which reflected her yearnings for personal affection and, in political terms, for the emancipation of her sex. "I never wish to leave you," she told Carlile in the spring of 1833, "and hope always to be near you, never to part until we are divided by death." She observed tenderly: "Heaven bless you, my love, anchor of my affection, and my hope, solace, and comfort of my life, inferior to none and without an equal." She credited him with helping her to develop as a woman and implored him to acknowledge her as his "wife" rather than as a "hole and corner" mistress. Less charitably from his point of view, she insisted that he try to speed up the date of his release from the Compter by paying the required fine and recognizances, acknowledging at the same time that "you will think me very weak, very unlike a Philosopher." "Is not sensibility, *too acutely felt*, a curse to human nature," she observed, "given us, for no other purpose, than to torture and distract us."[10]

Carlile, publicly brave on so many issues, would not accede to her request. He felt affection for Eliza (though not, almost certainly, of the same intensity that she felt for him), but his responses were limp and hectoring. Privately he accepted her as his "wife," assuring her that "in every respect I shall treat you as if there were no other Mrs. Carlile and as if you were my lawful as well as my good wife."[11] Yet he enjoined secrecy upon her, for fear that vicious rumors would begin to circulate about them and that his political position would be undermined.

In February 1832, one month after Eliza's arrival in London, he and Jane Carlile carried out the form of a "moral divorce." He agreed to make a £50 annuity available to his wife and sons and to give them the furniture in 62 Fleet Street, on condition that they move out of the house. He also transferred a portion of his printed stock to them in order that they would be able to start a bookselling business of their own. But Henry Hetherington and other reformers hostile to Carlile accused him of unceremoniously bundling his family out of their rightful home to accommodate the lustful demands of his mistress.[12] When Jane and the boys opened a small bookshop in Bride Lane in March 1832, they did so with the backing of Hetherington and other reformers, who were out to damage Carlile. It was a hurtful situation, alleviated only by the failure of Jane's business and her subsequent withdrawal from the public limelight.[13]

Central to these events, though never alluded to publicly, was Eliza's pregnancy. As an advocate of birth control who privately abjured both mistress and wife not to make use of the sponge because it was insufficiently respectable, Carlile should have anticipated this development. But when it did happen, it greatly complicated matters for him. As soon as Eliza's condition became known in the autumn of 1832, she was refused permission to visit him in the Compter, and although he tried unsuccessfully to persuade the gaoler to reverse this decision—sending obliquely phrased letters to the lord mayor of London and other dignitaries— he was less perturbed than Eliza.[14] Above all, he feared public exposure, which would be a humiliating setback to his professed qualities as a temperate, moral, "respectable" reformer. He counseled Eliza to obey the dictates of "philosophical love" and to have her baby quietly—and alone. "I cannot degrade myself so far as . . . to be food for the sport of my enemies," he wrote in an admonitory tone that resembled some of his earlier missives to Jane Carlile.[15] Eliza's expostulations were painful. She asked Carlile: "Will you have your Isis, a wild, romantic, loving, kind, affec- tionate creature, sometimes erring, sometimes weak, and making you a little angry at times, hoping, fearing, sincere, *faithful, unchangeable*, warm hearted, kind, generous, thoughtless but grateful, thankful for your kindness and sensible of your worth: Say, will you have me a woman? Or will you have me a Philos- opher?" She entreated him to try to get permission for her to have her baby in the Compter: "I wish I could kiss [your] hand, and press it to my bosom: it would make me so happy."

Eliza missed her family and friends, and, for the first time, was confronted with the eviscerating effects of poverty. "What has been gained by reducing me, to so much misery," she chided Carlile, "and, at a time too, when I require soothing, encouraging, and comforting." The birth of Richard Sharples, in April 1833, produced in her a state of depression that lasted for several weeks. "I cannot bear going out at all, I seem not to care for anything but your society, and if I have not that, I want nothing else. I want nothing else, and care for nothing else, and shall enjoy nothing else," she wrote.[16] Yet, during these months, Carlile maintained his aloof, "proper" disposition, refusing to provide the warmth and affection that Eliza craved.

The effects of Carlile's "moral marriage" to Eliza Sharples were to reverberate politically around the edges of his career for the remainder of his life. Unable to stem a malicious whispering campaign that began to take form while she was still pregnant, he decided to make a show of necessity by acknowledging their relationship openly. Accordingly, in September 1833, a little over a month after his release from the Compter, he published a statement in the *Gauntlet* (without referring to their child) in which he characterized his "moral marriage" as "one of the best, if not the very best marriage in the country." He told his readers, many of whom already knew of his changed domestic situation: "I am a radical reformer, and I have begun to reform at home in this matter. I have been unhappy, and without a home, under one marriage. I am now happy, and with a home, under another marriage."[17] Subsequently he described his relationship with Eliza as based on "the divine law of love and affectionate attachment."

Eliza's own acknowledgment of their union was more touching. In May 1834, she wrote a preface for an indexed edition of the *Isis* and signed it "Eliza Sharples Carlile." In a simple statement she affirmed that "nothing could have been more pure or moral, more free from venality [than our marriage]. . . . It was not only a marriage of two bodies but a marriage of two congenial principles, each seeking an object on which virtuous affection might rest, and grow, and strengthen." Conceding that their union lacked a legal basis, she insisted nonetheless that it was all the more binding and virtuous for being "of the soul." She appealed to the feelings of "charitable beings" to protect her from disagreeable comments: "I have intended well, and I am satisfied, conscientiously satisfied, that, whatever I have publicly done, has been well and usefully done, and will not license complaint until some Englishwoman does better."[18]

"Complaints," there were, unfortunately, a cascade of them, which emanated alike from reforming and conservative circles. One radical journal characterized their relationship as an "Immoral Marriage," while another, edited by a former vendor of Carlile, depicted Eliza as his "New Moral Mistress" and as "no better than a prostitute." Wherever Carlile and Eliza went, they were confronted by ribald allusions to their "marriage." In the *Poor Man's Guardian*, Hetherington referred to Carlile's "moral delinquency" (implicit in the reference was his authorship of *Every Woman's Book*) and, more woundingly, Taylor (with whom he had broken all ties) accused him of "taking other men's wives, and attempting to justify the doing so by new-fangled systems of the force of circumstances."[19] The political tragedy of this "moral marriage"—

with its exposure of a system that allowed little scope for sexual aberration and made divorce impossible for a poor man before 1857—is that Carlile had to expend so much time in justifying (his own phrase) "a private matter." It was enough to make a man more charitably disposed toward his fellow human beings than he was want to strike back in any way that he could.

Carlile's release from the Compter took place in August 1833, and once again Francis Place, whom he no longer saw regularly, was instrumental in bringing it about. Place had written to him in the previous year: "I dare not tell you the particulars I should like to tell you, because you either are too honest or too indiscreet to hold your tongue, or even to refrain from printing on such occasions, but I think there is a chance, a good one that you may be released."[20] But as on other occasions, Carlile refused to accommodate Place or any other reformer who sought to help him. As much as he wanted his freedom, he would not take the requisite steps toward achieving it by paying a fine or the recognizances demanded for his good behavior. Such a compromise with a detested legal system was unacceptable to him. "I will not yield up my mind to the power of greater ignorance," he told readers of the *Gauntlet*. Thus, while rumors of his impending release circulated during 1832 and in the early months of 1833, the two prescribed years of imprisonment stretched into thirty months. Finally, without any undertakings being given (as in 1825), the gates of the Compter swung open for Carlile, and he was at liberty to reweave the threads of his political and journalistic career.

Freedom produced as many short-term problems as it resolved. Notwithstanding the success of the *Gauntlet* and the excitement nurtured by the enrollment campaign, his following had been further eroded in the past two years. His "moral marriage," soon to be acknowledged publicly, lost him supporters, and the pot of infidel doctrine, on which his reputation as a radical reformer ultimately rested, had not been stirred to any appreciable extent since the "Isis" discourses in the early months of 1832. He tried, therefore, to bestir himself politically: to revive his morale and his economic fortunes. He reissued several stamped almanacs that had been withdrawn from circulation to forestall a government prosecution and announced plans to establish a London "church" for the "worship of the true christ," an institution that was intended to enable him to disseminate his allegorical theories more widely.

But he badly needed a regular lecture room and had not the money to lease one.

He attempted to regroup his London following. A meeting was convened at the Rotunda (which was hired for a single night), and before a crowd estimated at 2000, he scornfully denounced political reform, advocating in its place an amalgam of theological and educational changes. He felt uncomfortable in such a setting, however, and his speech was poorly delivered. The only saving note of the evening was an unexpected appearance by Taylor, who had been released from Horsemonger-Lane Gaol in July, after having given a bond for his good behavior, and who was then lecturing in the vicinity of Tottenham Court Road. Though the two men had not communicated with each other for nearly a year, Hibbert patched things together between them temporarily so as to present a facade of infidel unity to the public.[21]

London offered few compensations to Carlile in the months after his release. Funds were not easy to come by, and he was almost entirely dependent for support on the goodwill of a small number of loyal associates. Lacking regular lecturing premises, he decided to visit the provinces once more. This would enable him to establish infidel "chapels" and schools and to expand his publishing business. On the questionable assumption that many anti-excise volunteers still remained loyal to him, he published an address urging them to support his "moral allegory." He then attended several political meetings and, in September 1833, left London, accompanied by Eliza and their infant son. As on previous occasions, he was prepared to do intellectual battle with the devils of orthodoxy, in whatever guise they presented themselves to him.[22] He was willing to visit any reformers who agreed to help him with expenses and lodgings. Meeting rooms were less of a problem than they had been in 1829, when he toured with Taylor, because although restrictions might be placed in his way, he was ready to speak to audiences in any venue except public houses. His only proviso was that these audiences be restrained in their demeanor and attentive to his themes.

When Carlile left London he was considerably more messianic by temperament and conviction than he had been four years before. He was also embittered as a result of the ceaseless taunts directed at his "moral marriage." But in Bristol and Birmingham, his first two stops, he took a low-keyed, noncontroversial approach. He had prepared three general lectures, two dealing with the subjects of politics and morality and a third containing a full exposition of his allegorical views. Only the first two lectures, drawing extensively on Paine and on his own essays in the *Moralist*, were delivered in these cities, although he alluded to theological reform before a receptive audience of artisans in Birmingham's radical Lawrence Street Chapel.[23]

The explosion was timed deliberately to go off in Sheffield, a city with a tradition of radicalism where he had a small following led by Thomas Turton, a grinder, and P. T. Bready, a tractseller who was employed as his local agent. Carlile delivered all three lectures in the Sheffield Theatre to audiences consisting primarily of workingmen. And in his third, "infidel" lecture, delivered on October 3, he broke new public ground. Well publicized in advance, this oration was the first occasion when he openly preached his "New Christianity." Hitherto, he had confined the exposition of his moral allegory, with its recently acquired Christian symbols, to journals like *Isis*. Now he attempted in the flesh to win reformers over to his views. He asserted that religion was nothing more than a physical expression of the mental conflict raging within the human mind and that "the *word of God* signifies the *word of knowledge*, the knowledge of the physical and the moral God, the astral of the starry heavens and the earth." More contentiously, he described himself as a "happy christian, a philosophizing christian, a primitive christian": phrases that affected his audience in ways ranging from muted approbation to vocal dissent. Carlile concluded his lecture by declaring himself to be a messiah of reason, come forth to lead Sheffield's faithful to the promised land of knowledge. "I have risen again to stand before you," he announced, "and to show you the way to human redemption."[24]

Even from his own blinkered perspective, the reception was mixed. Several residents of the city asserted that the mental health of the lecturer had been demonstrated to be in imminent peril, while a group of clergymen organized prayer sessions to consider the disintegrating condition of his soul.[25] Nor did he win many new recruits to his cause. As Thomas Turton mournfully reported, his doctrines were too esoteric to gain wide acceptance. Still, if controversy and recognition were what Carlile pined for (and to a considerable extent this is what his career was about), he was successful. His message had been heard.

Acrimony trailed him as he left Sheffield and traveled to Barnsley where, according to a hostile observer, he refused to reply to the anti-infidel importunings of a local weaver.[26] After stopping at Huddersfield, a city where for many years he had commanded sizable support from groups of weavers, he went to Manchester, the place he knew best after London. In the 1830s, Manchester's textile districts were spawning all kinds of radical and millennial movements—reading groups, "scientific" clubs, political unions—and many of the artisans and mechanics who participated in these activities and who helped to define the cultural and political enthusiasms of the city were former or present supporters of Carlile.

The times, however, were beginning to pass him by. From the mid-1820s he had lost ground steadily to political reformers and social cooperators. He no longer appeared to have a "realistic" message to drive home; even the apocalyptic tone of his pronouncements fell, seemingly, on stony ground. There were too many alternative agitations on parade, including simple atheism of the kind he had once championed. In Manchester, Carlile delivered many lectures on religion and politics in Newhall's Room, which he hired for the duration of his stay of several months, but those who attended were not demonstrably sympathetic to his doctrines. The same was true in the city's hinterlands.[27] In Ashton-under-Lyne, a seedbed of religious unorthodoxy, large crowds turned out to hear him. But they were unreceptive to his Christian imagery and, notwithstanding a lengthy debate with local Wesleyans, he failed to win more than a few auditors over to his point of view.[28] Neither in Lancashire nor Cheshire did Carlile light anything that can be characterized as a political brush fire.

The only mildly encouraging event of this journey took place in October 1833 in Manchester, when he propounded the "truth of the gospel" before a "grand" convocation of "respectable" reformers. The response was warmer than it had been in Sheffield and Huddersfield and, just briefly, the future began to seem a little brighter. Then personal tragedy struck. Richard Sharples—the "child of united philosophy and love, the offspring of the sweetest of humane affections, of a marriage that was reason and reasonable, and therefore moral"—died suddenly of smallpox.[29] It was a lacerating event made harder for Carlile to bear by the charges and countercharges that continued to swirl about his "moral marriage." He and Eliza were to have three more children in the following years, but the death of their firstborn, who personified the strength of their union in its precarious early days, could not be endured easily, even by somebody as emotionally resilient as Carlile.

With his tour brought to a sudden end, he returned to London in a dejected mood. But as if to drown his misfortunes in an ocean of activity, he attended several political meetings and, in December, set off for Somerset, where for a fortnight he engaged in tumultuous debates and lectures. Bath was his base: an elegant Georgian city where the "Comforter" (as he now styled himself) could disseminate "the Gospel of Principle" amid physically congenial surroundings. Yet, even in Bath audiences taunted him for his "moral marriage" and his support for birth control. One speaker publicly burned a copy of *Every Woman's Book*, after describing it as "one of the vilest, most immoral, lewd and base publications that ever proceeded from the pen of man." In Bristol, "drunken religiosos" (Wesleyans) disrupted him when he attempted to propound his Christian allegory.[30]

Somerset was, clearly, unfavorable terrain for the kind of agitation that Carlile was attempting to stir up. He insisted that he had "set the brain of Bath a spinning of mysteries, and to an unravelling of their difficulties," and that his speeches offered an analysis of religion so bold and attractive as to prove irresistible. But, as was becoming evident, the reverse was true: the more he attempted to explicate his idiosyncratic blend of allegorical rationalism and Christian imagery to reformers, the less these ideas seemed to be blueprints for a better society.

A brief trip to the West Country in January and February 1834 provided confirmation of this depressing prognosis. To Plymouth, his first stop, he came bearing tidings about his intentions to lead the heathens to "a state of unity, amity, and peace, upon the very threshold of that earthly temple of the Lord which is called Christianity." He had, he averred, worked out "the great moral of the Christian Religion, which is resistance to evil." "I preach Christ and Christ crucified, and the surety of resurrection, and the glory of the ascension into heaven, under the mortality of the body and the immortality of the soul," he told a small group of Plymouth workmen.[31] He was a "prophet" able to dispense grace: "With the apostles I can say, that I have not wrestled against flesh and blood, but against principalities, against powers, against the rulers of the darkness of this world, against spiritual wickedness in high places. I am sure that I have the mystery of the Gospel revealed in me and I will go forth with its armour, and extend the revelation."[32] Yet how fallow was the ground! Little but contumely greeted him in Plymouth and in nearby Stonehouse and Devonport, where he came under attack from the local press. Returning to London a fortnight later, he was shaken by the fruitless sacrifices he had undertaken in pursuit of his goals. "Mine is an arduous task," he observed, "unsupported by others."[33] But like other reformers who are driven to increased effort by adversity, he was sustained by the inner assurance that posterity would confer just rewards on him and that he and those who believed in his cause would triumph eventually.

During the later months of 1833, the circulation of the *Gauntlet* declined sharply. Carlile, away from London for long stretches of time, was unable to maintain a tight control over the paper. The result was a journal of diminishing tautness and quality. However, the space given over to theological controversy increased, in proportion to his determination to reveal "the true principles of catholicity in the Christian religion." The essential point, he insisted, was that "true" Christianity must not be confused with the corrupt, debilitated product that had passed muster for 2000 years. His allegory was a redemptive message of reform: it was 'the poor man's gospel; the true peace on earth and good will among men." As he wrote in the *Gauntlet*: "Let God be worshipped as a fountain of knowledge—let the acquisition of knowledge be considered the only approach to God—let the church be a school—let every individual of every age be a scholar in that church—let that be done, and everything done beyond that in the Church will be trash and nonsense and waste of time."[34] It was taking a depressingly long time for his message to get across, but of its validity he had no reason to doubt.

In December, he commenced the *Political Soldier*, a journal that, because of its subject matter, is of uncommon interest. Subtitled *A Paper for the Army and the People*, the *Political Soldier* was a one-and-a-half-penny unstamped weekly whose aim was to inculcate a "rational sense of citizenship" among the soldiers. It printed accounts of wrongdoing in the army as reported by correspondents, in the same way that investigative factory journals of the early nineteenth century trained their resources on abuses in textile mills. The *Political Soldier* attacked "corruption" and immorality in the army and demanded an end to flogging and other forms of "military torture." Privately, Carlile regarded volunteer soldiers as "animal ferocity humanized."[35] But (in collaboration with Alexander Somerville who resigned as editor of the *Political Soldier* after the first number in protest at Carlile's "dictation"), he turned his attention to this subject to put to the test his belief that "good principles never die—are never defeated—will make their way among mankind in this era of printing, of criticism, and of discussion."[36] The demise of the *Political Soldier* after five numbers, because of a lack of readers, merely confirmed him in the view that religious issues had to take priority over all else if meaningful changes were to be carried out.

During 1834, Carlile's political path became increasingly strewn with obstacles. In February, he delivered a series of lectures on the "Sacred Scriptures" to members of the Westminster Rational School and General Scientific Institution, one of many groups of artisan reformers that met regularly in London at the time. His audiences were small, and his physical stamina, stretched to its limits for several years, began to show signs of wear. The novelty, too, of his Christian imagery was beginning to recede. Only about forty workingmen attended several Sunday morning sermons that he preached on Theobald's Road in the spring, whereas Taylor, discoursing in the same building under the pseudonym "Talasiphron" and with the aid of an "orchestra" and chorus, easily quadrupled that number.[37] Carlile continued unsuccessfully to search for a permanent lecture hall like the Rotunda where he would be able to "smite the Philistines of Constantine's Church, in all its ramified dissent." Under attack from some trade unionists whom he accused of having burned a copy of the *Gauntlet*, he resorted increasingly to apocalyptic imagery, as a way, perhaps, of transcending his personal despair. "We have reached the zenith of the hill of corruption," he told readers of the *Gauntlet* in one of that journal's last numbers, "and have now only to walk down into the plains of Paradise."[38]

After publishing two numbers of the *London Star*, a projected replacement for the *Gauntlet*, in April, Carlile left London on yet another extended journey to the provinces.[39] This time, accompanied by Eliza, he stayed away for almost six months. He visited East Anglia for the first time, northeastern England, the "heathen" outposts of Edinburgh and Glasgow, and familiar towns and villages in Lancashire and Yorkshire. But little support materialized. In Norwich, his first stop, he distributed a broadsheet in which he described himself as "invincible in Argument, exalted in Sentiment, and feared, envied, and persecuted by his natural enemies, viz. the Patrons of Political and Religious Frauds." Few workmen paid attention (it was a city with a reforming tradition but one influenced strongly by dissenting clergymen) and Carlile's only "victory" was a spirited debate with the Reverend Thomas Scott, an Anglican cleric who characterized him publicly as "one of the most foolish men the world has in it."[40] Bigger Christian game in the person of the Quaker reformer, John Joseph Gurney, eluded him, as did even a polite acknowledgment of his presence from many of Norwich's leading reformers.

Travelling to the northeast, he stopped briefly at Beverly and York, two puissant symbols of orthodox Christianity. Then, in May, he addressed a "very numerous assemblage" in Hull on behalf of James Acland, a quarrelsome local reformer who had recently completed a prison term of several months after a dispute with the Town Corporation.[41] Acland was a muckraking journalist—a breed of writer just beginning to emerge in the 1830s—who publicized parochial and borough grievances and, in so doing, laid himself open to numerous libel prosecutions. He lacked influential support among reformers, however, and Carlile could have had little reason to identify himself with Acland other than as a means of attracting an audience. Hull's municipal politics, to be sure, fell considerably outside the scope of his interests.

The remainder of the tour is shrouded in obscurity because Carlile did not elicit much newspaper coverage and because between March 1834, when the *Gauntlet* ceased to appear, and November, when *A Scourge for the Littleness of "Great" Men* commenced publication, he published no journal of his own. Almost certainly, he spent about six weeks in Newcastle, a city that he waspishly characterized as "the foul sepulchre of the Tyne." He delivered lectures in the Music Hall there but did not infuse his speeches with relevant political content and was, increasingly, forced to do much of his speechmaking on the open moors outside the city's boundaries, where he lectured free of charge to anyone who would listen.[42] Eliza's presence at his side evoked scurrilous references both to their "moral marriage" and to his advocacy of birth control. The *Newcastle Press*, a paper that supported some reform causes, referred to him as a "hoary lecher . . . [who] should be whipped and scourged out of the town."[43]

Mostly—when he was not being barracked—Carlile preached the "true doctrine of Christ as God." He contended that "Israel" was not a temporal place but "the intelligent and philosophical portion of the human race, pervading all nations, and belonging to no one more than to any other one." By means of scriptural and etymological references (the latter mostly drawn from Taylor's writings) he persevered in his view that the recurring Christ symbol was "a type of eternal principle, bodied forth from time to time in a variety of natures." The messiah, he maintained, was not to be construed as a literal entity; rather, and this was the gravamen of all his pronouncements, it was a spiritual deliverance from ignorance and moral evil, potentially resident in all human beings. "That which is to come is to be the reign of reason in the human mind," he stated, "after the overthrow of idolatry and superstition, religious dissent and sectarian churches."[44]

In specific terms there was little to show for his presence in Newcastle because the artisans and workmen who attended his meetings were much less interested in the "New Christianity" than they were in universal suffrage, factory reform, and the other political issues then being debated earnestly in radical circles. (Many of these reformers subsequently became active chartists and social cooperators.) Carlile also erred tactically when he quarreled with leading reformers, including Eneas Mackenzie, a printer and bookseller, and Charles Larkin, the editor of the *Newcastle Press*, whom he accused of "dishonesty and bad moral character." Larkin, a Roman Catholic, set his paper against Carlile, declaring him to be "the lowest, basest, most degraded, most infamous, most nefarious man alive," and trying to incite other reformers to think likewise.[45]

Such an atmosphere was not a felicitous one in which to disseminate freethought ideas, but Scotland (insofar as his movements can be pieced together) proved to be even more fallow terrain. Carlile spoke in Edinburgh, where in the 1820s he had commanded backing from zetetic tradesmen and artisans, and in Glasgow, a city whose squalid housing and poor sanitary conditions shocked him. "We saw [in Glasgow]," he wrote, "a state of human life than which nothing can be imagined lower."[46] A comment like this—reminiscent of his initial reactions to Liverpool in 1827—had its roots in feelings of revulsion for the new industrial system and, as well, in a contempt that he harbored for the "nonrespectable" poor. The latter were ineducable, he believed: some were "common criminals"; others moved trancelike in pursuit of the mirage of political upheaval; while still others (probably the majority) were indifferent to the dreadful conditions in which they lived. If Carlile was ever to forge a popular movement, he would need to win many of these workingmen over to his side. But there is little indication that he understood this, even on those few occasions when he made the attempt.

In October 1834, after delivering a series of lectures in the textile districts of the West Riding and south Lancashire, Carlile returned to London in a disheartened mood.[47] He then began to publish *A Scourge for the Littleness of "Great" Men*, a one-penny weekly journal, which survived until March 1835. The caustic comments in this paper reflected his frustration at his recent lack of political success and showed the extent to which his relationship with reformers in London and the provinces had deteriorated. For several years Carlile had attacked all forms of political association; such "impractical knowledge," he maintained, distracted reformers from the important objective of "power in knowledge." Now he began increasingly to vent his hostility toward trade unions because of their "nonsense of secret initiation and binding oaths." He printed exposés of trade union ceremonies in the *Gauntlet*, and accused the *Poor Man's Guardian*, which supported trade unions, of recommending "a common scramble for all existing property, and aiming to pull down everything to the level of his own character."[48]

Under attack from the *Poor Man's Guardian*, the *Pioneer*, the *Man*, and other radical papers for his attacks on political and trade unions and for his "apostasy" to the cause of infidelity, Carlile resorted to vituperation in the columns of *A Scourge for the Littleness of "Great" Men*.[49] He portrayed Henry Hetherington as a "poor, vain, contemptible, and talentless fool," while James Watson, with whom he had retained cordial relations until recently despite political disagreements, was depicted as "a viper, who has neither honour nor honourable memory, who can insult and rob the first and chief benefactor that he has had to put him in motion in his present business."[50] His choicest adjectives were, however, reserved for Taylor, with whom his relations had been terminated in the summer of 1833. Replying to Taylor's scarifying comments on his "moral marriage," Carlile claimed that his former comrade had given himself up to intemperateness and immorality. In September 1834, the two men were involved in an unseemly public fracas that led to assault charges being filed against Carlile by Taylor and to Carlile's admission in court that he had inflicted a "stamp mark of an honestly indignant resentment . . . upon an ungrateful villain's head."[51] It was a shabby ending to what had been for several years a constructive, dynamic partnership—uniquely so in the history of early nineteenth-century popular freethought.

Julian Hibbert's sudden death in January 1834 was a further blow to Carlile because it deprived him of the one close associate who could serve as a bridge to the working-class political community. (Upon hearing of Hibbert's death, Carlile described him as "the best specimen of human nature that I have seen, read, heard or thought of.")[52] Likewise, the death of Rowland Detrosier in the same year was damaging. Detrosier was the deist lecturer who had opened a Stockport church to him in 1827. In the intervening years he had become a brilliant interpreter of scientific and political subjects to working-class audiences, especially in Manchester where he founded the Mechanics' Institution. Carlile admired his talents—while disapproving of his theist views—and when Detrosier contracted an illness in the autumn of 1834, he lectured in his place on phrenology and allegorical Christianity at the Hall of Science, Islington, with the proceeds being given to Detrosier's wife and children. When Detrosier died in December, Carlile arranged to have his brain dissected, in emulation of the recent examples of Jeremy Bentham and Hibbert and prefiguring the contribution of his own brain to medical science.[53]

Carlile's knowledge of the inside of prisons, based on almost ten years of firsthand experience, was increased by an additional four months in the winter of 1834-35, as the result of an incident that once more confirmed his reputation as a determined battler for lost causes. The dispute involved the payment of church rates, a popular radical grievance during the early nineteenth century but one that had not been of much interest to Carlile since the 1820s. But he prided himself on a belief in freedom and principle, and when, in the spring of 1831, a church rate was assessed in the parish of Saint Dunstan's in the West (where his shop was located), he joined local householders in opposing it.[54] More than two years passed before Carlile and his associates were summoned to show cause why they should not pay the imposed rates. He refused at that time to make even a nominal payment of £4. He would, he stated, pay rates only to a "reformed" parish church, by which he meant one whose theology was based on his moral allegory.[55] Another summons was issued, and when Carlile again refused payment (several householders broke ranks at this time and paid the required sum), two seizures of his property followed: one, in January 1834, involving a confiscation of two gold watches and leading to the brief imprisonment of his shopman, and a second, in October 1834, involving the sequestration of 1200 almanacs and other printed stock.[56]

It was at the time of this second seizure that Carlile summoned up reserves of obstinacy. Claiming that his appropriated stock was irreplaceable, he fought back with all of his accustomed vigor. In his shop windows he installed two effigies linked arm in arm: one of a bishop, or "spiritual broker"; the other of a devil, or "temporal broker." The point was to illustrate the link between "Christian superstition" and "Devil worship." Boldly lettered placards were displayed in the shop windows, explaining the reasons for his "moral resistance" to the payment of church rates and calling upon all reformers in London to join him.[57] Inquisitive onlookers and politically conscious workmen began to gather around his Fleet Street shop to gaze at the effigies, and, as in his younger days, Carlile again began to pose as a symbol of private conscience in defiance of the myrmidons of church and state. As a result of this upsurge of publicity, the sale of his tracts increased considerably.

Punishment for such audacity could not long be evaded. In December 1834, a warrant was issued for his arrest as a "public nuisance," and he was brought to trial at the Old Bailey. He was exuberant and unrepentant. Coyly admitting to having been responsible for some "little annoyance to the neighbourhood," he maintained that his prosecution reflected official concern about the political dangers of having discontented crowds gather in the vicinity of Fleet Street. As if to confirm this reading of events, the prosecutor described him bluntly as "the lowest of the low." A relatively light penalty followed the inevitable verdict of guilty: a nominal fine of £2 together with sureties of £200 for good behavior for three years.[58] But in circumstances that required more than the usual quota of courage considering his deteriorating health and meager finances, Carlile refused to compromise. He would not consider paying the fine or the sureties; instead he opted for the Giltspur Street Compter, observing that he would rather "be mentally free in prison then mentally shackled out of prison." As he told readers of *A Scourge for the Littleness of "Great" Men:* "I am almost the creature of a prison, and really do not feel it to be a punishment."[59]

Carlile's return to the very same room in the Compter that he had occupied from 1831 to 1833 was a symbolic reminder of his continuing war with authority, which in varying forms he was to carry on to the end of his life. While in prison, he conjured up grandiose schemes, as in a tract that he wrote in January 1835 entitled *Church Reform.* In it he restated his belief that Christianity was based on both a human and a solar drama, that "man approaches and lives with God, as his mind expands in the accumulation of knowledge," and that Jesus is "a personification of the principle of reason, or of the knowledge of which the human being is a recipient, and without which he may have no salvation, has no relation to the idea of salvation, or any evil from which to be saved." He also explicated, for the first time, an interpretation of the doctrine of the trinity that was to become an integral facet of his "New Christianity." The "Father," Carlile maintained, represented existence; the "Son" stood for the "manifestation of knowledge and reason"; while the "Holy Ghost" was "the freedom of the human mind." He implored reformers to carry through a radical reform of religion within the present institutional forms of Christianity and incorporating this and other of his interpretations. "If I have been the chief of Infidels," he wrote in *Church Reform,* "I will atone for it in becoming the chief defender of revelation, and the faith, as it is in Jesus Christ, and not as it is in any Dissenting Church."[60]

Specifically, Carlile proposed that parish churches be converted into public schools, where the "mental birth and membership of Christ" would be taught and provision made for "the infirm and accidentally poor." Such a reformed church would, he believed, minister to "the physical and moral necessities of the people." He had alluded briefly to this theme in an unpublished letter to the bishop of London in November 1833, in which he described his proposed "christian church" as "a school for the people." But in *Church Reform* and other tracts that date from the mid-1830s, he became more insistent; he abjured the Tory prime minister, Sir Robert Peel, to restore tithes to their original "secular" purposes and to appropriate additional public money to the support of parish churches.

"Parish reform" was a subject that aroused as much controversy as any of Carlile's other proposals. He seemed to be standing conventional freethought on its head and to be taking up Christianity all over again. Was he, as some of his critics maintained, attempting to soften the debilitating effects of prison by coming to terms with its persecuting ideology? Were these proposals merely a linguistic compromise, as would seem to be indicated in a letter Carlile sent to Robert Owen in 1830, in which he wrote: "If we can then best lead that multitude from bad to better principles by such a hold on their noses, why should we withhold it? My judgment says—associate better principles with cherished names, particularly when etymology presents the warrant. Quarrel not with words."[61]

Neither interpretation does full justice to the Carlile of the second half of the 1830s, who seemed at times to be almost desperately in search of a cosmic interpretation of religion. Although he made use of some of the imagery and institutional forms of Christianity (as in his doctrine of the trinity and plea for "parish reform"), he never abandoned his belief in infidelity, as that word was employed in its nineteenth-century sense. The same kinds of radical changes that Carlile favored in the earlier years of his life—anticlerical and atheistic—he continued, albeit in a much modified way, to champion. His comments always favored a rough-hewn kind of political and economic justice and the destruction of religion in its traditional form. No explanation of Carlile that interprets his shifts as those of a compromiser or as part of a deliberate political strategy will suffice, for he was not a calculator. He was a complex, obdurate, impassioned man, driven by an inner conviction that the world could be made a better place in which to live if equality and social justice were achieved. His lengthy prison terms and failure to create a permanent infidel movement pushed him at times across a symbolic divide. But he never wavered in his commitment to radical reform.

Notes

1. *Isis*, 14 July 1832. See also *Cosmopolite*, 26 January 1833, where he describes his business as a "wreck."

2. *Gauntlet*, 24 February 1833. Previously he had characterized British policy in Ireland as intended "to train their dogs to war, to whet the appetite of their military hounds for blood, and to make it a common slaughter-house." *Prompter*, 15 October 1831.

3. *Gauntlet*, 26 February 1833. On the incident itself, see the hostile account by Gavin Thurston, *The Clerkenwell Riot: The Killing of Constable Culley* (London: George Allen & Unwin, 1967).

4. *Gauntlet*, 31 March, 7 April 1833.

5. This quote is from a letter in ibid., 5 May 1833.

6. Carlile sold his edition of Macerone's *Defence of Householders* at five shillings, but his son Thomas Paine published a four-penny abridged edition in 1839.

7. *Scourge for the Littleness of "Great" Men*, 18 October 1834; Carlile to the Lord Mayor of London, 11 March 1833, C.P.

8. *Isis*, 10 March 1832.

9. An informer claimed that Taylor helped Eliza to prepare her discourses, but this seems improbable. S.S. report, 12 March 1832, H.O. 64/12.

10. These quotes are taken from undated letters by Eliza in the C.P.

11. Carlile to Eliza Sharples, n.d., C.P.

12. *Poor Man's Guardian*, 1 November 1834.

13. The final advertisement for the business appeared in the *Poor Man's Guardian* in March 1833, but a year later Richard Carlile, Jr., had a shop at the same address.

14. See Carlile to the Lord Mayor, 26, 28 March 1833, C.P.

15. Carlile to Eliza Sharples, n.d., C.P.

16. Undated letters by Eliza Sharples in C.P.

17. *Gauntlet*, 22 September 1833. He described his relationship with Eliza as "pure in spirit." Carlile, *Letter to Charles Larkin*, p. 2.

18. *Isis*, preface, pp. v-vi.

19. The phrase "New Moral Mistress" is by Edward Hancock in *A Public Letter to the Noted Richard Carlile* (London: Edward Hancock, 1836), p. 14. For Taylor's comment, see *True Sun*, 1 October 1834. There are many unfavorable allusions in the radical press to Carlile's relationship with Eliza, as, for example, *Poor Man's Guardian*, 1, 15 November, 6, 27

December 1834. Interestingly, the *Man* attacked him on the basis that all "marriages," including his own, were irrational. *Man*, 8 September 1833.

20. Place to Carlile, 2 February 1832, C.P. Place asked a radical MP, Henry Warburton, to see Lord Melbourne, the Home Secretary, and to "do what you can." Place to Warburton, 22 February 1832, Add. Ms. 35,149, f. 22, Place Papers.

21. An account of the meeting is in the *Gauntlet*, 1 September 1833; *Cosmopolite*, 31 August 1833. In attempting to mediate, Hibbert wrote to Carlile: "As a friend of both parties, I must imagine that you are *both equally* to blame." Hibbert to Carlile, 17 August 1833, C.P.

22. He invited Taylor to accompany him, but the latter declined. Carlile to Thomas Turton, 19 September 1833, C.P.

23. See Richard Carlile, *The Substance of the Two First Lectures, Delivered in the Sheffield Theatre by Richard Carlile, on Politics and on Morals* (Sheffield: P. T. Bready, 1833). See also *Gauntlet*, 6, 13, 20 October 1833.

24. Richard Carlile, *A Full Report of the Third Lecture, Delivered in the Sheffield Theatre . . . on Religion* (Sheffield: P. T. Bready, 1833), pp. 8, 5, 9.

25. See, for example, *Sheffield Independent*, 5 October 1833.

26. *Leeds Mercury*, 26 October 1833.

27. There is an account of these lectures in the *Manchester and Salford Advertiser*, 19 October 1833. See also *Gauntlet*, 27 October 1933.

28. *Manchester and Salford Advertiser*, 29 October 1833.

29. Carlile announced the death in a black-bordered leader in the *Gauntlet*, entitled "Life, Death, Resurrection, and Ascension." 3 November 1833.

30. This tour was reported in the *Bath Herald*, 21, 28 December 1833, 4, 11 January 1834.

31. *Gauntlet*, 2 February 1834.

32. Richard Carlile, *The Respectful Address of Richard Carlile to the Inhabitants of Plymouth, Stonehouse and Devonport* (Devonport, 1834), p. 12.

33. *Gauntlet*, 9 February 1834.

34. Ibid., 29 December 1833, 5 January 1834.

35. *Political Soldier*, 21 December 1833.

36. Ibid., 4 January 1834. Somerville, who had been dismissed from the Scots Greys for circulating reform literature, told Carlile in his letter of resignation: "I must have the sole management of [the paper]; my will must be uncontrolled." Ibid., 14 December 1833. Carlile claimed that the dispute occurred because he would not pay Somerville a fixed salary.

37. S.S. report, 26 March 1834, H.O. 64/19. Taylor's "orchestra" consisted of four fiddlers and a French horn. For accounts of Taylor's

speeches, see *Philalethean* (by "Talasiphron"), 28 September 1833-18 January 1834.

38. *Gauntlet*, 16 March 1834.

39. I have been unable to locate any copies of the *London Star*, but there are references to it in Carlile's papers.

40. The *Substance of a Public Discussion, between Thomas Scott and Richard Carlile, after the Lecture on Theology, Delivered at the Free Mason's Arms, Norwich, April 23rd, 1834* (Norwich: Jarrold & Son, 1837), p. 12; Thomas Scott to Greeves, 10 December 1834, in *Scourge for the Littleness of "Great" Men*, 11 October 1834.

41. *Man*, 15 May 1834.

42. *Durham Chronicle*, 19 May 1840. See also *Carlile's Political Register* 30 November 1839; *Phoenix*, 26 February 1837.

43. *Newcastle Press*, 28 June 1834.

44. Carlile, *Respectful Address to the Inhabitants of Newcastle*, pp. 5, 6, 8, 16.

45. Carlile, *Letter to Charles Larkin*, p. 6; *Newcastle Press*, 28 June 1834. Larkin boasted: "The blow I struck was destructive. The man has never been heard of since." *Gateshead Observer*, 15 February 1840. Eneas Mackenzie, denying that he had been Carlile's agent, accused him of being "puerile and argumentative." *Newcastle Press*, 28 June 1834.

46. *Phoenix*, 26 February 1837. There is a reference to his visit to Edinburgh in his *Manual of Freemasonry* (1845 ed.), pt. II, p. xxii.

47. He was barred from several rooms in Bradford during the latter part of his journey. *Times*, 3 September 1834.

48. *Gauntlet*, 9, 30 March 1834; *Scourge for the Littleness of "Great" Men*, 8 November 1834. Given his views it is surprising that Carlile attended a meeting in July 1835 with Feargus O'Connor and Robert Owen to protest against the treatment of the six "Tolpuddle Martyrs." *True Sun*, 14 July 1835. I owe this reference to James Epstein.

49. The *Pioneer* accused him of being a "slanderer" and a "bigot" (7 September 1833) and of encouraging "marriages which are not legal" (17 May 1834); the *Man* attacked his "inexplicable" theories (29 September, 10 November 1833).

50. *Scourge for the Littleness of "Great" Men*, 22 November, 18 October 1834. Hetherington replied with bristling irony: "Towering Superiority! I shrink before the splendour of your stupendous intellect . . . of your surpassing penetration!" *Poor Man's Guardian*, 6 December 1834.

51. *Scourge for the Littleness of "Great" Men*, 4 October 1834. In a letter to Taylor in the same number, Carlile wrote: "If in any public assembly you play me these tricks of attacking any part of my career without consenting to hear my answer, when I am present, I will thrash you as I did at Westminster."

52. *Gauntlet*, 2 February 1834.

53. There are details of these lectures in *Scourge for the Littleness of "Great" Men*, 8 November, 13, 31 December 1834. See Richard Carlile, *Extraordinary Conversion and Public Declaration of Richard Carlile, of London, to Christianity* (Glasgow: H. Robinson, 1837), p. 15.

54. *Prompter*, 11 June 1831.

55. *Gauntlet*, 10 November 1833.

56. See the account in *Times*, 22 October 1834; *Carlile's Political Register*, 14 December 1839.

57. *Scourge for the Littleness of "Great" Men*, 25 October 1834; Carlile, *Church Reform*, pp. 88-89. George Julian Harney, the future chartist leader who was a vendor of unstamped periodicals at the time, stated that he placed the effigies in Carlile's shop window after the second seizure. *Notes and Queries*, 7. s. (IV), 8 October 1887.

58. Accounts of Carlile's prosecution are in *Scourge for the Littleness of "Great" Men*, 6 December 1834; *Times*, 22, 23, 24 October, 28, 29 November, 2, 18 December 1834.

59. *Scourge for the Littleness of "Great" Men*, 20, 27 December 1834.

60. Carlile, *Church Reform*, esp. pp. 89, 31-32, 75.

61. Carlile to Robert Owen, 13 June 1830, Robert Owen Papers, Co-operative Union Library.

11

THE NEW JERUSALEM

"I am not an atheist, not a blasphemer, not an infidel. I have not even a doubt of the goodness, genuineness, and catholicity of Christianity; and all that I am now labouring to show is other men's mistakes about it, so that we may put an end to religious controversy and all its baneful social effects. This I do, not by any religious conceits of my own, but by evidences tangible and triable by history and the sciences."[1] Carlile's words, voiced in September 1836, illustrate the path that he took in the late 1830s as he sought to turn the tide of popular radicalism away from chartism and cooperative socialism. These two forms of working-class protest gave expression to demands for political and economic democracy, and Carlile attempted to combat them by resorting to the language of Christian messianism. But the currents were running strongly against him; and he was forced to retreat ever more into an amorphous "millennium of the mind."

He by no means lacked energy for the struggle. If he was not any longer a "heroic" working-class agitator in the mold of Cobbett, Wooler, or Hunt, he was still a determined one. Between 1835 and 1839 he edited three journals, wrote and published several dozen tracts, spoke hundreds of times to groups of workers in London and the provinces, and, notwithstanding financial and health problems, maintained an involvement in the movement for radical reform that compared favorably with his earlier efforts. But he was not able to shape appreciably the contours of working-class radicalism. His followers were reduced in numbers and, increasingly, he was forced to engage in fruitless confrontations with reformers, while those whom he wanted to debate ignored him. At times, also, his allegorical discourses became so divorced from the political realities of the day as to make him seem almost a parody of his former self. He was not widely respected as a working-class leader nor, more damaging from his point of view, was he deemed worthy of denunciation by those who zealously tried to defend religion. In less than twenty years, events had turned nearly 180 degrees against him.

Shortly after his release from the Compter in February 1835, he reluctantly gave up *A Scourge for the Littleness of "Great" Men.* The Stamp Office had initiated a prosecution against him for publishing the journal without paying the required duty, and he lacked the resources to contest this action.[2] William Cunningham, to whom he owed a large sum of money, was unwilling to print the paper under these circumstances, and he could not find another contract printer to do the job. During the remainder of 1835, therefore, Carlile did not publish a journal and was unable to disseminate his views on a regular basis. At the same time other aspects of his publishing business languished. The small number of pamphlets that he issued were ineffectively distributed, Eliza having shown herself to be incompetent as a factotum publisher. And the refusal of other radical journalists to accept paid advertisements from him—including prominent working-class journalists such as Hetherington and Watson—compounded his difficulties.[3] Without adequate publicity it was impossible to sustain an interest in his ideas.

Carlile's desperate financial situation was at the root of most of his problems. Mounting debts led to a portion of his stock being assigned to the printing firm of Cunningham and Salmon, an action that he resisted in the courts for several years.[4] Except for the annuity from the Morrison bequest, which continued to be paid until his death, he was almost entirely dependent on private philanthropy, and there was precious little of this about. Hibbert's death had deprived him of his most loyal benefactor; other wealthy reformers who formerly had backed him now underwrote his chartist and socialist rivals, or, in the case of W. Devonshire Saull, supported infidelity but not the "peculiar" brand that Carlile was advocating. Carlile was reduced to hawking his dwindling stock of pamphlets and journals about the streets, an activity that, his supporters agreed, was as wounding to his dignity as it was irrelevant to the political problems of the day.

His health was also deteriorating. The asthmatic and rheumatic ailments that had affected him since his Dorchester days kept him in a state of constant pain. From the early 1820s he had imbibed crude mercury on a daily basis, a practice that he had endorsed politically in 1824 with the reprinting of Augustin Belloste's *An Essay on Mercury,* an eighteenth-century tract that was one of the first works to make the case for the corrective powers of mercury based on a need to "purify" the body. He now supplemented the intake of mercury with hot vapor baths and other home remedies. Self-treatment was an integral facet of working-class radical culture and a weapon in Carlile's political armory. It reinforced the individualistic quality of his radicalism while pinpointing the privileged nature of the medical profession, which he and many other reformers equated with corruption.[5]

His body did not respond to these treatments, however, and his illnesses frequently were accompanied by depression, of a type that alternated with "enthusiasms." Eliza could offer little solace at these times. Her bloom was beginning to fade for Carlile. He no longer saw her as a goddess of rationality; rather, somewhat pitilessly, he perceived her as a woman of limited ability who lacked the determination to pursue "serious" objectives. "I mark that she has no study in philosophical matters," he confided to his friend Thomas Turton, "and on that I think much depends."[6]

In spite of these problems, he lectured whenever and wherever he could during the spring and summer of 1835. He leased a small room near Temple Bar for this purpose and propounded his allegorical ideas on a weekly or semiweekly basis. He tried to persuade his audiences of the validity of his fundamental insight: that true reform was predicated on a "second birth" of mind. But he made little headway, his listeners consisting either of the "converted" who sought no additional illumination, or the recalcitrant who found his presence stimulating but were impervious to allegorical theories.

In an effort to refute the arguments of his critics, Carlile began to simplify his allegory, substituting starker imagery for cumbersome detail. He described Christ as "the principle of reason" and the Church of England as "a school . . . for revelation without mystery." Christianity, he contended, was a fusion of "the general drama of human morals [combined] with the annual tragedy of solar physics." More controversially, he sought to "prove" his interpretations by citing scriptural passages, particularly from the

Pauline epistles. This self-validating technique laid him open to the charge of having returned full cycle to the starting point of Christian prophecy.

Toward the end of 1835, at a time when he confessed himself to be "a wreck in purse and health," Carlile took a step that, double-edged in its effects, enabled him to shore up his strength for the battles that lay ahead.[7] He allowed the lease on his shop at 62 Fleet Street, which was due for renewal, to lapse, and in its place he leased a small cottage on Enfield Highway in a country district ten miles northeast of central London. This meant a severing of his direct ties with the metropolis. He had to transfer his publishing business to his son Alfred, who had recently opened a shop at 183 Fleet Street, and to give up his Temple Bar lecturing room.[8] But, as Carlile reluctantly concluded, he could no longer afford to spend most of the year in London, where the winters had become physically unendurable and where he lacked the solitude necessary for productive work.

Enfield gave him the opportunity to "retire altogether" into a quieter life and to lecture on an impromptu basis whenever there was a demand for his services. It was a difficult move for him psychologically—and in political terms damaging—because it reduced his contacts with London artisans and workingmen, who were a major artery of his support. But Enfield, as he had anticipated, allowed him time for reflection and study, and it eased somewhat the strain on his finances (he paid only £20 annually for the cottage.)[9] It also encouraged him to try once more to extend his influence into districts of the Midlands and the North, where he believed he stood a good chance to bring the working classes around to his side.

For several months Carlile reveled in the simple life offered by Enfield. He lavished attention on a small vegetable garden and walked daily in the countryside. By means of intensive reading he sharpened some of his allegorical insights. And occasionally he lectured in and around Fleet Street, staying the night with friends in Bloomsbury, or taking an omnibus part of the way back to Enfield after his lecture and then walking the remaining distance. He had lost none of his enthusiasm for political combat. By temperament he was still—as he had been for nearly twenty years—a radical artisan, trying to bring about reform by a mixture of (mostly) individual mobility and (relatively little) social engineering. Life in Enfield enabled him to husband his resources for future confrontations at a time of considerable personal difficulty.

By the spring of 1836, Carlile began to exert himself more forcefully. Early that year, Eliza gave birth to their third child and first daughter, Hypatia (Julian Hibbert, the second of their sons to be given that name, was born at the beginning of 1835), and this acted as a signal for him to rebel once more at the constraints of marriage. "I have committed the last of my follies in adding a daughter to my family," he told Thomas Turton. "I am now about to end my days in wisdom." He wanted to rejoin the world of radical politics and to win support from "respectable" workingmen. He felt "ripe and ready" to persuade the "rational" poor to join his infidel movement. If they could be aroused from their torpor and their minds sown with enlightened arguments, they would, he was certain, be able to improve their lives drastically.[10]

In August, Carlile traveled to Brighton, his first provincial port of call in nearly two years. It was a town previously unknown to him, whose reforming artisans and mechanics had never demonstrated more than a sporadic interest in infidelity. Though he stayed for more than five weeks and tried to arouse enthusiasm for his views, he was not notably successful. However, his high spirits were very much in evidence during this time. He expressed a willingness to share, with believers and reprobates alike, "the freedom of my present state of mind for the public good." His salutations to the inhabitants of Brighton were offered "in the sacred name of Jesus Christ." More humbly, he pleaded for "an end to religious controversy and all its baneful social effects."[11]

That Carlile's views were not popular soon became clear. Anglican and dissenting clergymen made scurrilous comments about him, and he was denied permission to use the town hall on the particularly frustrating ground that "the principles of Mr. Carlile were so well known." To this he could only respond: "Am I to be rejected now I offer conciliatory explanation of the progress of my mental labours and no more offense?"[12] But he was not easily put off. He had drummed up advance publicity by inserting five letters in the *Brighton Theatrical Observer*, and he now hired a small room near the center of the town, where he conducted a series of meetings. When the weather permitted, he also addressed outdoor gatherings along the Parade and at congenial sites available to him. His message, though phrased in messianic terms, was "moral" and temperate. He declared himself to be "wholly, and in every respect a Christian," and his expectations for the future were summarized in this way: "To hasten the promised time of peace and good will among mankind, which has never yet been . . . and to speedily obtain for every man the culture of his own vine, and his own fig tree, unsurrounded by any circumstances of life." "The expert Messiah of the Jews and Christ," he stated, "was the power and principle of science working beneficial changes in the human mind"; while "true religion [consisted] of good morals as to individuals, and good politics as to a nation."[13]

Carlile's unabashed advocacy of Christian rationalism disquieted many potential supporters. Although his views had been changing slowly during the previous decade, he was now perceived by many reformers as having undergone a sudden conversion to orthodox Christianity. Particularly resented was his practice of citing scriptural passages to reinforce his views. Thus, while controversy accompanied Carlile wherever he set foot in Brighton or adjacent parts of Sussex during the summer of 1836, he cannot be said to have achieved any concrete results.

In November he was on the move again, this time to Manchester, which he used as the base for a series of peregrinations across the north of England during the next few months. His aim, as he told Thomas Turton (who held a large stock of his printed tracts in Sheffield and parceled them out as the need arose), was an "activation of the human mind universally."[14] Eliza and their two children remained behind in London for the first time, but Thomas Paine Carlile, his seventeen-year-old son by Jane Carlile who described himself as an "assistant Missionary in the cause of Our Lord and Saviour Jesus Christ," accompanied him to help with the distribution of tracts and the making of arrangements.

The visit to Manchester, fully laying to rest any rumors that Carlile had lost his zest for political combat, proved to be the most frenetic of his life. For more than eight weeks he traveled ceaselessly through Lancashire by coach and on foot, visiting weaving villages and mill towns, offering himself as a messiah of rationalism, and trying to create a blaze of support where, by all odds, the tinder was uncommonly dry. He hired a room in

Manchester to plead for "mental principles." "I am the same man still," he told those who came to listen, "but with more knowledge, on better ground."[15] He tried to win supporters away from the suffrage and cooperative movements, both of which were rapidly gaining ground in the industrial north. Several long-time disciples (including his former shopman, William Campion, who owned a "circulating library" in Manchester) assisted him with the sale of pamphlets, with which he reported some success. But the political situation was generally bleak.

Carlile also attempted to win over adherents in Yorkshire, particularly in Sheffield where he twice lectured successfully in the Music Hall, notwithstanding attacks directed against him by local Methodists.[16] (Before one lecture he collected the relatively munificent sum of £27 in receipts at the door.) Elsewhere, however, the situation was less encouraging. In Huddersfield, he spoke six times in a room that his son described as more akin to a "pig sty" than a hall of free discussion. In Barnsley, local constables prevented him from leasing a theater in the town, and when he finally coaxed an antagonist, the Reverend Tully Crybbace, into debate at another site, he was barracked steadily by a hostile audience, an incident that evoked expressions of bitterness from him.[17] At the beginning of December he experienced a polite reception from a "crowded" audience in Bolton's Town Hall. But his rejection of "profane history" did not sit well with his listeners, and he was attacked subsequently in the local press by a lecturer on science who conceded to him a measure of "learning, talent, and candour," while pointing out numerous etymological "errors" in his theories.[18]

After abruptly terminating the tour in December for personal reasons and returning to London, Carlile, during the next two months, commenced two more publishing ventures: still another revised edition of the *Manual of Masonry*, which had last been issued in 1831, and a four-penny weekly journal, the *Phoenix: or, the Christian Advocate of Equal Knowledge*, that appeared for the first time in February 1837. The changes in the *Manual of Masonry* show further how Carlile's thought had changed and the degree to which he had repudiated Taylor. In the section dealing with the Royal Arch and Knights Templars Degrees, all references to sun worship and the "physical" origins of religion were deleted. In their place Carlile substituted the theme of "mental rebirth," which he defined as "the incarnation of God or Christ in man." He described man as "a creature to be improved by cultivation" and affirmed that "knowledge of things is the source of improvement; and . . . time is the material to be properly used to that end." Apocalyptic imagery was very much in evidence. He characterized himself as the "prophet" of "the greatest of all the advents that have yet blessed the human race" and "the best and most enduring soldier of Jesus Christ, that the Church has produced within these last fifteen hundred years."[19]

These ideas were worked out in even greater detail in the *Phoenix*. Calling for the establishment of a "Catholic Christian Church" based on the "principle of reason," Carlile reiterated his belief that biblical names stood for "principles, or Gods . . . that never die, but are eternal." Superstition, "the master evil of this and every other country," must be destroyed, he affirmed; while science, that is, the "church of christ," had to be substituted for it. Then and only then would a "New Jerusalem" of knowledge emerge, which would bear witness to the most critical reform of all: "the conquering of the physical or animal passion, with regard to all excesses, by the intellectual culture and exercise of the moral and rational powers."[20]

But if workingmen were to be won over to his side, more than cloudy rhetoric was needed, and here Carlile was notably deficient. He lacked sufficient funds to hire a lecture room in London, where he could continue on a regular basis the "Christian" disquisitions that he had commenced in the north. He admitted that he was in a cleft stick: that he was "positively and absolutely shunned by a great majority" of radical reformers and that the political world was dominated by a mixture of venality and ignorance.[21] But he would not give up. For the first time he turned to outdoor speaking in London, taking out a formal license as a preacher so that he could speak on religious subjects. He began to frequent the environs of Regent's Park, addressing anyone who was prepared to give him some attention. On cold, wet evenings (abundant, it seemed, in the early months of 1837), he was to be seen at his accustomed spot in the park, attempting to create "rational" human beings out of "ill-mannered" idlers.[22] It was a task that required uncommon fortitude and, sometimes, a modicum of physical courage.

When, because of steady losses, the *Phoenix* had to be given up after five numbers, Carlile seemed to have reached the end of his rope. Chartism had begun to develop a national political base, and there was a groundswell of working-class support for universal suffrage, the ballot, annual elections, and other democratic political demands. Both the newly organized London Working Men's Association and the East London Democratic Association were active, and, shortly, the Six Points of the "People's Charter" were to be drafted. A new generation of radical leaders was coming to the fore, among them Feargus O'Connor and Bronterre O'Brien; and Carlile (who knew both men) was distrustful of their "extreme" egalitarianism. Even the "moral force" chartism of William Lovett and his artisan-dominated London Working Men's Association was, in his view, suffused with the rhetoric of class conflict. It contradicted the tenets of self-help and voluntary moral choice, goals that Carlile insisted were essential.

During these trying months Enfield offered consolations. Its serenity and remoteness from political conflict encouraged him to reflect upon the meaning of his West Country boyhood. In such a preindustrial setting the cause of "rationality" stood a better chance of making headway than it did in London or the turbulent cities of the north. Yet, as he understood, effective organization could alone bring about an end to injustice and privilege, and the struggle remained to be fought in the poorer districts of urban and industrial centers. The polarities of rural and urban life—with their respective cachets of individualism and cooperation—had somehow to be reconciled in the political world.

In June 1837, Carlile received an unexpected boon when a successor to Julian Hibbert appeared on the scene. His new bene-factress was Sarah Chichester, an eccentric backer of "lost causes" who lived in Painswick, Gloucestershire, with her sister, Mrs. Welch. The two "Ladies" (even in his private correspondence Carlile did not identify them for almost two years) bestowed considerable largesse upon him, giving him hundreds of pounds between 1837 and 1840, and aiding his family, which was increased in size in June 1837 by the birth of a second daughter, Theophila. They fortified his belief that by means of messianic imagery and allegorical insights, it was not yet too late to bring about decisive reform.[23]

Once more, Carlile undertook to carry his doctrines into the farthest reaches of the country. "I must begin my new career with the new reign," he told Turton in June, on the day of Queen Victoria's accession to the throne. There was much to be gained by another provincial tour, he insisted. While his prospects in London were thin, he felt certain that he would be able to recharge the aspirations of his provincial supporters who would otherwise drift inevitably into chartist or socialist agitation. The provinces also offered the likelihood of increased sales of his tracts. The welfare of his family was of little concern to him. He left Eliza and their three children in London and for the next eight months traveled to different sections of the country, carrying on an extensive correspondence with Sarah Chichester and Thomas Turton, while largely ignoring the claims of his own family.

Norwich was the first major stop on his journey. The response there, in August 1837, was encouraging. Before an audience estimated at 1000, and in the presence of the mayor and other dignitaries gathered in Saint Andrews Hall, Carlile debated the merits of his "Christian allegory" with a Baptist preacher named John Green. The account of their discussion (which lasted two nights) does not support his ebullient claims of victory, but it indicates that a fair amount of excitement was generated. Before the largely skeptical assemblage he proffered the claim that "Christ was never manifested bodily in individual humanity" and that the apostles "preached Christ and Christ crucified, Christ dead and Christ risen, as a Spirit, and not as a body," evidence for which, he maintained, was to be found in the Pauline epistles. The path to reform was by means of "the cultivation of the human mind," he maintained, a conclusion too inexact to satisfy either his numerous detractors in the audience or a small, devoted group of disciples who were present.[24]

If Norwich was a partial success (taking into account the extensive press coverage that the debate received), Lancashire, next on his itinerary, offered much less political solace. Carlile had to contend with the usual problems: inclement weather, fatiguing coach journeys, grinding poverty, and, on this occasion, incessant squabbling with other reformers. And these problems were compounded by the successes of his rivals. Weavers, artisans, factory workers, and mechanics were giving their support increasingly to chartism and socialism, and they were not, seemingly, to be deflected from this course by a lone reformer whose voice was no longer strong enough to carry across open market squares and whose message was couched in so many obscurities as to make it almost incomprehensible.

Carlile's preaching license allowed him to speak at outdoor sites, but the prefix "Reverend," which he now attached to his name, further tarnished his image in the eyes of reformers, as did the initials "M.B.A.A.S." (standing for Member of the British Association for the Advancement of Science), which he occasionally affixed to his name. During this tour he became a member of the British Association and spent a week attending its annual meeting in Liverpool.[25] He tried to establish his claims as a "scientist"—the only true one in England, he averred—but the members of this august body were decidedly unimpressed by his pronouncements. They refused him a hearing (and took the same step a year later in Newcastle), a decision that confirmed his opinion that scientists as currently defined were exemplars of superstition.

Once again, Manchester became the focus of Carlile's activities. He remained there from October 1837 to the spring of 1838, lecturing to groups of infidels in a "chapel" on Shude Hill and making whirlwind visits to nearby villages and towns. The city itself was politically unruly, and Carlile clashed repeatedly with reformers. In November, he confronted Feargus O'Connor at a meeting and attacked him for advocating universal suffrage. Shortly afterward he engaged in a blistering three nights' debate in Hyde with the talented chartist orator, George Rayner Stephens. Rejecting Stephens's condemnation of the New Poor Law Act of 1834, which had prescribed a workhouse test for relief in place of the prevailing system of outdoor assistance, Carlile urged that "parish reform" be adopted as the only feasible means of rectifying social and political injustices. His theological insights were not well received, however, and he made little headway against Stephens. He admitted that the preponderantly working-class audience backed Stephens overwhelmingly and that he had been outmaneuvered in debate. He even expressed a sneaking admiration for Stephens's forensic abilities. "Taking [Stephens's] character together, I like it," he told Turton.[26]

Lancashire's socialists proved to be even more intractable than its chartists. They managed the local "halls of science," which Carlile needed to hire for his speeches, and their itinerant lecturers challenged him constantly. On several occasions, he reported, socialists heckled him mercilessly from an adjoining part of a market square while he was trying to preach his "New Christianity." They accused him of having "no object but pennies" and of prostituting himself "for mercenary considerations, instead of devoting [his powers] to the unfettered advocacy of the truth." (These allusions, decidedly unfair, were to his unavailing efforts to charge a small admission fee for his outdoor lectures.)[27] Carlile clashed several times with Lloyd Jones, a leading Owenite "social missionary" whom he accused of being a member of a "class of mad projectors" and of propounding a potpourri of sense and nonsense. Less animated though equally fruitless were his exchanges with John Finch, an Owenite propagandist from Liverpool whose millennialist imagery bore a resemblance to his own.[28]

Day after day throughout the winter months of 1837-1838, Carlile trekked into the outer reaches of Manchester in search of followers. He spoke to "respectable" audiences in Saddleworth, was applauded by members of a working-class discussion group in Oldham, and engaged in a four nights' debate with socialists in Stockport.[29] (Some Methodists succeeded in barring him from speaking in the Stalybridge Town Hall.) And in weaving villages like Mosley, he was reduced to the customary expedient of outside preaching, all indoor sites being closed to him. Despite his poor health, his energy was prodigious. In December, he claimed to have spoken ten times in eight days. Large audiences were attending his outdoor meetings, he told Turton, and he had reason to expect that his ideas might soon begin to catch on.[30]

Sarah Chichester and Mrs. Welch continued to shower gifts on him and his family. "They have made me rich!" he blurted out excitedly after receiving a modest token of esteem from them.[31] He decided to remain indefinitely in Manchester, offering Eliza the consolation of a brief visit at Christmas and the prospect of a closer involvement with his future plans. He wanted her to return to the lecture platform as a resurrected "Isis" disseminating his insights to the heathen multitudes of the industrial north. They would become joint apostles of moral and political redemption, in emulation of his partnership with Taylor. Fearful of public embarrassment, Eliza demurred, and Carlile harshly criticized her. His public objectives counted above all else with him, and he was prepared to sacrifice personal relationships for the sake of abstract good. Once his ideas were accepted, or so he insistently proclaimed, private and public benefit would merge into one.

Sarah Chichester's backing enabled him to issue several pamphlets from Manchester during the winter of 1837-1838. These appeared under the imprint of his son Thomas Paine, who was now established as a bookseller there. The most interesting tract was a *Dictionary of Some of the Names in Sacred Scripture Translated into the English Language, (Showing that They Are Names of Offices, Principles and Attributes of Deity)*, which was the first (and only) installment of a long-projected history of the concept of "God." The *Dictionary* was not as comprehensive as intended, but several of Carlile's etymological illustrations—for example, *Jacob* meaning "Supplanter by Pursuit of Knowledge," *Daniel* meaning "Judgment of God," *Levi* meaning "Under the Tie" of religion— offer channels into his thought processes. He also amplified some of his general themes. The Jews, he wrote, were "the philosophers and scientific men of ancient times" who, having given the Scriptures "a national orientation," fraudulently passed them off as of divine inspiration. The principles of human salvation were explained in terms of the trinity: that the material reality of a "Father" and "Son" produced a "Holy Ghost," which was a synthesis of human achievement.[32]

The other pamphlets that Carlile published in Manchester provided similar analyses of religion. Adopting the pseudonym "A Catholic Minister," he attacked the Reverend Hugh Stowell, an old opponent, for advancing a system of national education based on Bible study. After mockingly describing himself (in *A Letter to the Reverend Hugh Stowell*) as "that notorious character, and formerly avowed Infidel of the most daring kind," Carlile attacked Stowell's schemes on the admittedly unusual ground that "the Catholic spirit of the Bible" had not yet penetrated into modern readings of Scripture. In substitution for conventional biblical analysis, he called for a revival of the "ancient universal science" of interpretation. This alone, in his view, would provide the basis for a proper educational system.

In *A Letter to the Right Reverend Father in God the Lord Bishop of Norwich* (1837) and *A Letter to the Reverend Isaac France* (1837), Carlile delineated his doctrines more fully. "The cultivation of the human mind, in all science," he wrote, "is the one thing and only thing needful to human salvation from all present evil and all future punishment."[33] "National schools of science," conducted by "truly Christian schoolmasters in a truly Christian Church," had to be organized to provide public instruction. In this way, the Church of England would be transformed into an institution of pedagogical value, not as it now is, "a Theatre or Play House or School of Industry and Superstition."[34]

Stripped of its apocalyptic baggage, Carlile contemplated a world in which intellectual and moral considerations would count for more than political ones. But his formulation was too vague to wean more than a handful of discontented workers away from the shibboleths of chartism and economic cooperation. As was made clear on many occasions, he was not capable of forging an effective movement with well-defined political objectives. He distrusted "organization," and as a speaker he lacked an intuitive ability to respond to the ebb and flow of feeling in an audience. His small band of disciples continued, therefore, to fragment in the direction of more popular causes, and Manchester, it became evident, was not to be "the City of Peace that is hoped for by wise and good men, to arise out of the improvement toward perfection of the human race by scientific education." Carlile told Turton early in 1838 that he had not addressed any large audiences since Christmas. "I find it difficult to get my income from preaching," he admitted. Despite one well-received debate with a Unitarian minister from Salford with whom he had sparred previously, he could foresee "little hope of bettering things."[35]

Unable to hold his Shude Hill "congregation" together, Carlile redoubled his efforts to win support in other parts of Lancashire at the outset of 1838, selling tracts and debating with chartists, socialists, and a handful of dissenting clergymen—in short, engaging in any activity that might promote his cause. Few gains accrued to him. After a brief visit to Birmingham, he returned to London in the spring, satisfied that he had garnered some publicity by his travels and had coaxed a few opponents of his allegorical views into direct confrontation but ineffably pessimistic about the future. He had been abused and shunned—though not, perhaps, as frequently as on previous occasions—and had failed to deflect the sentiments of significant numbers of working-class reformers away from chartism and socialism.

In April, with the aid of Sarah Chichester, he commenced still another weekly journal, the *Church*. This paper survived for eight numbers and had a weekly circulation of about 500. In format and content it was similar to his other journals: personal in style and dedicated to an explication of his allegorical theories, it emphasized the merits of a national church founded on "scientific" principles. His losses on the *Church* were about £40, though some of this was underwritten by his son Alfred, who was now a publisher. "The speculation is [Alfred's]," he informed Turton, "the labour of editing is mine."[36]

During 1838 Carlile was subject to oscillating emotions. At one moment he felt confident enough to slay the dragon of ignorance and superstition; at the next he was downcast about the possibility of making any gains. Private assurances to Turton (with whom he corresponded almost daily) that "I am very happy and very much at ease in my mind" were quickly followed by mournful complaints that "my exertions bring me no money."[37] As always, however, the more vilification and abuse that Carlile endured, the greater was his determination to push on with new schemes and enterprises.

In June he visited Wisbeach, a Cambridgeshire market town where he had established a tiny "mission" in the previous year. James Hill, the atheist editor of the *Star of the East*, an Owenite journal, was well-disposed toward him and allowed him to insert two letters in his newspaper in which he contended that the Bible is "the Garden of Spiritual Principles for the culture of the Soul" and that "covenant, command, law, injunction, exhortation and Gospel or Mystery of the Godhead is the *one thing needful* to the human race."[38] Nothing of political substance occurred in Wisbeach, however, and after returning to London and confronting once more the reality of dwindling attendances at his lectures, he revived his plan to bring Eliza before the public. She was induced by him to give two lectures in London on the subject of phrenology— in Carlile's words, "to see if she can excite any interest in the country." The experiment was a failure. And although, subsequently, Eliza lectured in several other cities, the possibility no longer existed that popular support could be marshalled beneath her banner.[39]

Between November 1838 and August 1839, Carlile made two final trips to the north of England, attempting almost single-handedly to stem the tide of working-class support for chartism and socialism. Both movements were, he reiterated, likely to bring about soulless mechanical equality: chartism by virtue of its

demagogic political formulations, socialism because of its cooperative panaceas. To preserve the true spirit of reform it was necessary
to war against them, he believed; and so he moved vigorously
across the north of England, visiting Tyneside and Cumberland for
the first time and many familiar areas as well. He hurled political
anathemas at hostile orators. And wherever he went, he preached
the gospel of peace, brotherhood, and "moral righteousness."

Carlile was generally less antagonistic to socialism than to
chartism. He described cooperative economic schemes as "castles in
the air" that led inevitably toward a "milk-sop, effeminate life,
through which a man has nothing to call his own, and in which the
noble spirit of independence is molten down by the tyranny of rules
and regulations." Such projects obstructed individual advancement
and the reform of social institutions.[40] But, at the same time, he
expressed some admiration for Robert Owen and his disciples.
They were "certainly the best sect in the country," he commented in
February 1837. Owen (whom he met on three occasions) was an
"intelligent and rational" reformer in the ennobling tradition of
Socrates, Plato, and Cicero; his doctrines were commendably
antichristian, even messianic.[41]

Yet he resented the treatment meted out to him by local socialists
who denied him access to speaking halls. In *A View and Review of
Robert Owen's Projects; or the Manspel, According to Robert
Owen, Criticised by the Gospel, According to Richard Carlile*, a
one-and-a-half-penny tract that he published in 1838, he gave vent
to these feelings. "I received from [Owen's followers] the most
rancorous, lying, insidious, villainous, and cut-throat conduct that
could be expected from any associated fiendishness of the human
character," he wrote. Cooperative proposals were a hobbyhorse,
which, unfortunately, was likely to be ridden "as long as there is a
shilling left to pay for a show, or a feed to be obtained from
lingering hope, and new proselytes."[42]

If Owenism was an irritant to Carlile, chartism, which had
developed into a formidable movement of working-class political
protest by the spring of 1838, was a veritable abomination. He
conceived of it as arising out of the "pothouse politics" of Henry
Hunt, who had died in 1835; masses of workingmen were "be-
deviled, be-priested, and be-fooled by every Tom Fool that appeals
to their low taste." They did not comprehend that "national education in rationality" was the only secure basis for political refor-

mation and that "the Parrot-cry of universal suffrage," even if adopted into law, would not enhance the quality of their lives by one millimeter.[43] As he commented in a letter to Daniel O'Connell: "You seek to be rid of a bad master; I, of a bad servant."[44]

Carlile elaborated his case against chartism in three articles, which appeared in February and March 1839 in the *Operative*, a journal edited by Bronterre O'Brien, who was his most implacable foe among the advocates of universal suffrage. (Their quarrel dated from the early 1830s when O'Brien, then editing the *Poor Man's Guardian*, had attacked him in personal terms.) Agreeing with O'Brien that a monoply of landholding was "the master evil in this country," Carlile nonetheless rejected the suffrage ideas of the chartist leaders. A democratic franchise, he asserted, was "a folly, mockery and imposture" which would change nothing; the chartist convention then meeting in a hotel near Charing Cross, London, was a "profit-mongering, poor-robbing project." He insisted that injustices could be ended only when a "superstitious state of mind was eradicated." Parish reform—"the two edged sword of the Lord and of Gideon"—was absolutely necessary: "Let the corn laws be abolished, and the people get and manage their tithes, and who will, may hold and cultivate the land."[45]

A visit to Cumberland in the autumn of 1838 proved particularly heavy going. In Cockermouth, Whitehaven, and other towns in the county where there were few radical workingmen, he was attacked as a "notorious infidel," in spite of his insistence that he was now a "martyr-like" proponent of the gospel of reason.[46] The city of Carlisle presented him, seemingly, with a better opportunity to gain some support. There, at a "Grand Chartist Demonstration," he confronted two well-known opponents, Joseph Rayner Stephens and Feargus O'Connor. When Stephens, in a famous formulation, described chartism as a "knife and fork" question, Carlile challenged him unsuccessfully to a debate. He maintained that the number of participants at the meeting was considerably fewer than reported and that the rhetoric of the two chartist leaders was ludicrously disproportionate to the occasion.[47] He also attended church services for the first time publicly in Carlisle, so as to affirm symbolically his "return to the fold." This dramatic gesture was intended to underlie his proposal that the poor should occupy parish churches on Sunday mornings and reestablish their rights to vestry control. Although some Scottish chartists began to move in this direction early in 1839, "parish reform" was a line of attack that, in the view of most working-class freethinkers, entirely undercut Carlile's "infidel" message.[48]

By December 1838, his health was failing badly. He told Turton that "I must keep by the fireside, for two or three months and nurse myself carefully."[49] The winter was harsh, and there seemed little that he could do to contain the political turbulence of the working classes. Even his two patronesses were beginning to distance themselves from him. Although prepared occasionally to donate small sums of money to support the "New Christianity," they were much more interested in cooperative schemes, including the establishment of a Fourierite school and community at Ham Common under the leadership of J. P. Greaves.[50] Carlile's pamphlet business, which was conducted by his son Alfred, was unremunerative and, as he told Turton in March 1839, "the bulk of my stock is scattered about in different friends' houses in London; but nothing of it sells to produce any return."[51]

Still, he mustered strength to essay one more journey to the provinces, which began in May and lasted for nearly six months. He concentrated on Yorkshire and Lancashire, the two leading centers of chartist and cooperative agitation and the areas outside London that he knew best. Characterizing himself as a "bold, honest, and wise man, a Republican in Politics, and a man of Science or Israel in Religion," he attacked both movements tirelessly, giving his immediate attention to whichever one had greater support in the locality he was visiting.[52] In Hull, Sheffield, Leeds, Bradford, and elsewhere he encountered vehement opposition, and he responded in kind. As he informed Turton in June: "I will go on, if I walk from town to town and village to village confined to bread and water."[53]

Doncaster and Wakefield were the northern towns most receptive to his doctrines. Assisted in the former by J. B. Levison, a reformer who operated a phrenological museum, Carlile spoke several times in the Market Place and participated in a well-publicized debate with local chartists. His ideas were assuredly not "all the talk" of the town as he claimed, but he sold some copies of the *Dictionary* and other pamphlets and aroused a fierce response in the local press. Equally encouraging from his point of view was the reaction in Wakefield. There, in the Market Place, he preached for about a week, speaking on one occasion amid "a smart shower of rain . . . which I, standing sheltered and wrapt up in the spirit, did not discover until the business was over." He lectured on phrenology and religion to members of the chartist Working Men's Association and to his delight discovered that they were not as hostile to him as he had supposed. After selling twenty-five copies of the *Dictionary* in Wakefield instead of the anticipated ten, he expressed renewed hope for "this wicked world." "With the Bible in my hand, I can go anywhere, without the least sacrifice of principle," he told Turton. "It is a magic book on human ignorance."[54]

There were other peaks—as well as numerous troughs—on this final expedition to the north of England. In Leeds, where "the highest state of excitement" prevailed, Carlile denounced socialism in a debate with Lloyd Jones before an audience of 1500 people jammed into the Music Hall.[55] Several noisy outdoor meetings followed in Bradford, as did "large" gatherings in Bolton Market Square and Rochdale churchyard. And in August, at Batty's Circus in Manchester, he and Bronterre O'Brien confronted each other for the first time publicly, an incident graced, according to newspaper accounts, by perfervid chartist rhetoric and impassioned claims for the "New Christianity."[56]

Under attack from chartist newspapers, including the influential *Northern Star* (which, in Carlile's words, was made up of "vapid speeches, beer house resolutions, and quack and filthy advertisements"), he repeatedly expressed disdain for the leaders of chartism.[57] Some of them—former supporters like James Watson, Lawrence Pitkeithley of Huddersfield, and Peter Bussey of Bradford—had been led astray inadvertently, he believed; others, including O'Connor, who was the "first Radical Fiddler in England," were unscrupulous demagogues without any redeeming qualities.[58] In *An Address to That Portion of the People of Great Britain and Ireland Calling Themselves Reformers*, a two-penny tract that he issued in Manchester in July, Carlile attacked the recent chartist riots in the Birmingham Bull Ring. They were destructive of human happiness, he wrote, because private property was essential to the good of society. "All Charters, from Magna Carta down to the new 'Peoples' Charter', have been in relation to popular welfare and improvement mere waste paper," he observed.[59] But his own proposal—for "rational reform" by means of the occupation of parish churches—remained tantalizingly vague.

The summer of 1839 was a climactic period for Carlile. It was his final attempt on the hustings to reverse the direction of popular radicalism. In Sheffield, where the response to his speeches was tepid, he depicted himself as David struggling against the modern Goliath of political and social injustice; elsewhere he adorned himself in the symbolic attire of a nineteenth-century Christ figure who was vouchsafed to the poor to preach the gospel of reform to them. He believed himself capable of preparing masses of people for temporal and spiritual paradise. What was needed was "reason and love, peace and good-will," and, specifically, "a scientific church and a mind-improving sabbath."[60] Then, and only then, would corruption and privilege disappear.

Moving through the textile districts of Lancashire by coach and on foot in the summer and early autumn of 1839, Carlile was roundly attacked by freethinkers for abandoning infidelity and by conservatives for advocating it. Most of his challenges to clergy-men went unnoticed. In Bolton, he was barred from speaking in the public theater; and in Halifax, he was compelled to address a small group of his disciples on an open moor about a mile from the town center. Almost everywhere he went the situation was depressingly similar: bruising poverty and a paucity of converts. As he confided to Turton: "Penny lecturings are not worth attending to and more than Penny Admissions are undermined as extravagant money settings."[61]

After a fortnight of lecturing in Birmingham's Lawrence Street Chapel, where he attacked Thomas Attwood's revived Birmingham Political Union, he returned to London in mid-October. He sought to keep up a facade of resilience and good cheer, but his spirits were inconsolably dampened by recent events. "It is no fair play any more," he observed, while vowing to continue his struggle against the "money changers of the temple."[62] He participated in a second debate with O'Brien, when, according to Carlile, he forced the chartist leader to retreat from his more "extreme" positions. And he engaged in a heated discussion with Charles Southwell, an Owenite, which he described as between an advocate of "science in the church" and an opponent with a brain less phrenologically de-veloped who was content to "talk, talk, talk; nothing but talk." Lacking adequate facilities for lecturing, Carlile was continually at the mercy of socialists who often denied him the use of their rooms.

He was, he admitted, reduced to "grubbing."[63]

The only significant contribution that he made to working-class politics during these months was the publication of still another journal, *Carlile's Political Register*, which was issued in two-penny weekly numbers for nine weeks beginning in October 1839.[64] In this paper he repeatedly condemned universal suffrage. It would "abate nothing of the beggary, misery, wretchedness, rags, filth, disease and discontentment of the poor; it would not add one shilling to any man's wages, not advance his liberty of speech or action in any way." He pleaded—as he had done for several years—for true radical reform, that is, for a "scientific" church. He urged the multitude, living in abject ignorance and poverty, to reclaim their parish churches and voluntarily pay tithes for their upkeep. The resulting "common church or school of science" would eliminate all artificial distinctions (including the class tensions that informed chartism and socialism); it was the key to political salvation and the "only basis of human equality." Expressed in the vernacular of his "New Christianity," a "unity of mind must precede human salvation, as the principle of true liberty and righteousness."[65]

The publication of the *Political Register* illustrates the extent to which Carlile's language and thought had become infused with millennialist formulations, both as a mechanism for allowing him to cope with personal reversals of fortune and as a means of inducing others to share his vision of the future. He urged Queen Victoria to appoint a commission to examine various scriptural interpretations. The results of such an examination would, he was certain, result in the acceptance of his theories and allow for the transformation of mankind into a "living temple, or worthy receptacle of the spirit of God, or of God as spirit." Sensation, perception, and reflection would merge into a blend of "physical, moral, and mental power," and Victoria would become "queen of Israel: to be crowned on Zion: to triumph over the Philistines and to overthrow the idolatrously mighty, the priests of the earth."[66] Toward the end of 1839, Carlile wrote: "I have since discovered and made [the people] feel and act by that feeling, that God almighty was highly pleased with what I was doing, that he had given me all manner of encouragement to go on, that he had in expressed approbation of my conduct taken up his residence in my head and is now in me fighting against my enemies."[67] There could be no greater stimulus to personal effort than this. But clarity and political concentration were receding ever further behind a curtain of rhetoric.

Notes

1. *Brighton Herald,* 17 September 1836.

2. He paid £12 in costs to the Stamp Office. He believed that Jane Carlile and his sons were instrumental in getting the journal suppressed. Carlile to Thomas Turton, 14 January 1835, C.P.

3. Carlile informed Thomas Turton that after much urging, John Cleave had agreed to receive paid advertisements from him. Carlile to Turton, 7 May 1835, C.P.

4. *Scourge for the Littleness of "Great" Men,* 7 February 1835. There are references in Carlile's papers to these debts and to his suit against the printing firm of Cunningham and Salmon.

5. *Republican,* 30 July 1824; *Lion,* 9 May 1828. The importance of self-treatment to radical artisans was expressed by Carlile's shopman, Richard Hassell, when he wrote: "There are few diseases but are of our own acquiring." *Newgate Monthly Magazine,* September 1824. See also Bruce Haley, *The Healthy Body and Victorian Culture* (Cambridge, Massachusetts: Harvard University Press, 1978).

6. Carlile to Turton, 8 December 1837, C.P.

7. Ibid., 19 November 1835, C.P.

8. Alfred's shop was on the site of the old Sherwin-Carlile shop. Alfred Carlile to Thomas Turton, 2 May 1836, C.P.

9. In March 1836, he added a second cottage to his property at an annual cost of £8. There is a copy of the deed in C.P.

10. See his letter to Thomas Turton, 2 June 1836, C.P.

11. Richard Carlile, *The Letters . . . to the Inhabitants of Brighton, with a Syllabus of His Course of Seven Lectures* (London: Richard Carlile, 1836), p. 3; letter in the *Brighton Herald,* 14 September 1836, reprinted in *Phoenix,* 5 February 1837.

12. Letter in *Brighton Herald,* 25 August 1836, reprinted in Carlile, *Letters . . . to the Inhabitants of Brighton,* pp. 4-5.

13. *Phoenix,* 5 February 1837; *Brighton Gazette,* 25 August 1836. See also Carlile, *Abstract, Embodying the Evidences, of the Lectures Delivered . . . at Brighton.*

14. Carlile to Thomas Turton, 11 November 1836, C.P.

15. *Phoenix,* 19 February 1837. After attending a lecture by Carlile, a reporter for the *Bolton Free Press* commented: "We left the room as wise as when we entered it." 10 December 1836.

16. The *Brighton Patriot* claimed that he was driven from the city by Methodists. *Phoenix,* 5 February 1837. For an account of his Sheffield

lectures, see *Sheffield Independent,* 19 November 1836.

17. Thomas Paine Carlile to Thomas Turton, 8 December 1836, C.P.; *Phoenix,* 12 February 1837. The *Leeds Intelligencer,* 26 November 1836, claimed that after the debate with Crybbace, the audience passed a resolution declaring Carlile's theories to be "utterly unphilosophical and irrational."

18. *Bolton Free Press,* 10 December 1836; *Bolton Chronicle,* 10 December 1836; *Phoenix,* 5, 12 February 1837.

19. Richard Carlile, *Manual of Masonry* (1837 ed.), pp. iv, viii, xx, xxii.

20. *Phoenix,* 5, 12 February 1837, 5 March 1837.

21. Ibid., 5 March 1837.

22. Ibid., 12 February 1837; *Times,* 6 February 1837.

23. Carlile referred to Sarah Chichester as "another Julian Hibbert" in an undated letter, c. summer of 1837, C.P.

24. See *Report of the Public Discussion between the Rev. John Green and the Rev. Richard Carlile* (1837); *Norfolk Chronicle and University Gazette,* 26 August 1837. Just before Carlile arrived in Norwich, Sarah Chichester predicted "the dawning of a bright Day Star, which will progressively illumine the darkness in which the majority of the British population is so woefully benighted." Chichester to Carlile, 6 September 1837, C.P.

25. Carlile to Thomas Turton, 5 October 1837, C.P.

26. There are references to these attacks on O'Connor in *Bolton Free Press,* 3 April 1841, and *Carlile's Political Register,* 30 November 1839. For his contacts with Stephens, see Carlile to Turton, 4 April 1838, C.P.; Richard Carlile, *An Address to That Portion of the People of Great Britain and Ireland Calling Themselves Reformers, on the Political Excitement of the Present Time* (Manchester: T. P. Carlile, 1839), pp. 6, 16.

27. Carlile to Turton, 8 December 1837, C.P.; *New Moral World,* 23 December 1837.

28. See Lloyd Jones, *A Reply to Mr. Carlile's Objections to the Five Fundamental Facts as Laid Down by Mr. Owen (An Answer to a Lecture Delivered in his Chapel, November 27th, 1837)* (London: A. Heywood, 1837). For a study of Finch, see R. B. Rose, "John Finch, 1784-1837: A Liverpool Disciple of Robert Owen," in *Transactions of the Historical Society of Lancashire and Cheshire,* 19 (1958), pp. 159-184.

29. Carlile to Turton, 18 December 1837, C.P.; Richard Carlile, *A Letter to the Rev. Isaac Newton France, Curate of St. George's Chapel, on his Paltry, Unchristian and Dishonourable Attempt to Deprive me of the Use of the Town Hall, Stalybridge* (London: Alfred Carlile, 1837), pp. 4-5.

30. See his advertisement in the *Northern Star,* 17 March 1838.

31. Carlile to Turton, 8 December 1837, C.P.

32. Richard Carlile, *A Dictionary of Some of the Names of the Sacred*

Scriptures Translated into the English Language, Showing that They Are Names of Offices, Principles, and Attributes of Deity (Manchester: T. P. Carlile, 1837), pp. iii-iv, vii-viii.

33. Carlile, *Letter to the Rev. Isaac Newton France,* p. 7.

34. Richard Carlile, *A Letter to the Right Reverend Father in God the Lord Bishop of Norwich, on His Unwise and Uncalled For Concession to the Dissenters* (Manchester: Abel Heywood, 1837), pp. 15, 19.

35. Carlile, *Dictionary of Some of the Names,* p. 20; Carlile to Turton, 1 March, 4 April 1838, C.P.

36. Carlile to Turton, 4 May, 12 July 1838, C.P. I have been unable to locate a copy of the *Church,* but there is information about it in C.P.

37. Carlile to Turton, 12 June 1838, C.P.

38. *Star in the East,* 7, 23 June 1838. Hill described Carlile's theories as "hazy, misty, indistinct, and useless."

39. Carlile to Turton, 12 July 1838, C.P. He had intended that Eliza speak under the pseudonym of "Mrs. Clay", but she spoke under her own name.

40. *Prompter,* 12 February, 19 March 1831; *Isis,* 1 September 1832. Carlile had described retail cooperatives as "pepper and salt chandlers' shop associations." *Lion,* 16 October 1829.

41. Carlile, *Abstract, Embodying the Evidences, of the Lectures Delivered . . . at Brighton,* p. 12. He described Owen as "a great and a good man" who was right in everything except "community of goods" (*Carlile's Journal for 1830,* 21 January 1830) and praised him at an 1835 meeting for having "infinitely more of [moral courage] than I ever possessed." *New Moral World,* 16 May 1835.

42. Richard Carlile, *A View and Review of Robert Owen's Projects; or the Manspel, According to Robert Owen, Criticized by the Gospel, According to Richard Carlile* (London: Alfred Carlile, 1838), pp. 11, 13.

43. *Carlile's Political Register,* 2, 9 November 1839.

44. Carlile to Daniel O'Connell, c. January 1843, C.P.

45. *Operative,* 3, 17 February, 3 March 1839. He referred subsequently to the chartist leaders as "men who can fight in their cups and faint when they are sober." *Carlile's Political Register,* 2 November 1839.

46. *Cumberland Pacquet,* 6, 13 November 1838. This newspaper described him as one of "these itinerant and vagabondizing swindlers."

47. There are accounts of the meeting in *Carlisle Journal,* 27 October 1838; *Carlile's Political Register,* 30 November 1839.

48. The incident is described by Carlile in *Besley's Devonshire Chronicle,* 13 October 1840. On "Christian Chartism," see Alexander Wilson, *The Chartist Movement in Scotland* (New York: Augustus M. Kelley, 1970), pp. 138-50, and the interesting chapter, "Labour Churches," in K. S. Inglis,

Churches and the Working Classes in Victorian England (London: Routledge and Kegan Paul, 1963), pp. 215-49.

49. Carlile to Turton, 18 December 1838, C.P.

50. On Ham Common, see W. H. G. Armytage, *Heavens Below: Utopian Experiments in England, 1560-1960* (London: Routledge and Kegan Paul, 1961), pp. 171-83.

51. Carlile to Turton, 22 March 1839, C.P.

52. His description of himself is in an advertisement in the *Northern Star*, 6 July 1839.

53. Carlile to Turton, 7 June 1839, C.P. In Sheffield, he made a stir by challenging some clergymen to debate the merits of his allegory with him. *Sheffield Iris*, 4 June 1839; *Carlile's Political Register*, 14 December 1839.

54. Carlile to Turton, 6, 13-14 June 1839, C.P.; *Leeds Times*, 22 June 1839.

55. Carlile to Turton, 21 June 1839, C.P.; *Leeds Times*, 6 July 1839.

56. On the Bradford meetings, see *Leeds Times*, 29 June 1839; for Rochdale, see Carlile to Turton, 17 July 1839, C.P. There is a reference to his debate with O'Brien on Alfred Plummer, *Bronterre: A Political Biography of Bronterre O'Brien, 1804-1864* (London: Allen & Unwin, 1971), p. 121. See also *Carlile's Political Register*, 19 October 1839.

57. Carlile, *Address to That Portion of the People*, p. 13.

58. *Durham Chronicle*, 16 May 1840.

59. Carlile, *Address to That Portion of the People*, pp. 1-2, 6. He commented: "Political reform . . . is not to be worked by weapons of iron and lead. It is a work of improved brain and improved manners." *Regenerator, and Advocate for the Unrepresented*, 26 October 1839.

60. Richard Carlile, *On Going to Church, or the Grounds and Reasons, on Which the People May Be Thereby Benefited, at the Present Crisis, Stated* (Manchester: A. Heywood, 1839), p. 5.

61. See Carlile to Turton, 11 September, 3 August 1839, C.P.

62. Ibid., 22 October 1839, C.P.

63. *Carlile's Political Register*, 9 November, 7 December 1839; Carlile to Turton, 22 October 1839, C.P.

64. He also contributed a few articles to the *Regenerator, and Advocate for the Unrepresented*, a short-lived chartist journal published by his son Thomas Paine.

65. *Carlile's Political Register*, 19 October, 2, 23 November 1839.

66. Ibid., 16, 23 November 1839.

67. Ibid., 7 December 1839.

12

THE FINAL YEARS

The collapse of the *Political Register* in December 1839 marked one more stage in the decline of Carlile's fortunes. Although he continued to write prolifically for the press during the final years of his life, he was unable to commence another journal until January 1843. And the *Christian Warrior, or New Catholic Church Militant,* which lasted for four numbers, appeared only a few weeks before his death. "Being neither Tory, Whig, Radical, Socialist nor Chartist—I find I am nobody and nothing," he observed in February 1840.[1] It was a poignant commentary on his situation. As he noted sardonically in a letter to Turton: "My reward is to be in heaven."[2]

During these final years Carlile remained at Enfield for long stretches of time. There were few paying audiences left to him. The small number of London artisans and laborers who were willing to pay a penny or twopence to listen to him were insufficient to cover his expenses. He tried to improve his prospects by seeking paid employment, even going so far on one occasion as to reply to an advertisement for lecturers by the Society for the Diffusion of Useful Knowledge, an organization of middle-class educationalists that was decidedly hostile to his views. His efforts to secure remunerative employment were unsuccessful, however, mostly because of his "notoriety" as an infidel agitator. He rejected invitations from reformers in Norwich and Newcastle to undertake speaking tours of their areas, foreseeing that financial problems would overwhelm him and that the final vestiges of his hard-won "respectability" might have to be relinquished. As he observed with more than a trace of sarcasm: "I have twice exited Norwich without costs."[3]

From October 1840 to May 1841, Carlile, despite many difficulties, continued to lecture on a regular basis. He entered into a limited leasing arrangement for the Hall of Science in Gray's Inn Road, which was controlled by socialists. This gave him a platform from which to popularize his ideas, and it enabled him to sell some tracts. And although illness compelled him to cancel some of his scheduled engagements, he spoke almost weekly for seven months to "small but respectable" groups of workingmen.[4]

The themes of these lectures were grandiose. Discoursing on topics such as "Religion is Vice" and "God is a Principle of Intellect," he informed his audiences that the "Gospel of the Lord and Savior Jesus Christ is the Mystery of the Use of Letters" and that the Bible was a "volume of mental and moral science whose leading characters illustrated principles and not human history." He enlarged upon the "genuine Spirit of Truth," human knowledge, which informed the universe. This spirit was, he emphasized, "the only comforter, the only redeemer, the only saviour: the Christ, not yet fully come; but he or that Spirit which is to come, to restore the golden age, the parliamentary reform, the Charter, the Republic, the millenium [sic] of Saints, the heaven, etc." The "stolid ignorance and vice of human authority" would be destroyed as soon as the majority of people advanced to a state of knowledge in which "the created mind rules the animal passions."[5]

Carlile sketched in his vision with gusto, sparing neither himself nor his listeners an iota of enthusiasm on the subject. Yet always the conditional tense loomed large. Regardless of how attractively phrased his speeches were, he could not impart to them a sense of political reality. Almost perversely it seemed, the more he declaimed about the universality of his moral allegory and the "Jerusalem of the mind," the smaller his audiences became. The conclusion, as he admitted in a petition to the House of Commons in May 1841, was inescapable: he had been "condemned in the end even by those who had applauded and cheered him in his career."[6]

In March 1841, he suffered a stroke. His speech became slurred, and he found it difficult to lecture. Accordingly, he terminated his lease at the Hall of Science—a likely decision anyway given the hostile feelings of local socialists toward him. Refusing to take professional medical advice, he treated himself with a large number of home remedies—many of them supplied by a friend, Charles

Roach Smith, who was a chemist—putting his faith, in his own words, in the "Lord Jesus Christ." He felt unable to shape events. "I have so enlarged in body that my usual cloaths will not cover me," he told Turton in April.[7]

But although Carlile never fully overcame the effects of this stroke and was partly incapacitated for the remainder of his life, he made a temporary recovery in the summer of 1841, which he likened to the "second birth" of the prophet Mohammed. He began to take part in outdoor meetings in Regent's Park, London, in the company of Emma Martin, a freethinker whom he described as "the cleverest woman I have met yet." Martin's views differed markedly from his own. She would have no truck with allegorical interpretations, proffering instead an antireligious theory based on the alleged fusion of earth and water. Yet, for a time in the autumn of 1841, she and Carlile were companions in arms, jointly denouncing Christianity and emphasizing the need for a reform based on individualism, a position condemned by the many socialist speakers who frequented the park. Martin's vibrant oratory drew audiences of 300 to 500 workingmen nightly, a comparative avalanche of recognition for Carlile that resuscitated his flagging spirits.[8]

Taken together, however, the political barometers were distinctly unfavorable to him. His efforts to conduct meetings with speakers other than Martin ended in failure. And on his own he could not attract large audiences, partly because his impaired speech accentuated his deficiencies as an orator. Carlile's only real successes were in the company of Emma Martin, and because of personal differences (less overt than with other reformers) their political association ended after two months. In a letter from Sheffield, Turton reminded him that most reformers had "little or no relish for spirituality or Allegory." But Carlile remained undaunted. "I must persevere," he wrote back. "I have a pleasure in it; while disappointment does not fret me."[9] He believed that the salvation of the human race was at stake, and he prided himself on being "the first man within the era of printing, that has rested on the Bible as a source of truth, to be defended as a science, or that has made anything rational of it as a whole."[10] Under no circumstances would he allow personal considerations to dilute the vigor of his commitment.

If Carlile's lecturing followed a jagged path during these final years, his journalism acquired an unexpected shape. Without a paper of his own (attempts to revive the *Political Register* in the spring of 1840 were abortive) and in need of an income, he began to write paid newspaper articles in 1840. This became a regular practice, which he pursued with intermittent success until the autumn of 1841. It was not an edifying activity after so many years of independent journalism, and, somewhat abashedly, he characterized it as "grubbery." But it had compensations. For more than a year it provided him with a weekly income of about thirty shillings in circumstances that were not overly demeaning either to his political principles or his "respectability." And it gave him the opportunity to "insinuate" his views into newspapers and journals that would otherwise have been closed to him.

During 1840 and 1841 Carlile was employed by the *Durham Chronicle*, a weekly stamped newspaper, and by *Besley's Devonshire Chronicle*, a newspaper published in Exeter. He contributed numerous unsigned leaders and articles to both papers. He also contributed many paid articles to the *Durham Advertiser*, which was the leading competitor of the *Durham Chronicle*, and to the *Dundee Chronicle*, whose proprietor terminated the relationship after several months when Carlile began to express his views too strongly. Less regularly (and without compensation), he contributed articles to the *Bolton Free Press* and the *Morning Advertiser* and to a smattering of provincial and London journals, including the *Cheltenham Free Press*, the *Morning Herald*, the *Times*, and the *Sun*.

The most important of Carlile's professional employments was with the *Durham Chronicle*. From April 1840 to March 1841, he received a pound weekly from the owner and editor of the paper, John Harding Veitch, for writing three to four weekly leaders or essays of about 1000 words each.[11] The hiring of a London journalist to "edit" a provincial newspaper from several hundred miles away was not as unusual as it may seem. With a local printer and subeditor on hand to put the paper together, it was a way of assuring the proprietor that there was a continual supply of leaders and political analyses available to him for publication. In most provincial newspapers commentary took a back seat to advertising and national news anyway (the news was usually copied from the

London papers), and in the event of a story for which the "editor" was unable to provide an article, local writers could be hired to fill the gap, or the proprietor himself might hurriedly compose a leader. The "editor's" contributions—in this case Carlile's—would then be held over to the following week.[12]

What was odd about Carlile's relationship with the *Durham Chronicle* was not the distance from which it was carried on but the fact that his identity remained unknown to the proprietor during most of his employment. This stratagem was successfully devised by Thomas Prout, a London intermediary, and accepted by Carlile who understood that his name was emphatically not a recommendation for newspaper work. "I have lost two papers merely by the knowledge of my hand writing," he confided to Turton in February 1840.[13] Yet it proved to be a satisfactory arrangement for both Veitch and his "editor." Carlile fulfilled his prescribed tasks with skill, composing weekly leaders in a restrained, fluent style and invariably submitting them on time. And all the while readers of the paper never guessed who their illustrious contributor was.

An analysis of Carlile's contributions to the *Durham Chronicle* and the other journals for which he worked professionally during 1840 and 1841 poses some difficulties. His opinions necessarily had to be tailored to fit a miscellany of issues, some of them of no particular interest to him. More jarring was the need to hew to the editorial line of the owners of the journals, which in the case of the *Durham Chronicle* meant support for the political ambitions of the earl of Durham, a moderate reformer, and endorsement of a substantial role by government in social matters, a position that conflicted with his own preference for individualism. Among the subjects that he commented upon in his leaders for the *Durham Chronicle* were repeal of the corn laws and a reduction of taxation, both of which he favored; a further extension of the franchise; rumored Jewish "blood rituals" in Damascus (which gave him an opportunity to comdemn the antisemitism of some chartist agitators); and the Near Eastern crisis of 1840-41, which involved conflicting claims by Britain, France, Egypt, and the Ottoman Empire. On this foreign policy issue Carlile appealed simplistically to the "Gospel of Peace," maintaining that war was "a manifestation of human madness—a concentration of destructive elements—a passion struggling for chaos."[14]

His comments on social issues for the *Durham Chronicle* were an admixture of his own views and those of Veitch. Though an advocate of classical political economy and the laws of supply and demand, he adjusted his opinions to conform to the collectivist leanings of the newspaper. Personal incentive, he told the paper's readers, was the basis of reform, but intervention by government was necessary if a substantial measure of social justice was to be achieved. Thus he endorsed "sound social economy" in place of "flippant liberalism, or heartless libertism," and he gave strong support to Lord Ashley's proposal that children under the age of fourteen be prohibited from working in coal mines. "A slavery in our cotton mills, and other infant labour," wrote Carlile, is "more humanly disgraceful than even the Negro slave trade." More in line with his own convictions was his emphasis on the need to "spiritually educate" the poor through the aegis of a reclaimed national church. On a drainage of buildings bill then being debated in Parliament, he expressed opinions that must have struck readers of the *Durham Chronicle* as distinctly idiosyncratic. Such a measure was to be commended, he affirmed, because its enactment would signify the "beginning of the restoration of the Jews, and a preparation of the second advent of the Saviour CHRIST, in the sense in which cleanliness is a necessary part of godliness."[15]

Although his articles in the *Durham Chronicle*, *Besley's Devonshire Chronicle*, the *Durham Advertiser*, and other journals often had to be trimmed or diluted, many of the positions Carlile took were not far removed from those he advocated when editing his own journals. Frequently, for example, he embraced "blood and thunder" imagery, as in his references to a "synagogue of Satan," or a "true Christ" that was "latent as fire in a Lucifer match." And "New Christianity" themes worked their way into many of his leaders. Writing in the *Durham Chronicle*, in April 1841, he described religion as "the wisdom of mankind working through righteousness, making a constant appeal to public judgment, and freely challenging public opinion." Christianity, he commented, was "the second birth of the human race," while Christ was "the Spirit of Liberty—that is, of the truth and virtue by which a good man is made free."[16] He confided to bemused readers of one of his provincial papers that "the state of mind desirable to be reached is that of *Jerusalem, the state or city of peace, rest and*

love—the holy city, or heaven, or church of *the true Israelite.*"
There was as yet "no realized advent, no epiphany, no church of
Christ to accouchere, and nurse the second birth of the human
race." But as he told the readers of *Besley's Devonshire Chronicle,*
redemption was at hand: "The Messiah, the promised seed, was
not to be carnal but spiritual. We are yet waiting for that spirituality, and shall wait, shall never reach it until we have the right
understanding of these sacred [secret] mysteries and the true
revelation of them." By implication he was the "Saviour to
come . . . for which we are waiting, hoping, and exercising our
faith."[17]

Carlile also alluded frequently in his paid writings to his suggestion that the people reestablish control over their parish
churches. Christianity in its original state was "the noblest institution that human wisdom has devised," he observed, but it had
been debased into "a system of money-changing." He proposed to
restore it to "the noble spiritual provision of our ancestors": by
confiscating tithes and other church revenues and applying the
funds to the feeding of the poor (an "improvement of the mind and
condition of the whole people"), and by rewarding "spiritual
industry." He composed a paean to this ideal national church: "Of
stone and cement—of brick and mortar churches—we have
enough. But where is the spiritual, the Catholic Church, to embrace
the souls of the whole people?" When reconstituted, this church
would be without "sects, schisms, divisions, creeds, catechisms, or
dissent, [and] would encompass all human hope and
aspirations."[18]

Whenever the opportunity arose, Carlile urged the repudiation
of the chartists, with their "currency crotchets and Poor-law
pasquinades." The insistent clamor of political demagogues
hampered the cause of reform, he maintained, while a "change of
mind" would bring about a permanent improvement in the
condition of mankind. To work for universal suffrage and other
institutional changes before disseminating "spiritual education"
was, in his opinion, to "seek a community without mental communion." The proper course was evident: the cultivation of
morality and science, "communicable, by teaching, between man
and man." Science, as he reminded his readers, "belongs to the
Christian religion and its mysteries, as the constituent principle of
the greater teacher—OMNISCIENCE!"[19]

Using the pseudonym "A Searcher After Truth," Carlile wrote an interesting series of articles for the *Bolton Free Press* in the early months of 1841, which were in response to letters from Colonel T. Perronet Thompson, a prominent anti-corn law reformer and member of Parliament. In more restrained terms than was his wont, he stated that the key to reform was to be found in the "creation of mind" and the "uneducating, unpauper-sustaining application of the church property." Purity of conviction must be the overriding goal of mankind," to be achieved by eradicating the "spiritual corn laws" (orthodox religion) since these withheld "the bread of life from the people." When challenged by Thompson to explain how he proposed to bring about a revolution in society without prior political changes, Carlile retreated into "scientific" ambiguity. "The people in vestry are the church," he told readers of the *Bolton Free Press,* and they have the power to bring about all essential transformations. He reiterated his belief that the Jews of the Old Testament were "the progenitors of the spiritualities, not of the corporalities, of the human race" and that the Bible was "the best book in existence for human existence."[20]

Paid journalism provided Carlile with a weekly income of more than a pound for almost two years and enabled him to propagate his opinions a little more widely. But it was stultifying, unedifying work for a reformer of such passionate convictions. He resented the small change of daily compromise that was necessary if his identity was to be kept a secret. And he was distressed at having to fob off his supporters with indirection and anonymity and at having to put in abeyance plans for a weekly *Political Warrior,* which would declare open war on all "sects" and delineate the merits of Christian allegory without fear or favor of any kind.[21]

During the final years of his life Carlile read omnivorously, considerably increasing his knowledge of comparative religion and becoming familiar with writers not previously well known to him. He immersed himself in the thought of Plato and his interpreters. In the 1820s, he had incorporated into his theories the Greek concept of the logos. But it was not until the late 1830s that he began to read Plato with any intellectual awareness. When he did so he discovered much of uncommon interest, including discussions of the nature of reality that bore directly on his theories. Plato's writings strengthened his belief in a single unifying religious truth, a conception that was enhanced by familiarity with the work of

Ralph Cudworth, a seventeenth-century neo-Platonist.[22]

Significant also was Carlile's interest in Emanuel Swedenborg's writings. Swedenborg was an eighteenth-century Swedish philosopher whose ideas contained "spiritual" and supernatural elements. And although throughout his life Carlile ridiculed Swedenborg's views—describing them on one occasion as representing "a lower state of mind"—he began at this time to concede certain parallels between Swedenborg's interpretations and his own. Both analyses sought to overcome sectarian disharmonies by appealing to universal allegorical symbolism. In the *True Christian Religion*, Swedenborg employed phrases such as "the foundations of the New Jerusalem" and "a literal sense of the word," which can be found almost verbatim in Carlile's writings. The affinities between the interpretations and phraseology of the two men are such—the former being "orthodox," the latter "infidel"—that one historian, G. D. H. Cole, mistakenly describes Carlile and Swedenborg as precursors of modern theosophy.[23]

During these years Carlile's interest in phrenology increased. His writings became peppered with phrases such as "mark of the beast" and "mark of the lamb". Phrenology, he affirmed, was "a most interesting, family, fireside science," symbolizing as it did the principles of man's "second birth" and the power for good that he would be able to exercise by means of "scientific" knowledge.[24] Man's encephalic organs had to be cultivated, he stressed, to insure the triumph of virtue over vice and the dawn of the spiritual millennium. "The only possible Temple of God," stated Carlile, "is the cultivated head of man, and . . . in man's head, all good and evil prevail." In the *Christian Warrior*, which appeared at the beginning of 1843, the link between phrenology and messianic prophecy was fully delineated. The Bible, Carlile wrote, had no temporal reality: "All is Gospel, all phrenology, relating to the cultivation of wisdom, God, or good, in the head of universal man, as the only means of salvation." The brain was a microcosm of life: "The head of man is calvary, the cross, the sepulchre, the locality of the crucifixion, resurrection, and ascension to Zion of Christ as a spirit there incarnated."[25]

Likewise, "animal magnetism," a new interest, consumed much of Carlile's time. Mesmerism (as it is better known) originated in France in the late eighteenth century and then spread to Britain.

Almost everywhere it was regarded as a reforming science. Free-thinkers were drawn to it by its supposed ability to illuminate the complex material relationship between mind and body, while other reformers were impressed by the medical and therapeutic claims made on its behalf. In the late 1830s, as a result of the popularizing activities of John Elliotson, a professor of medicine at the University of London, it gained a large following in Britain. Itinerant lecturers and propounders of medical cures regaled audiences with "demonstrations" of its powers, while volunteers were induced to take part in public hypnotic experiments. (In the late 1840s, a few years after Carlile's death, mesmerism began to be known by its modern name of hypnotism.)[26]

Carlile found mesmerism attractive for several reasons. First, any self-help panacea that promised to alleviate his physical ailments was welcome. Mercury had clearly not done the job for him after almost twenty years of trying, nor had he been helped by prussic acid, purging, "steaming the body with boiling herbs," or any of the treatments that he had begun to resort to on a regular basis. Mesmerism and its offshoot, the galvanic battery (a "shock apparatus"), held out exciting therapeutic possibilities.

More important to him, however, were the intellectual attractions of this "science." Carlile saw it as offering a potential key to the moral allegory of religion, more promising even than phrenology with which in his mind it was closely linked. Just as freemasonry had given him entrée into the inner sanctums of ancient religion and mythology in the 1820s, and more recently the Pauline epistles had provided documentary "evidence" for his allegory, so mesmerism had an essential role to play. According to Carlile, it represented a practical working out of the "second birth" of knowledge, when mind would be able to control body. Once the physical basis of life was brought under control by a revivified moral power—exemplified mesmerically by a "strong" will dominating a weaker one—then a spiritual utopia would be at hand.

Throughout his life, Carlile had been fascinated by the image of electrical power (as had many other reformers) and mesmerism, which he described as a "manifestation of the divisible powers of the two sets of nerves: those of sensation and those of will and motion," fit securely into this pattern.[27] With its help he sought to explain the origins of life, postulating the existence of a galvanic fluid that was transmitted to the body by the brain. What is sensation, he asked, but "physical electricity?" What is emotion, or sexual attraction, but "varied magnetic actions of the body?"[28] Believing in an endemic connection between mesmerism and electricity, he experimented during the last years of his life with a small battery, treating himself daily and allowing his beard to grow in the belief that hair was "a conducting power between the electricity within and without man." From time to time he publicly demonstrated the use of this battery to his followers.

In November 1841 (at a time when he was immersed in the writings of mesmerist theorists such as Elliotson, the Reverend Hare Townshend, J. C. Colquhoun, and Amariah Brigham), Carlile arranged for W. H. Halse, a self-styled "Professor of Animal Magnetism" from Torquay, to give public demonstrations in Chancery Lane.[29] Among the first of their kind to be held in London, these exhibitions were attended by many reformers and persons of a scientific bent, including W. Devonshire Saull, Taylor's former patron who was now a prominent London free-thinker. The performances did not make any money for Carlile, and he and Halse quarreled; yet when Eliza became ill in the following year he sent her to Devon to be cured mesmerically by Halse. Mesmerism never provided Carlile with the all-encompassing interpretation of human behavior for which he was searching, but he praised its usefulness right up to the end of his life. It was, he wrote in April 1842, "a key to many of the difficulties of ancient history and its language, and is the first modern attempt to elucidate the science of the soul."[30]

The winter of 1841-42 was particularly cold, and Carlile rarely ventured out of Enfield. When he did so it was to participate in debates with socialists and chartists, encounters that left him emotionally drained and physically exhausted. Britain, it seemed to him, was not one whit nearer to perfection than it had been two decades before. He was having difficulty breathing as a result of his congested lungs and was hampered by the effects of his stroke. "One of the most likely things you have to hear of is my sudden death," he told Turton in January 1842. Yet he continued to battle, trying almost desperately to recapture some of his earlier buoyancy. His illnesses wore him down, but, he reported, "in the heat of discussion, I throw this off." And although his hands shook when he tried to write and he had little physical energy left, he remained adamant in the belief that his "heart has never quaked or quailed."[31]

Poverty remained the chief incubus. With the loss of all of his remunerative journalism by the end of 1841, he could no longer make plans even to the next day for fear that he would not have the requisite funds to see them through. Sarah Chichester now refused to help him, and little assistance was forthcoming from other sources. He was, as he observed in May 1842, "in the dumps for want of money."[32] Thomas Prout, an apothecary who had helped him to find work as a paid journalist, sent small sums of money and tried unsuccessfully to raise a public subscription on his behalf. But his only other regular benefactor was his trusted confidant Thomas Turton, who plied him with saucepans, razors, and other handmade gifts, eliciting the somewhat jocular observation from Carlile that "you are as generous in physicalities as I am in spiritualities."[33]

Notwithstanding his virtual withdrawal from political agitation, he restored himself to a position of visibility in reform circles for several months in the summer of 1842, by supporting George Jacob Holyoake in his defense against charges of blasphemy. Holyoake, an atheist and Owenite social missionary who was subsequently to become a leader of the secularist movement in Britain, had been indicted for blasphemy because of a lecture given at the Cheltenham Mechanics' Institution in which he had attacked the building of churches as a profligate use of public money. While preparing for his trial, which was to be held in Gloucester, he conducted a speaking tour of London, and it was then that he met Carlile.[34] The two men developed a genuine respect for one another. Holyoake rejected the "New Christianity" in its entirety but affirmed his admiration for Carlile's earlier "infidel" views and for his courageous efforts on behalf of a free press. For his part Carlile admired the twenty-four year-old Holyoake's integrity and stubbornness. "I like all but his socialism," he commented after their first meeting Asked by Holyoake to help him prepare for his trial—which was to become the focus of considerable publicity in radical circles—he accepted with alacrity, pausing only long enough to borrow twenty-five shillings from some London friends to cover his traveling and living expenses.

Carlile's support for Holyoake, and the public part that he

played during the trial, derived primarily from his lifelong hatred of the "political" crime of blasphemy. Having been a prominent victim himself, he never ceased to rail against prosecutions that were, in his opinion, a pretext for stifling free discussion. "Whatever had been brilliant in human genius and virtue, taking cognizance of human actions, finding fault and stating it," he wrote, "has by the stolid ignorance and vice of human authority, been accused and punished as blasphemy."[35] In allegorical terms, blasphemy trials were "the same everlasting gospel mystery or drama of divine principle [of Jesus] played over again." Because he saw himself as "indisputably, the moral and political leader in the struggle for free discussion," he was prepared to undergo whatever sacrifices were necessary to protect and uphold this right.[36]

In July 1842, he traveled to Cheltenham where he remained for about two months. While there he lectured many times and engaged in rancorous discussions with socialists, chartists, and clergymen.[37] He also provided important assistance to Holyoake. He gave him legal advice before and during the trial, visited him regularly in Gloucester Gaol, and raised subscriptions for him among his own followers.[38] Cheltenham was a prim town with a small working-class population, and Carlile could not have anticipated winning many converts to his cause there. But he nonetheless worked hard at it.

To maintain a facade of "respectability," he stayed in a "splendid lodging" near the center of the town and, in his public speeches, professed to "mediate" between orthodox Christians and atheists, whom he referred to as "sectarian not Catholic." He denied that he had renounced the basic tenets of infidelity. But he asserted that "science in the Church is the form of my politics and theology," and he described Holyoake—a self-proclaimed atheist—as a "good Christian." Stated Carlile: "I revere Christianity . . . as the science of human wisdom, morals, and love."[39] In August, he published a "Declaration of Principles," which summarized his main themes. The "true spirit and science of Christianity," he affirmed, "was all that is necessary to human salvation," provided that it was used to combat the "evils of the world." "Through the last seventeen hundred years," he wrote, "man has not been saved, is not now saved; but the condition of the multitude of the labourers grows more and more deplorable, from the joint starvation of body and soul in the prevalence of idolatry, precisely as the predicted cause and consequence in the Bible."[40]

While such an interpretation was in his view incontrovertible, it did not enhance his reputation among Holyoake's atheist followers, who were further antagonized by a series of letters that he wrote for the *Oracle of Reason,* a journal managed by Holyoake's close associates. In an article entitled "What Is God?", Carlile attacked atheism, proffering the claims of "trinitarian Christianity" in its place. He described the Bible as "a volume of important truth" and primitive Christianity as "the birth of wisdom in man." "For five and twenty years past, nobody has moved, but your humble servant," he complained bitterly in the *Oracle of Reason* in an article that appeared several months after Holyoake's trial.[41]

Because he voiced these opinions in their own journal, Carlile was denounced by working-class atheists. Charles Southwell and William Chilton, both associated with the paper, accused him of seeking to "theise and christianise in his peculiar way and with his peculiar interpretation" and of being "thoroughly crazed by excess of vanity." (Carlile's pointed reply was that "they who are fond of depicting abominations must have a mind suited to them.")[42] Holyoake was gentler in his rebuke. He acknowledged the seminal contribution that Carlile had made to the history of popular free-thought while reiterating that the "Bible is unworthy the compliment and science is polluted by its contact with religion." Subsequently the *Oracle of Reason* ceased to accept contributions from Carlile, and, even more than previously, he stood branded by working-class freethinkers as an apostate to the cause of infidelity. It was an accusation that badly damaged his reputation.

While in Cheltenham, Carlile tried to carry his message beyond the environs of the town. He addressed a crowd of "not less than three thousand people" on Radborough Common, Stroud, after-ward telling Holyoake: "Paul, at Mars Hill, in Athens, was not more in his glory, nor did he preach better christianity, but the same."[43] Three lectures that he gave in Sheffield in the socialist Hall of Science were less well received, and in Sidmouth and other parts of Somerset (which he visited after leaving Cheltenham in late August) attendance was sparse. But in Bristol, where he spoke repeatedly in the final two weeks of September, he scaled a peak of messianism.

The tone of his Bristol visit was set by a broadsheet that announced the consecration of a Hall of Science for "Christian Purposes" in the city. Challenging "all the preachers of the Gospel" to meet with him, Carlile professed that his aim was to show that the Bible is "not a Book of limited, local and temporal history . . . but a Book of Spiritual Principles" and that "the Physiological and Phrenological Law and Covenant for the *Salvation* of the Human Soul clearly explained by the rules of science, [is] in harmony with all modern physical and moral science."[44] He attacked the new triumvirate of socialists, chartists, and churchmen in a series of lectures (how much like kings, lords, and priests they were), reiterating that the Bible alone held the key to human prosperity. "Every thing of human salvation, present and future, is provided for by the doctrines of the inspired pages of the Bible, understood as revelation, or the science of God in man," he stated. His message was one of "moral and scientific" redemption. And in calling for a "Church truly Catholic" to be built in Bristol, in which "Christ is taught, as a spirit for universal incarnation," he told his working-class listeners: "I behold the angelic, benevolent, virtuous and lovely, cultivated head of man, which becomes the teaching power of nations and the saving grace of God."[45]

These were the final addresses delivered by Carlile outside of London. In October he was back at his cottage in Enfield, worn out by poverty and contemptuous of the feckless behavior of a populace that had rejected decisively his "spiritual" call to arms. Man is "full of evil," he wrote; he is the creature of the devil. Several London supporters continued to give him financial aid, including Thomas Prout and Alexander Morrison, an old subscriber to the *Republican* who, having rejected Carlile's doctrines for more than fifteen years, quietly returned to the fold.[46] But most reformers shunned him and his views. Francis Place, with whom he had revived a desultory acquaintanceship in June 1841, refused to help, "until you give up talking such nonsense as you have written to me." And Sarah Chichester, while expressing concern about his health and the state of his "soul," was preoccupied with the building of socialist communities, having recently published a translation of some of Charles Fourier's writings.[47]

With his lecturing at a standstill and his health deteriorating (he persisted in his refusal to consult a doctor), Carlile felt shunned and isolated. "I find it necessary," he declared, "to live entirely within myself, to have no society but books, no recreation but reading."[48] His name no longer set political waves into motion. He wrote unsolicited letters to daily and weekly newspapers signing them with noms de guerre such as "Cato," "Theophilus Clay," and "A Christian," but few of these letters found their way into print.

In March 1840, Carlile composed the *Unitarian or Socinian and Social Catechism*, a tract intended for use in connection with his proposed "Rational Religion of the National Schools." In it he described himself as a "most firm and conscientious believer in the doctrine of the Holy Trinity" and attacked the favorable treatment given to Unitarians at the expense of "real Christians" like himself who were forced continually to make sacrifices.[49] But he was so discouraged by a lack of public support that he advised his son Alfred not to print it for fear that the name Richard Carlile (or even a decipherable pseudonym) would damage Alfred's business prospects.[50] When a group of socialists reprinted his Stockport *Sermon on the Mount*, first issued in 1827, in garbled form and without acknowledging its paternity, there was nothing he could do but express contempt for them. "They are making a merit of the produce of that brain and experience, which up to this time, as a sect, they have laboured to suppress and destroy," he complained.[51]

Eliza became ill toward the end of 1842, and Carlile agreed to find other accommodations for her. Somewhat astringently (their relationship had lost most of its warmth by this time) he summarized her plight as follows: "She is heartily sick of the poverty of Philosophy—she has had her martyrdom that way—as often without money as with it."[52] Julian Hibbert, their seven-year-old son, had been sent to a socialist school in 1840, and in November 1842, Eliza, Hypatia, and Theophila moved to Devon where they remained until Carlile's death in February of the following year.

Carlile's disenchantment with the world increased during these final months of his life. People know "but little of what a struggle my life has been," he told Turton. He complained that "my publications have had their five hundred peculiar readers, but they have been lost to the world at large." Only one hope remained, and that was to persuade Sarah Chichester to continue her support of him. All of his activities hinged upon renewed contacts with her, "whether I shall be a beggar or a Gentleman." The verdict was soon in. Sarah Chichester and her sister would give him no support. "At this time my prospects are absolutely blank," he admitted at the beginning of January 1843. He felt "empty of life," noting that "nothing but my own science of my own body keeps me alive."[53]

There was always, however, one more reserve of energy left in Carlile, one final attempt to turn the tide of events in his favor. "The iron has been made to enter my soul," he commented. "It sealed my heart; but it brought no submission." Thus despite the desperateness of his situation, he managed to commence another weekly journal in January 1843, the *Christian Warrior*, which was to be the last effort on the part of a beaten warrior to express a radical political vision and to try to wrest the torch of reform away from its present leaders. By selling off remnants of his old tracts, he scraped together money for the journal. And by sheer combativeness, he kept the paper going for a month with a readership that did not exceed 300 to 400 weekly.

Predictably enough, the *Christian Warrior* is the most self-indulgent of all Carlile's journals, making little pretense at addressing itself to the public issues of the day and slipping into messianic gibberish in its final pages. The quote on its masthead from the Book of Daniel ("The Stone that Smote the Image became a great mountain and filled the whole earth") indicates the tenor of many of its observations. Its apocalyptic imagery merely accentuated the gap between Carlile's private despair and his affirmation of principles. He referred to the "cultivation of a three-Godded head for Universal man," described the brain of man as "the only Palestine of the Bible," and characterized Solomon as "the perfected man, the Prince of Peace and Hero of love, in the order of Israelitish progression."[54] Yet for those prepared to make a sympathetic effort to understand the plight of the early nineteenth-century poor as seen through the eyes of one of their better-known political leaders, there remains something in the pages of the *Christian Warrior* that commands respect. The journal trumpets the conviction that man can achieve perfection by means of reason. He is "an atom of changing matter," wrote Carlile, "a mortal organization, and is, of himself, the entire world of spirit in life, not in death." Knowledge was a "spiritual" microcosm of human life, which must be used temperately and effectively. The "cultivation of wisdom" was the true messiah and the basis for "a better church, a church of science and not of superstition, for the better education of the people."[55]

In the *Christian Warrior*, Carlile emerged as a full-blown Christ figure who was fated to carry the burden of man's political sins across time and to undergo a modern crucifixion on his behalf. Just as the Pontius Pilates of the Liverpool ministry had imprisoned him in the 1820s for defending free speech, so now, at the end of his life, he—"an honest lover, searcher after, and utterer of truth"—was being destroyed by the pressures of the multitude. But he delineated a vision of the human potential for good: of a "Garden of Eden" filled with "art, science, love, and all virtues." Will you, he asked Daniel O'Connell, "join me in a struggle, an agitation, for a pure Catholic Church, as the only way to reform of parliament, to provision for the poor, to the divorce of all disastrous unions, and the repeal of all bad laws?" And, in words that were among the last he wrote, he stated: "My spirit is on Mount Pisgah, seeing the promised land in the distance. I may not reach it, but I have seen it."[56]

On February 10, 1843, less than two weeks after the final number of the *Christian Warrior* appeared, Carlile died. He had been a fighter to the end, having recently made arrangements for a series of public "conversations" with opponents of his moral allegory to be held on condition that "ill-mannered idlers" be kept away. His death resulted from a bronchial infection, and, fittingly enough, it occurred on Fleet Street, in a shabbily furnished room occupied by his son Alfred. A handful of friends and supporters were present when he died, and according to the "official" account which they spread, he rose deftly to the occasion. His final words are reported to have been: "I have gone neither to the right nor to the left. My aim has been to accomplish one great purpose."[57] Even if apocryphal (as seems likely), no better words could have been chosen to round off a frustrating, though spirited and unusual political life.

Within days of his death, Carlile's body was removed to St. Thomas's Hospital, where his brain was dissected. He had made provision for this previously, having decided (in emulation of Bentham, Hibbert, Detrosier, and other reformers) to "let science make what science can make of it." Death, he maintained to the end, was nothing but the evaporation of bodily motion. No fuss should be made over it. Only scientists should concern themselves with the dead, so as, by studying and analyzing the composition of the brain, to be able to add to the stock of human knowledge.[58]

Carlile had requested that he be cremated, but this wish was ignored by his family and friends who interred him in Kensal Green Cemetery, a burial ground in northwest London where many of his reforming contemporaries were also laid to rest. On February 26, the day of the funeral, the weather was piercingly cold. Snow began to fall before daybreak, and by afternoon, as a cortege of several hundred mourners left Fleet Street and began a slow perambulation to Kensal Green, the greyish-white flakes had turned to steady drops of rain. As the procession wended its way through streets once so familiar to Carlile, only a small number of bystanders took notice.[59]

Yet controversy pursued him literally into the grave. As the mourners filed into Kensal Green Cemetery, walking past imposing monuments to the "poorer" section, an incident occurred that illustrates the ambivalent, disputed nature of Carlile's legacy to reformers. A clergyman advanced toward the funeral party and insisted on performing a Church of England service at the graveside, which was on consecrated ground. At this "provocation" Alfred and Richard Carlile, Jr., withdrew, along with some other mourners. They insisted that their father had lived and died an enemy of Christianity and that his "conversion" to the "New Christianity" had been one of nomenclature rather than substance. It was a sacrilege to his memory, they insisted, for a despised clergyman to pretend to intercede on his behalf with a "god" whom he had steadfastly refused to acknowledge. Only when the clergyman had departed, after conducting the service, did they return to the burial site. Yet, while this altercation was taking place, other friends and associates of Carlile remained in their places, apparently less certain about how to react.

Notes

1. Carlile to Turton, 2 February 1840, C.P.
2. Ibid., 26 February 1840, C.P.
3. Ibid., 6 August 1840, C.P.
4. Ibid., 3 February 1841, C.P.
5. Ibid., 31 December 1840; *Durham Chronicle*, 26 September 1840, 9 January 1841.

6. Carlile to Turton, 27 March 1841, C.P.

7. Ibid., 21 April 1841, C.P.

8. Ibid., 6, 19 October 1841, C.P. For a summary of her views, see Emma Martin, *Religion Superseded, or the Moral Code of Nature Sufficient for the Guidance of Man* (1850?) and *A Funeral Sermon, Occasioned by the Death of Richard Carlile, Preached at the Hall of Science, City Road, London* (1843).

9. Carlile to Turton, 16 June 1840, C.P.

10. Letter from Carlile to *Times*, 25 December 1840. There is a copy of this unpublished letter in the Carlile Papers.

11. For information about the *Durham Chronicle*, see Maurice Milne, *The Newspapers of Northumberland and Durham* (Newcastle-upon-Tyne: Frank Graham, 1971), p. 50.

12. In the 1850s Thomas Frost "edited" the *Birmingham Journal* and the *Shrewsbury Chronicle* while living near London. Frost, *Forty Years Recollections: Literary and Political* (London: S. Low, Marston, Searle, and Rivington, 1880), pp. 120-32.

13. Carlile to Turton, 26 February 1840, C.P.

14. *Durham Chronicle*, 26 September 1840.

15. Ibid., 8 August, 18 July, 5 September 1840, 20 February 1841.

16. Ibid., 23, 2 April 1841, 17 October 1840, 2 January 1841.

17. Ibid., 5 December 1840, 2 January 1841, 22 July 1840; *Besley's Devonshire Chronicle*, 8 February 1842, 29 September 1840, 27 October 1840.

18. *Durham Chronicle*, 14 November, 11, 25 April, 9 May, 26 December 1840.

19. Ibid., 9 May 1840, 25 April 1841, 15 June 1840.

20. *Bolton Free Press*, 13 February, 15, 22 May 1841; *Morning Advertiser*, 8 May 1840.

21. There is a reference to a projected *Political Warrior* in a letter from Carlile to Turton, 15 June 1841, C.P.

22. See Ralph Cudworth, *The True Intellectual System of the Universe* (London: T. Tegg, 1845, orig. pub. 1678), esp. ch. 5, sec. 3.

23. The reference to a "lower state of mind" is in *Christian Warrior*, 7 January 1843. The quotes from Swedenborg's writings are from his *The True Christian Religion: Containing the Universal Theology of the New Church* (London: W. Newbery, 1847), ch. 4. Cole links Carlile with theosophy in Cole, *Carlile*, reprinted in Michael Katanka (ed.), *Writers and Rebels* (London: Charles Knight, 1976), p. 95.

24. *Durham Chronicle*, 25 July 1840; Carlile, *Abstract, Embodying the Evidences, of the Lectures Delivered . . . at Brighton*, p. 14.

25. *Christian Warrior*, 7 January 1843.

26. Mesmeric exhibitions were popular until mid-century after which

time they came to be associated with less "scientific" kinds of public instruction. See Parsinnen, "Popular Science and Society," pp. 12-14; Fred Kaplan, "The Mesmeric Mania: The Early Victorians and Animal Magnetism," *Journal of the History of Ideas,* 35 (1947), pp. 691-702.

27. *Christian Warrior,* 21 January 1843. Elliotson ascribed its effects to "a peculiar power, to a power acting . . . constantly in all living things, vegetable and animal, but shown in a peculiar manner by the processes of mesmerism." *Human Physiology* (London: Longman, Orme, Brown, Green, and Longman, 1840), p. 685.

28. *Christian Warrior,* 21 January 1843. In her "Isis" lectures, Eliza Sharples described the brain as a "self-acting galvanic pile." *Isis,* 12 May 1832.

29. Carlile to Turton, 19 August 1841, C.P. The key texts in addition to Elliotson's *Human Physiology* were Amariah Brigham, *Remarks on the Influence of Mental Cultivation and Mental Excitement upon Health* (1832); J. C. Colquhoun, *Isis Revelata: An Inquiry into the Origin, Progress, and Present State of Animal Magnetism* (2 vols, 1836); C. H. Townshend, *Facts in Mesmerism* (1840).

30. *Besley's Devonshire Chronicle,* 19 April 1842.

31. Carlile to Turton, 4 March, 11 April 1842, C.P.

32. Ibid., 23 May 1842, C.P.

33. Ibid., 3 January 1842, C.P.

34. Holyoake Log Books, Bishopsgate Library; *Oracle of Reason,* 30 July 1842.

35. *Cheltenham Free Press,* 15 February 1840. Carlile signed this letter "A Christian."

36. *Oracle of Reason,* 3 September 1842; Carlile to M. Q. Ryall, 11 July 1842, Holyoake Papers, Co-operative Union Library.

37. Carlile to Turton, 29 July 1842, C.P.

38. See George Jacob Holyoake, *The Last Trial for Atheism in England: A Fragment of Autobiography* (London: Trübner, 1871), p. 88; Joseph McCabe, *Life and Letters of George Jacob Holyoake* (London: Watts, 1908), vol. I, pp. 78-82. There are letters in C.P. describing the assistance he gave to Holyoake.

39. Carlile to Turton, 27 July 1842, C.P.; *Oracle of Reason,* 3 September 1842.

40. *Cheltenham Free Press,* 6 August 1842.

41. *Oracle of Reason,* 22 October, 26 November 1842.

42. Ibid., 15 October, 26 November 1842; Carlile's reply is in ibid., 29 October 1842.

43. Carlile to Holyoake, 1 September 1842, Holyoake Papers, Co-operative Union Library.

44. A copy of this broadsheet is in the Bishopsgate Library.

45. "A Letter from Richard Carlile to the Inhabitants of Bristol," 19

September 1842. Copies are in the Bishopsgate Library and in the Holyoake Papers, Co-operative Union Library.

46. Morrison presented Carlile with a gold watch and told him: "You may just as well try to reconcile a burnt-out stick to the building of a man of war, as the bible to science—Read Immortal Paine." Morrison to Carlile, 21 November 1842, C.P. Another supporter, Logan Mitchell, committed suicide at the end of 1841. Mitchell's views (similar to those of Taylor) are summarized in a book he published anonymously, *The Christian Mythology Unveiled, in a Series of Lectures by a Forty Years' Cultivator of the Earth, and Follower of Nature* (1842). A revised edition of this book was published by the Freethought Publishing Company in 1881 as *Religion in the Heavens; or, Mythology Unveiled.*

47. Place to Carlile, 7 August 1841, C.P. In an article written in 1836, Carlile described Place as "a prodigy of useful, resolute, consistent political exertion and indefatigable labour." *Monthly Magazine*, 21 (1836), pp. 454-56. Sarah Chichester's book, published under the title *The Phalanstery; or Attractive Industry and Moral Harmony* (1841), was based on a precis of Fourier's writings by Madame Gati le Gamond. Chichester was elected president of "The British and Foreign Society for the Promotion of Humanity and Abstinence from Animal Food" in 1843. *New Age*, 1 December 1843.

48. *Christian Warrior*, 21 January 1843.

49. Richard Carlile, *Unitarian or Socinian and Social Catechism* (New York: G. Vale, 1846), pp. 7-8.

50. Carlile to Turton, 27 March 1840, C.P. The tract was published in New York in 1846 at the urging of Richard Carlile, Jr. G. Vale, the publisher, told its readers: "We do not admire the style, but give it as an exhibition of Mr. Carlile immediately preceding his death." Carlile, *Unitarian or Socinian*, p. 4.

51. Carlile to M. Q. Ryall, 11 July 1842, Holyoake Papers, Co-operative Union Library.

52. Carlile to Turton, 19 December 1842, C.P.

53. *Oracle of Reason*, 8 October 1842; Carlile to Turton, 1 November 1842, 24 January 1843, C.P.

54. *Christian Warrior*, 14 January 1843.

55. Ibid., 7, 14 January 1843.

56. Ibid., 28 January 1843.

57. Alfred Carlile to Turton, 10 February 1843, C.P.

58. The dissection is described in *Besley's Devonshire Chronicle*, 7 March 1843 (reprinted from the *Morning Advertiser*); *Times*, 16 February 1843; *Lancet*, 18 February 1843. See also Brook, *Carlile and the Surgeons.*

59. For accounts of the funeral, see Joseph Harris to Thomas Turton, 28 February 1843, C.P.; *Times*, 27 February 1843; *Weekly Dispatch*, 5 March 1843.

EPILOGUE

Why the disagreements about Carlile, even among those who knew him best? The intensity of feeling? The unwillingness of many reformers to acknowledge a proper debt to him? There is no doubt that, politically, he lost his way in the late 1830s. He failed to harness the discontents of the British working classes to a realistic program at a time of crisis and political unrest. After giving a considerable stimulus to popular freethought by making Paine, d'Holbach, and other "infidel" writers nearly household words among the working classes, he did little more in the area of religious controversy than to disseminate theories that lacked a wide basis of support. Many artisans and mechanics who initially supported him turned increasingly to socialism and chartism. He became isolated, a lone voice seeking to express a rationalistic view of politics in apocalyptic imagery.

But if Carlile was not an effective leader of a political movement of the working classes and if few of his ideas have had a long-term impact upon reformers, the achievements of this "plain, matter-of-fact, ungarnished-narrative, no-struggling, no-secrecy sort of man" are not to be underestimated. Few other nineteenth-century reformers have made as much of a virtue out of poverty and struggle as did Richard Carlile. The greater the obstacles, the more he struggled to overcome them; the more intractable the issues—whether birth control, freedom of the press, antiscriptural theology, phrenology, mesmerism—the more resolutely he attempted to debate them and to make them part of the public consciousness. As he affirmed: "If my body be in chains, so long as I have a mind, that mind shall be free. I will endeavour to make others free."[1] Carlile's shifts of position, particularly on the subject of religion, cost him many followers. But how else except by political isolation could his uncompromising individualism, the quality that most deeply shaped his personality, be spotlighted?

As to the seeming confusions about his purpose, these do not detract from a basic consistency. Carlile's ideas ran the gamut of interpretations on freethought and on many other issues. Yet he never purported to be a theorist. He was an activist, a doer, less concerned to proffer concrete solutions to specific problems than to insist upon discussing issues whenever he chose to and wherever the need arose. He battled hard during his lifetime for the right to dissent from orthodox "truths." And, on a personal level, he sought to meld past and present so as to increase the scope of individual freedom. Messianism became his chosen means of expression: to quote a historian writing in another context, he espoused a "secularized version of the everlasting struggle between good and evil, light and darkness, God and Satan."[2] The important thing, though, is that Carlile took risks that few other reformers were willing to take, endured harsh punishments for his defiance of authority, and helped immeasurably to extend the boundaries of discussion and debate. He had, in his own words, a "passionate desire to do good and to leave the world better than I found it."[3]

Richard Carlile may be regarded as a prototypical nineteenth-century working-class reformer. At a time when the British legal system was heavily biased against the poor, he fought to bring about reform, neither giving nor receiving quarter from those whom he regarded as his enemies. He championed with deep conviction almost all of the tough issues of his day. If his solutions were sometimes crude, and his journalism and speechmaking fell short of the highest standards (sometimes even those he set for himself), the attempt was, nonetheless, worthwhile. Other reformers were stimulated to action by his efforts. And, almost certainly, without Carlile the resistance to political change in Britain would have been more sustained and effective.

This is the meaning of his life, its basic consistency. To illustrate it one can do worse than reprint the "epitaph" he composed for himself a decade before his death: "I have extended the freedom of the press, promoted the freedom of discussion, excited public inquiry, dared the very jaws of despotism, given up my body, a sacrifice as far as its motive liberty is in question. I have lessened the conceits of kings and priests and lords—I have lessened their powers. I have given birth to mind, and if I die today, I shall leave the aggregate man better than I found him."[4] With Carlile's many faults in mind, it is the case that few reformers can convincingly say as much about themselves.

Notes

1. *Republican*, 19 December 1823.
2. Oliver, "Owen in 1817," p. 179.
3. Carlile, *Church Reform*, pp. 77-78.
4. *Gauntlet*, 4 August 1833.

CARLILE'S FAMILY

Jane Carlile died in the summer of 1843 and was buried in Kensal Green Cemetery. Richard's three surviving sons by Jane became publishers and newsagents. Neither Alfred nor Thomas Paine was particularly successful. But Richard, Jr., moved to the United States in 1846 and was elected to the House of Assembly of the state of Wisconsin. He died in New York in 1854, of ship fever contracted after a visit to London.

Eliza Sharples lived in extreme poverty in London from 1843 until her death in 1852. During the final three years of her life she resided at a former temperance hall at 1 Warner Place, Hackney Road, in East London. With the assistance of several of Carlile's supporters she established a coffee house and newsroom at this address. Charles Bradlaugh, the future MP, then in his teens, lived briefly with the Sharples family at this time.

Carlile's three surviving children by Eliza migrated to the United States. Julian Hibbert, trained as an engineer, was killed in the American Civil War. Hypatia and Theophila left London together in 1852 with the aid of reformers. Hypatia married Elias Cooke and died in Chicago in 1923. Theophila married a Scottish tailor, Colin Campbell, who became the first socialist candidate for governor of the state of Wisconsin. In 1899, while living in Chicago, she published the biography of her father, *The Battle of the Press as Told in the Story of the Life of Richard Carlile.* She died in California in 1913. Her daughter, Mrs. Norman Stevens, came into possession of Richard Carlile's personal papers and donated them to the Henry E. Huntington Library, San Marino, California, in 1937.

BIBLIOGRAPHICAL ESSAY

In recent years there has been a growing interest in British working-class radicalism and labor studies. Professional organizations in Britain and North America have come into existence for the express purpose of advancing such studies. The Society for the Study of Labour History, with its base in the North of England, has produced several local offshoots and, since 1961, has published a *Bulletin*, which prints articles and reviews on aspects of radical history, as well as documents and oral testimony from participants in labor movements. More scholarly (and committed to writing socialist history) is the *History Workshop Journal*, published since 1976 by an "Editorial Collective," which emerged from the annual History Workshops organized by Raphael Samuel of Ruskin College. Though by no means limited in its coverage to Britain, the *History Workshop Journal* is a major source for articles on working-class radicalism. Useful, also, are two older journals: *Past and Present*, which is still the best journal concentrating on social history, and the fine *International Review of Social History*, published three times a year in Amsterdam. *Labor Studies*, an American quarterly, occasionally publishes an article or review dealing with an aspect of British radical history. Other periodicals of value include *Social History*, the *Journal of Social History*, the *Radical History Review*, *Science and Society*, and more specialized journals such as *Feminist Studies* and the *Victorian Periodicals Review*.

If the creation of new organizations and the establishment of journals dedicated to radical studies indicates an increased interest in the subject, so too does the publication of major reference and bibliographic works. The two most important of these in recent years have been the *Biographical Dictionary of Modern British Radicals: Volume I: 1770-1830*, edited by Joseph O. Baylen and Norbert J. Gossman (Hassocks, Sussex: Harvester Press, 1979) and the *Dictionary of Labour Biography*, edited by John Saville and Joyce Bellamy, volumes 1-4 (London: Macmillan, 1972-1977). *The Biographical Dictionary of Modern British Radicals* is projected as a three-volume edition covering the period up to 1970. It is as comprehensive as its contributors and sources allow it to be considering that each volume is a self-contained chronological entity. Notwithstanding inadequate indexing and cross-referencing, it is the most significant addition yet made to radical studies. More definitive though less focused (there is no chronological or subject pattern to any volume), the *Dictionary of Labour Biography* is intended to give a broad framework to labor studies. Each volume extends well into the twentieth century and includes biographies of many trade unionists and political activists who can by no means be considered radical. Two additional *Dictionary* projects, still in their infancy but certain to include much useful material on British radicals, are the *Dictionary of Unbelief*, being edited by Gordon Stein and to be published by Greenwood Press, and the *Dictionary of Victorian Journalists*, to be edited by Joel H. Wiener.

In addition to the dictionaries, several excellent bibliographies have been published in recent years, including: J. F. C. Harrison and Dorothy Thompson, *Bibliography of the Chartist Movement, 1837-1976* (Hassocks, Sussex: Harvester Press, 1978), a superb compilation, which lacks only skilful annotations to make it definitive; Norbert Gossman's impressionistic but helpful "Definitions and Recent Writings on Modern British Radicalism, 1790-1914," *British Studies Monitor*, 4 (1973), pp. 3-11; and the lengthy bibliographies appended to J. F. C. Harrison's *Robert Owen and the Owenites in Britain and America: The Quest for the New Moral World* (London: Routledge and Kegan Paul, 1969) and to Edward Royle's two-volume history of secularism, *Victorian Infidels: The Origins of the British Secularist Movement, 1791-1866* (Manchester: Manchester University Press, 1974), and *Radicals, Secularists and Republicans: Popular Freethought in Britain, 1866-1915* (Manchester: Manchester University Press, 1980).

Those wanting to learn more about Richard Carlile's radical environment are best advised to turn to E. P. Thompson's landmark study, *The Making of the English Working Class* (London: Victor Gollancz, 1963), which traces the development of class consciousness during the formative years of the early nineteenth century. This work of humanistic Marxism (for want of a better term) has been attacked on the Left by orthodox interpreters of Marx such as Perry Anderson, *Arguments with English Marxism* (London: Verso, 1980), and on the Right by students of working-class politics such as Malcolm I. Thomis, *The Luddites: Machine-Breaking in Regency England* (Newton Abbot, Devon: David & Charles, 1970) and (with Peter Holt) *Threats of Revolution in Britain, 1789-1848* (London: Macmillan, 1977), who see working-class industrial and political objectives as separate and maintain that Thompson exaggerates the likelihood of revolution. But notwithstanding its many critics, *The Making of the English Working Class* remains easily the best book on the subject.

The theoretical problems of class formation and radical consciousness tackled by Thompson, and by that other doyen of British radical studies, Eric Hobsbawm—see especially *The Age of Revolution, 1789-1848* (Cleveland, Ohio: World Publishing Company, 1962), and *Labouring Men: Studies in the History of Labour* (New York: Basic Books, 1964)—can be pursued in the following books: John Foster, *Class Struggle and the Industrial Revolution: Early Industrial Capitalism in Three English Towns* (London: Weidenfeld & Nicolson, 1974); Robert Q. Gray, *The Labour Aristocracy in Victorian Edinburgh* (Oxford: Clarendon Press, 1976); Geoffrey Crossick, *An Artisan Elite in Victorian Society: Kentish London, 1840-1880* (London: Croom Helm, 1978); and Patrick Joyce, *Work, Society and Politics: The Culture of the Factory in Later Victorian England* (New Brunswick, New Jersey: Rutgers University Press, 1980). Each of these books makes a distinctive contribution to the debate about what happened (or failed to happen) to class consciousness and working-class radicalism after the demise of the chartist movement in the 1850s. Why, for example, did a powerful Marxist tradition not take firm root in Britain? Why did Britain not experience a political revolution in the nineteenth century as did so many other European countries? Does the existence of a "labour aristocracy" (the term used by Hobsbawm in his essay "The Labour Aristocracy in Nineteenth-Century Britain," reprinted in *Labouring Men*, pp. 272-315) explain the fragmentation of the working class? Or was the latter, as Patrick Joyce argues, subtly co-opted into a reformist position by means of an internalization of capitalist values? Also worth consulting for theoretical insights are Francis Hearn, *Domination, Legitimation, and Resistance: The Incorporation of the English Working Class* (Westport, Connecticut: Greenwood Press, 1978), a study influenced by the writings of Herbert Marcuse, which emphasizes the importance of myth in the formation of class consciousness; and Zygmunt Bauman, *Between Class and Elite: The Evolution of the British Labour Movement, A Sociological Study*, translated by Sheila Patterson (Manchester: Manchester University Press, 1972), a more conventional Marxist analysis. There is also much to be learned from Trygve Tholfsen, *Working Class Radicalism in Mid-Victorian England* (London: Croom Helm, 1976).

If scholarship and historical imagination are of as much concern as theoretical analysis (as they should be), those interested in British radicalism will turn to Asa Briggs, *The Age of Improvement, 1783-1867* (London: Longmans, 1959), an impressive general synthesis of nineteenth-century British history, which includes a lot of material on the working class; R. J. White, *Waterloo to Peterloo* (London: William Heinemann, 1957), limited in scope but eloquent in delineating the aspirations of the radical poor; John Stevenson, *Popular Disturbances in England, 1700-1870*

(London: Longman, 1979), containing detailed studies that add considerably to an understanding of popular unrest; and E. J. Hobsbawm and George Rudé, *Captain Swing* (London: Lawrence and Wishart, 1969), the first major study of the "Swing Riots" of 1830 since J. L. and Barbara Hammond's classic *The Village Labourer, 1760-1832: A Study in the Government of England before the Reform Bill* (London: Longmans, Green, and Company, 1911). In a class by themselves are the writings of Gwyn A. Williams, a brilliant Welsh scholar who roams across continents and disciplines in pursuit of those nameless multitudes who achieved a "point of breakthrough" in history. Williams's latest book *The Merthyr Rising* (London: Croom Helm, 1978), deals with a minor political rebellion in Merthyr Tydvil in 1831 led by the legendary Dic Penderyn. But it contains so many insights and imaginative conjectures that it must be set alongside Thompson's book as a classic study of popular unrest.

Of the chief radical figures of the early nineteenth century, few have been well served by biographers. Only three such biographies are better than run of the mill: A. R. Schoyen, *The Chartist Challenge: A Portrait of George Julian Harney* (London: Allen and Unwin, 1958) is a first-class study of a minor Chartist leader; Cecil Driver, *Tory Radical: The Life of Richard Oastler* (New York: Oxford University Press, 1946) presents a finely-etched portrait of a leading factory reformer; and R. K. Webb, *Harriet Martineau: A Radical Victorian* (New York: Columbia University Press, 1960) contains numerous insights into the idiosyncratic side of radicalism. There is a poor biography of Feargus O'Connor by Donald Read and Eric Glasgow, *Feargus O'Connor: Irishman and Chartist* (London: Edward Arnold, 1961), but this has been partly superseded by James Epstein's *The Lion of Freedom: Feargus O'Connor and the Chartist Movement, 1832-42* (Manchester: Manchester University Press, 1982). Alfred Plummer's *Bronterre: A Political Biography of Bronterre O'Brien, 1804-1864* (London: George Allen & Unwin, 1971), re-creates little of the texture and excitement of the chartist years. Two studies of William Cobbett—G. D. H. Cole, *The Life of William Cobbett* (London: W. Collins Sons, 1924), and James Sambrook, *William Cobbett* (London: Routledge & Kegan Paul, 1973)—lack definitiveness on the political context of his life and his qualities as a journalist. But they have been superceded by a new biography of Cobbett by George Spater, *William Cobbett: The Poor Man's Friend,* 2 vols. (Cambridge: Cambridge University Press, 1981). John W. Osborne's *John Cartwright* (Cambridge: Cambridge University Press, 1972) is more of an analysis of "old radical" ideas than a study of the man. Finally, there are no up-to-date biographies of George Jacob Holyoake, William Lovett, Henry Hetherington, James Watson, and, most striking of all, Henry "Orator" Hunt. In histories of British radicalism Hunt is invariably depicted as a mindless demagogue (and, indeed, there is little evidence that he was a man of any intellectual substance), but he is a key personality in early nineteenth-century radicalism and deserves a major study.

On the political side of radicalism, much remains to be done. In addition to the books already cited by Thompson, White, and Read, those interested in the period will want to look at Olive Rudkin, *Thomas Spence and His Connections* (London: George Allen & Unwin, 1927), still the best study of the Spencean agitators of the post-1815 years; Joseph Hamburger, *James Mill and the Art of Revolution* (New Haven, Connecticut: Yale University Press, 1963), which is too critical of the National Union of the Working Classes but, nonetheless, a work of impeccable scholarship; John Stevenson (ed.), *London in the Age of Reform* (Oxford: Basil Blackwell, 1977), which includes good essays on the Queen Caroline agitation and other events in London radical politics; and Carlos Flick, *The Birmingham Political Union and the Movement for Reform in Britain, 1830-1839* (Hamden, Connecticut: Archon Books, 1978), a book that is narrow in scope but useful. Joel H. Wiener, *The War of the Unstamped: The Movement to Repeal the British Newspaper Tax, 1830-1836* (Ithaca, New York: Cornell University Press, 1969), and Patricia Hollis, *The Pauper Press: A Study in Working-Class Radicalism of the 1830's* (London: Oxford University Press, 1970), cover in detail the important battle of the unstamped press of the 1830s with which Carlile was peripherally involved. A recent book by I. J. Prothero entitled *Artisans and Politics in Early Nineteenth Century London: John Gast and His Times* (London: Dawson, 1979), which focuses on the shipwrights' union and its leader John Gast, promises more than it delivers but is a perceptive treatment of radical and artisan attitudes. Several important articles should be consulted as well: Asa Briggs, "The Language of 'Class' in Early Nineteenth-Century England" in *Essays in Labour History*, edited by Asa Briggs and John Saville (London: Macmillan, 1960); Terry Parsinnen, "The Revolutionary Party in London, 1816-1820," *Bulletin of the Institute for Historical Research*, 45 (1972), pp. 266-82; T. M. Parsinnen and I. J. Prothero, "The London Tailors' Strike of 1834 and the Collapse of the Grand National Consolidated Trades' Union: A Police Spy's Report," *International Review of Social History*, 22 (1977), pp. 65-107. A recent important book is J. Ann Hone, *For the Cause of Truth: Radicalism in London, 1796-1821* (London: Oxford University Press, 1982).

On the Chartists, who loomed so large in Carlile's life, there is a plethora of important studies. Dorothy Thompson, *The Early Chartists* (London: Macmillan, 1971), provides a solid introduction to the subject. Mark Hovell, *The Chartist Movement* (Manchester: Manchester University Press, 1918), and Julius West, *A History of the Chartist Movement* (London: Constable, 1920) are in tandem still unsurpassed on the overall history of the movement. Asa Briggs (ed.), *Chartist Studies* (London: Macmillan, 1959), contains a series of innovative local studies (some of which have been superseded); and G. D. H. Cole, *Chartist Portraits* (London: Macmillan, 1941), is remarkably sound in its balanced treatment of Thomas Attwood, Joseph Rayner Stephens, William Lovett, and other chartist leaders. Two recent general histories of chartism are: David Jones, *Chartism and the Chartists* (New York: St. Martin's Press, 1975), a lucid interpretative book that makes the point that chartism was permeated by religion, at least outside London and Leeds; and J. T. Ward, *Chartism* (London: B. T. Batsford, 1973), a comprehensive if dull analysis of chartist leaders and events. David Williams, *John Frost: A Study in Chartism* (Cardiff: University of Wales Press, 1939), is an outstanding account of Welsh chartism, while Alexander Wilson, *The Chartist Movement in Scotland* (Manchester: Manchester University Press, 1970), is adequate on Scottish chartism.

Owenism as a constituent element of British radicalism has been less systematically studied than chartism. The best book on the subject is J. F. C. Harrison, *Robert Owen and the Owenites in Britain and America*, which has been cited for its impressive bibliography. This comparative study, written by a leading authority on the period, suffers only from an attempt to fit economic cooperation into a constricting millennialist framework. Margaret Cole's rather thin biography of Owen—*Robert Owen of New Lanark* (London: Batchworth Press, 1953)—is the best modern account of his life, but it must be supplemented by two earlier studies: Frank Podmore, *Robert Owen: A Biography* (London: George Allen & Unwin, 1906) and G. D. H. Cole, *The Life of Robert Owen* (London: Frank Cass, 1965, first published in 1925). To celebrate the bicentenary of Owen's birth, two important collections of essays dealing with his life and influence were published in 1971: John Butt (ed.), *Robert Owen, Prince of Cotton Spinners* (Newton Abbot, Devon: David & Charles, 1971), and Sidney Pollard and John Salt (eds.), *Robert Owen, Prophet of the Poor: Essays in Honour of the Two-Hundredth Anniversary of His Birth* (London: Macmillan, 1971). The latter volume, which is the better of the two, includes two articles of exceptional merit: Eileen Yeo, "Robert Owen and Radical Culture," which examines the (too often overlooked) cultural dimensions of popular history; and W. H. Oliver, "Owen in 1817: The Millennialist Moment," which captures the quintessence of cooperative imagery and feeling at a time when the discontented poor were receptive to extreme rhetoric.

Millennialism itself, and the cast of mind that affected Carlile so deeply in his final years, has received exemplary treatment by J. F. C. Harrison in *The Second Coming: Popular Millenarianism, 1780-1850* (New Brunswick, New Jersey: Rutgers University Press, 1979). Once again, however,

Harrison tries too hard to show that millennialist thought was the primary lever in the movement for radical reform. A number of general studies of millennialism (none of them dealing directly with Carlile) shed light on this nineteenth-century phenomenon and, specifically, on what it was that compulsively drove Carlile toward his "New Christianity" in the late 1830s. The best of these studies are: Norman Cohn, *The Pursuit of the Millennium* (London: Secker & Warburg, 1957), an illuminating analysis of millennialist thought by way of a study of mass movements; Christopher Hill, *The World Turned Upside Down: Radical Ideas during the English Revolution* (London: Maurice Temple Smith, 1972), which deals with radical sects and revolutionary beliefs during an earlier period of social crisis; and Eric Hobsbawm, *Primitive Rebels: Studies in Archaic Forms of Social Movement in the 19th and 20th Centuries* (New York: W. W. Norton, 1965, originally published in 1959), which contains a set of uncommonly stimulating essays on millennialist movements in Spain, Italy, and elsewhere.

The final major aspect of nineteenth-century radicalism that impinged directly upon Carlile's life is freethought, and although there are many books and articles dealing with British freethought, few give adequate attention to the early part of the nineteenth century. Most of the published works concentrate on the later years when Holyoake and Charles Bradlaugh were struggling for control of the secularist movement and freethinkers like Carlile and Taylor were beginning to recede into popular memory. Edward Royle's two-volume history of freethought (*Victorian Infidels* and *Radicals, Secularists and Republicans*) is, for example, excellent, but it mostly skips over Carlile and his contemporaries. J. M. Robertson's *A History of Freethought in the Nineteenth Century* (London: Watts & Co., 1929), though dated, is still a work of impressive scholarship. David Tribe, *100 Years of Freethought* (London: Elek, 1967), is somewhat hagiographical but well written and perceptive in its treatment of the later decades of the nineteenth century. Susan Budd, *Varieties of Unbelief· Atheists and Agnostics in English Society, 1850-1950* (London: Heinemann, 1977), and Colin Campbell, *Towards a Sociology of Religion* (London: Macmillan, 1971), contain some trenchant insights but are sociological rather than historical analyses of freethought. Joseph McCabe, *A Rationalist Encyclopaedia: A Book of Reference on Religion, Philosophy, Ethics, and Science* (London: Watts & Co., 1948) comes as close as any other book to providing definitive source material on freethought and freethinkers. Finally, there is a general history of British freethought, John Edwin McGee, *History of the British Secular Movement* (Girard, Kansas: Haldeman-Julius Publications, 1948), that is useful if not entirely satisfactory.

INDEX

About the Author

JOEL H. WIENER is Professor and Chairman of the History Department at the City College of New York. His previous books include *Great Britain: Foreign Policy and the Span of Empire* and *The War of the Unstamped*.